Brain Plasticity

How the Brain Learns through the Mind to create INTELLIGENCE

By

Roy Andersen

The Moving Quill Publishing House.

MQ

Disclaimer:

The author and the publisher will assume no liability nor responsibility to any person or entity with respect to any loss or damage related directly or indirectly to the information in this book. Neither the author nor the publisher will provide any remedy for indirect, consequential, punitive, or incidental damages arising from this book, including such from negligence, strict liability, or breach of warranty or contract, even after notice of the possibility of such damages. Neither the publisher nor the author accept any responsibility for the actions of another based on the information in this book..

ISBN: 978-1-0685296-9-6

A CIP catalogue record for this book is available from the British Library.

I would like to dedicate this book
to
Professor/Dean Emeritus David Martin.
Gallaudet University, Washington, D.C.

It seems like a thousand years ago since I first thought to study what intelligence actually is. I have dedicated most of my life to this quest. A very, very long time ago, I wrote to the Dean of Education at Gallaudet University in America, asking if he could kindly help me with some wording. David, as a stranger, wrote back and since that time has given me very great support, confidence and guidance. I can honestly say that without the encouragement of David with his extensive background of work in cognitive education, I doubt that I would have had the confidence to complete my work. His kindness and the time he gave me will always remain close to my heart. With my greatest respects to this very good man, I dedicate this book, which opens up a great understanding to what the environment of intelligence is. By this understanding, we may better realise how the feature of intelligence in the human being is far more open to development than we are currently aware.

Thank you David.

Acknowledgements

There is not space here to mention all the many people I have ironed out my thoughts with in the twenty years it took me to complete these books. To those I mention here, and to many others, I am profoundly grateful for their time, generosity, and the great friendship they have shown me.

Prof. / Dean Emeritus. David Martin. Gallaudet University. U.S.A.
Prof. Søren Nørby. Denmark.
Prof. Mads Hermansen. Nordic School of Public Health. Sweden.
Prof. Freddy Bugge Christiansen. Arhus University. Denmark.
Prof. Albert Gjedde. Arhus University Hospital. Denmark.
Prof. Rik Drummond-Brydson. Leeds University. England.
Prof. Jorn Bundgaard Nielsen. Arhus University. Denmark.
Dr. Paul Harris. Southern College of Optometry. U.S.A.
Prof. Cosimo Di Magli. The Anne Frank School. Italy.
Prof. Harry Chugani. Wayne State University. U.S.A.
Prof. Laming. Cambridge University. England.
Prof. Martha Constanine-Paton. MIT. U.S.A.
Prof. Carla Shatz. Stanford University. U.S.A.
Prof. Derek Forest. Dublin University. Ireland.
Ms. Claudia Krenz. U.S.A.
Ms. Leigh Collinge. Australia.
Ms. Sara Lappi. U.S.A.
&
My Personal Gratitude for your love, support and help:
Dr. Irina Andersen Ph.D
Dr. Gini Andersen. Ph.D.
Ms. Naomi Andersen

What the Experts say:

“The books of Roy Andersen are important books that should be read by every parent and educator in the world. They represent a real breakthrough in our understanding of what intelligence is and how it develops, and the importance of changing the ways students are both parented and educated. Roy is doing for learning the work that is as significant as was that done in the past by such figures as John Dewey. These are must-reads for both parents and educators alike.”

Dean Emeritus/Professor David Martin Ph.D,
Gallaudet University, Washington, DC.

“Roy's series of books clearly and methodically map out exactly how students learn. He isn't afraid to address head-on the many mis-conceptions that are plaguing our society and thus having a negative impact on our students’ learning.

Parents and educators who read these books will not only have a better understanding, but will also be inspired to change in their attitudes and preconceived notions on how students can excel in their learning.

If you've ever wanted to unravel how student's learn, then these books are the answer you have been looking for! They should be mandatory reading for every parent and educator.”

Erin Calhoun. National Institute of Learning Development. USA

“The most important books I have ever read about a child’s intelligence.”

Prof. Tatyana Oleinik. Pedagogical University. Ukraine.

"Roy Andersen's deep understanding of children's behavior gives a new perspective to parents and educators in directing and re-directing student potentials -- where their unique individualities can be given proper attention to shape their creative ideas into reality. Andersen's books are really a heart touching narration of his experiences in dealing with children who need empathy and understanding. Educators and parents alike may use these books as the basis for learning -- to create a genuine culture of assisting children in the optimum development of their full potential."

Prof. Marinel Dayawon Ph.D. Assoc.Dean of Education.
Isabela State Univ. Philippines.

"Roy Andersen's research and writings provide deep insights into the minds of children. His works are always easy to read and understand. His books are assets that are good material for professional development on every teacher's table."

Daniel Tay Xiong Sheng. Visual Mapper and Educator. Singapore

"I could not imagine the existence of such a completely different perspective for education, and the way it could be offered to new generations. The book kept my attention from the first to the very last page. Highly recommended not only for teachers, but essential for all parents."

Elias Aloupoyiannis. Ministry of Administrative Reform. Athens.

"Your observations on the way "education" is delivered, and all the things that are wrong with the current model of public education, are an eye-opener. It's plain to me that many of your proposals are not only well-reasoned, but absolutely necessary if we are to achieve any semblance of an egalitarian society in which every child can develop to his or her full potential."

Dr. Sara Lappi Educator USA

“We may have significant policies in education, but if we do not understand how the mind of the learner works our education will forever give us the wrong output. Roy Andersen has dealt with the issues of the learner and the learning process in great detail, and his books should inspire every stakeholder in education.”

Olive Wambui. Senior Assistant Director.
Institute of Curriculum Development. Kenya

“Dear Roy, What you have done should reach out to all the parents, parents-to-be and other practitioners such as kindergarten teachers, primary and secondary teachers. You have done extraordinary work!

Chun Hong Zong. Educator. China

"These books should be in the library of each school in every corner of the world. They should also be part of the syllabus in the institutions who are offer child psychology, and teacher training diplomas and degree programs, or at least they should be the part of a refresher course."

M.Imran Khan. CEO AIMMS Universities. Middle East.

"These are wonderful books in which teachers are invited to develop motivation in their pupils through a new and creative way to teach. I like how they explain how parents have a pivotal role inside the school system and in the family to develop intelligence in their children. Roy Andersen suggests very interesting ideas to reach the heart of children in their path to learn. This work is a real masterpiece of modern education.”

Nicoletta Lastella, Feuerstein trainer, Sviluppo Cognitive. Italy.

"Roy, I would like to thank you for sharing your passion, heart, brilliance, and intellectual journey with me. I am very much enjoying your knowledgeable perspective on some very important challenges.”

Dr. Christopher John. Psychologist. USA.

"These books are never dull, not even for a moment. Beautifully written! Roy has written in such a way that anyone can pick up his books and understand where he is coming from and where he is going in his thoughts, that offer profound insight into what is wrong with school, and why we need to change the ways we are preparing our children for the world they will live in.
I would recommend that ALL educators read his books, especially "Teacher, Parent, Child," as they will definitely be refreshed and challenged to re-think their position as teachers in these challenging times."

Rachel Wong. Principal. Malaysia

"Roy....thank you! I started reading the first bits and was immediately hooked (this does not happen often, maybe once a year, I'm SUPER fussy about books, I've read too many...). You are a fantastic writer, not just because your info is of obvious high quality (just skimming a bit made that obvious) but the way you write too - it's warm and entertaining and easy to read - no wonder you have such high applause from your critics!"

Lydia Cooper. Graphic Designer and Mother of 3, South Africa.

"These are very important and interesting books, with lots of valuable points for parents and teachers. They bring learning and education to a whole new level. Well done!"

Prof. Mads Hermansen. Educational Psychologist Denmark.

"After reading your book, I felt I was sitting in your Lecture, and could ask any question? I wouldn't feel uncertain about asking, because you write in a manner for all to understand. Anyone can embrace, and grasp easily the knowledge you share from your mind. Your work has so much distinctive influence upon us all. You make us realize what we need to do to help children, and how we can do it."

Denise Nakata. Educationalist Japan.

A Personal Introduction by Roy Andersen

A new type of thinking is essential, if mankind is to survive and move toward higher levels.
Albert Einstein

Despite a great number of changes in education, we still process children in school more than we educate them. Why?

The simplest answer, although this is not openly discussed today, is that school sees the ability of the child to be more or less limited by the genes they inherited, and it is upon its understanding of this that children are processed. Yet, what most do not realize is that this impression of an inherited intelligence is only one that evolved out of a serious political struggle in the 19th century.

Education clings to this reasoning because by doing so it can most economically fulfill its purpose, which is to produce a citizen who will take either a manager or a managed role in work and in society. While this design fitted the operational needs of the 19th and 20th centuries, it could bring serious troubles to us in this century, because it limits the real potential of the individual as they face a world dominated by artificial intelligence.

From the 1970s and as our understanding of the brain developed, we became increasingly aware of the effects of the environment on the intelligence of people. The media took this up and started talking about how IQ can be affected by certain food, causing the term IQ to became a household name as a substitute for the word intelligence. Yet, we make a great mistake when we refer to intelligence as IQ. They are not the same.

IQ, or rather the intelligence quotient, is only a belief that intelligence can be measured. It is only the name of a test. It gives no understanding of how intelligence can form or indeed what it is. So, when we use the term IQ we innocently enforce this reasoning that intelligence is determinable, that it is measurable, and that it has a limited quality within each individual according to the value they are thought to have inherited. This book will show you why this belief is wrong.

Indeed, over a thousand case studies have proven that if an individual's perspective of their environment can gain a deep enough change, then so will their level of intelligence. This ability to develop brings into question what we think the environment of intelligence is.

The environment of intelligence is far more complex and far, far more determining than it is thought to be. It follows from this that intelligence is not what we think it is, and certainly not what school thinks it is as it processes our children.

What we need to grasp from this, is that the planned use of the citizen in society is based on their performance in education, and that this performance is far more a factor of political and social planning than we believe it to be.

Through the many books I have written, which are said by experts in education around the world to be some of the best written about School, Society and Learning, I have tried to offer thoughts how we can all help the global child be better prepared for the A.I. world that will await them.

Brain Plasticity,
The Illusion of School,
Ben Learns to Get Smart,
The Illusion of Education,
Intelligence: The Great Lie,
Teach Better, Learn Better,
Five Ways for Better Grades,
Memoirs of a Happy Teacher,
For Parent For Teacher: Mediation,
What Every Parent and Teacher Should Know,
Are we Educating our children for a Working World
that will not want them ?
&
The Real Dangers of A.I. The Struggle of Man to Survive by Natural
or Artificial Intelligence - A New Role for the School.

Through the above books (and more have since been written), we have sought to raise our understanding of what intelligence is, how it develops and how, with this understanding, we can better educate all children in every country.

As our story unfolds in this book, we take references, accounts, and incidents from the social and educational frameworks of many lands without bias. Throughout the 20th century we could still describe the child in America as different from the child in England, or the child in India, but by the first decade of this 21st century we were already thinking of the global child.

Our story then, is not a story about one people of one nation. It is a story of all people, and the common troubles and dangers their children may come to face as this new century unfolds.

All we are about to discuss in this book will explain exactly why school fails today, and why our children fail to understand better the lessons that will determine the role they will later come to play in the global society. This is so because education still centres its operations about a 19th century understanding of intelligence, which never recognised the reality of brain plasticity. Our previous book *Intelligence: The Great Lie* explained why, and so why intelligence and the concept of the brain not being "plastic" underlay a great political purpose.

Let us move, then, to understand why and how the human brain is far, far more able to alter its construction, by the mind driving neurons into new networks of understandings, than our earlier scientists ever thought possible. After all, . . .

The intelligence of a person describes only their history,
not their potential.

Roy Andersen

Table of Contents

Brain Plasticity

How the Brain Learns through the Mind
to create
INTELLIGENCE

by

Roy Andersen

Introduction

When we think upon something, we tend to think of it as it appears and not so how it came to be. You may, for instance, look upon a tree and wonder at the beauty of its form, much less than wondering how it grew from a seed and struggled through many seasons to be as it now appears. This is what we do. We think in such general terms as things appear to us in the present.

By the same general reasoning, we think that parents come together to create their baby. The baby grows inside the mother, is born and lives its life. In its very early years, the baby is very dependent on its parents to survive in all manner. As the baby grows to become a toddler, then child and so adolescent, they need less and less support from adults. While they are a baby, we notice how cute and lovable they are. Once the infant begins to gain mobility and is beginning to learn to interact with the world, we notice their personality and then how they respond to information they are given. Once they enter the educational system, they begin to be compared to other children and so become more and more classified as the years pass by — based upon what is thought to be their intelligence.

In all this, we seldom stop to think how the human being actually gains any of their intelligence. We simply notice how they perform and accept their action for what it is. Very seldom do we stop to think of all the factors in their life that have caused them to develop the way we witness them. We much less stop to think how and when all these factors, which make them who they are, took place or why they did. Consider how we are little aware that the adoration we feel towards a new born actually comes from a gene coding, having the singular purpose to create a bonding process to ensure the survival of the infant.

However, should this bonding process break down, the development of the infant can be impaired. After all, a baby may not smile if deprived of love nor a toddler walk or talk until far beyond their normal age for doing this if they are badly treated by a parent.

This way of thinking to readily accept what we see, causes us to think of the baby as having arms and legs, a heart, lungs and a brain, which all work the way they do. The baby's brain works. It thinks and it learns, but then we hear the term Brain Plasticity and wonder what it means?

It means, we know, that the brain is adaptable to learn, but we have always known the brain can learn, so why have such a term?

The term Brain Plasticity actually arose late in the 19th century, when scientists discovered that the brain is made up of cells **'that learn'** to connect to each other. This may seem natural to us today, but at that time all public interest was on how intelligence came to be. The standing belief, then, and as we shall see still persists today, is that the individual's intelligence is greatly related to the intelligence of their family line. This reasoning caused intelligence to be seen as a relativity stable feature, coming from a stable and so a 'fixed' brain. The term 'plasticity' challenged this reasoning.

At that time, a whole new and busy industry called psychology was in motion. Largely because of the political drives behind their science, psychologists viewed the brain as an inborn feature and were only interested in how the brain of each responded to test questions so the individual could be routed to the best job for their intelligence. The construction of the brain was left to experts in medical science to investigate, who looked upon the brain as a lifeless anatomical feature. As a consequence of this, the term 'plasticity' little became realized to what it could mean.

It was only once our technology developed in the 1970s and we could 'look into the operation of the brain,' that this term resurfaced. As we came to monitor how parts of the brain related to environmental experiences and physically changed in its structure through this that the term brain plasticity began to become a household term. Yet, still today, few understand what this term really means.

The purpose of writing this book about brain plasticity was a natural consequence to my previous book, *Intelligence: The Great Lie.* In the writing of that book, I spent a number of decades researching over the past 200 years in our understanding of intelligence. Through this, we were able to reveal the extensive lies, fraud and misrepresentation of data at the highest levels of psychology, to convince civilization that intelligence is more or less determined by a family quality purely as a means of social stratification. Intelligence tests grew through this belief to open or close doors of opportunity for children according to their family line, as a means to maintain the status quo.

Through this manner, individuals were, as they still are but to a lesser extent, promoted or hindered from progressing in their society according to their family's social level, political interests, religion, ethnic background and, as we know too well, the color of their skin.

As we concluded that book, we saw how there is absolutely no evidence that the quality of genes that are inherited, limit the ability of the individual to develop their intelligence. It arose from this that it is not possible to measure intelligence and therefore that neither the concept of IQ nor that of the nature/nurture debate has any basis to exist.

It has long been believed that an act of intelligence is composed partly from an inherited quantity and partly through developed experiences, although no one has ever proven this relationship. However, we were able to explain in *Intelligence: The Great Lie,* how a misunderstanding arose in this belief of a two part ability, and that the actual role of the genes is merely to provide a design for this feature to exist and for it, then, to be decided wholly by environmental experiences.

On the face of it, this goes directly against tradition. However, if we see this for what it truly is, a political invention in a time of very great political crisis and, then, see how the genes we inherit for language, just as for emotion and so to know of something and how it moves, among a host of very many other human features and capabilities, which are not decided by the qualities of genetic inheritance, we may be more open in our thoughts.

It is to discuss what these life experiences are and how they develop the individual's intelligence through the environment, which is far, far more complex than we may have imagined, that I wrote this book to explain how and why the brain is 'plastic' in its construction and life long development. You can learn anything at any age, if the desire is there for it.

I may bring small insight into much of what we will discuss, if I now inform you that the brain is brought into a photo-design through a genetic plan, but then becomes constructed very much through environmental experiences. This is to say that the physical wiring of the brain changes according to the thoughts moving through it.

One form of these environmental experiences relate to the mind. So, by the behavioral and language experiences of the individual, each will perceive the meaning of information differently, to some lesser or greater degree, and through these experiences mentally bring the axons of neurons together to form circuits of understanding. While their mind is actively doing this, it is also affecting the production levels of various neurotransmitters to either hinder or accelerate the signals moving through these networks — according to their emotional state.

It is not, then, that the brain is fixed with all neurons in place, and works much the same as those of an individual's ancestors. It is rather that brain cells grow, axons spread through the information they receive, as coordinated by the mind, to join other brain cells or neurons. As neurons connect with each other to create circuits of memory and understanding, so the individual is able to recognise and determine the meaning and consider purposes to the information they focus upon. It is through this very individual processing that the cerebral cortex (the higher brain) in any family is totally, totally different and caused to be so through their very personal experiences.

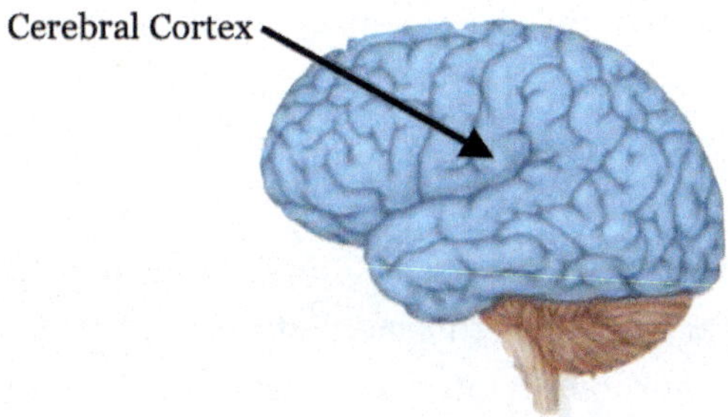

However, to many people the brain is still seen as 'an inherited' grey mass that just seems to work, so it is necessary to layout how we have been able to so far understand how it comes to be constructed through environmental forces. In time, we shall look into this through understanding the construction of the visual system, which is an essential part of the intelligence process.

It may be that gene codes pull in amino acids to build proteins to build the relevant neural cells, but as we shall find these cells require signal information from the environment to pull them into an operational visual system. Thus, it is the coding of the genes that allow the conditions of the environment, to determine the efficiency of the visual system in its creation. This is a very important point to note for later on, when we shall examine this construction in detail. However, many years later in life, the psychological profile of the individual can be brought about by environmental situations to deteriorate this visual system. We are far more a part of the 'living' environment than we generally think.

As we may begin to see, it can be confusing to understand what the term the environment means when we talk about the brain. When we use the word environment in this context, we refer to the food and liquid we digest that produces chemicals that move to the brain giving it energy and material for reconstruction.

We also refer to the mind's perspective of the world and so how information is recognised by language and how this information is selected by emotional sensitivity to be relayed to memory circuits in the brain, where it seeks to match related information to extend neural networks. We also refer to how emotional drives alter the production of neurotransmitters and how this accelerate or hinder the passage of signals through neurons. By all these factors of the environment, new brain cells can grow, just as existing brain cells extend their connections (their axons) to other brain cells, causing networks of understanding to be built-up.

The traditional view of the brain sees the mind to be consequence of it. However, if we move away from this Western based understanding, towards a more Eastern spiritual understanding, we see the mind as a consequence of the universe living and interacting with the brain and so the body as a whole. Once we do this, we can understand better how the mind subtly controls the body. We can, for instance, recognise how psychosomatic illness stems from mental perspectives of the environment and so how stress can be a killer!

Further in this book, we shall examine instances of abused children, who were found to have lesser number of nodes on the dendrites of their neurons, due to hormonal action caused by the stress they incurred, which hindered the action of their brain cells to process information. While great interest has been given to the effects of stress created by the mind's perspective of environmental issues, few understand how it is able to repair certain bodily functions and reverse illnesses through positive mind affirmations. As we shall see, it is the mind that drives physical changes in the brain to cause, what we now call, brain plasticity.

It is only by considering how the mind learns to interact with the environment that we may come to understand the ability of the brain and so of intelligence. When the mind does not "see" the environment, the ability of the brain to think decreases. This was clearly brought home when children were discovered in Romanian orphanages in the 1990s. Because they were raised with virtually no love or care, they were found to have almost zero intelligence. We shall discuss this later in our book.

As we move through the many pages ahead, we will examine work by scientists who have been able to prove the true plasticity of the brain in how it is actually formed and thereafter continues to function throughout the life of the individual — through the mind's interaction with the environment..

Therefore, imagine if you will that rather than thinking of the brain as a grey mass that simply works, that you instead think of it as a living, vibrant mass of neurons actively searching for new connections and being assisted or inhibited in their effort through changing levels of neurotransmitters, as the mind balances interests against insecurities.

To expand upon the meaning of Brain Plasticity, we devise here the term *The Brain Environment Complex* to emphasize the importance of how the environment is interrelated with the brain in its basic construction, operation and thereafter how that construction can be modified through environmental information. We shall examine many cases of this shortly. Yet, we also wanted this term to set a working principle that would explain how gene coding can have the purpose of enabling a feature to exist, without causing that feature to be necessarily limited or restricted to a normal variation in that code.

This is to say that when gene codes reproduce as new cells are made or when they mix at conception in the creation of a baby, they are known to shuffle or mix and even mutate. This "mixing" is reasoned to create a variation in the gene code. It is further reasoned that this variation in gene coding creates variations in qualities of intelligence, so that some are born smarter than others. However, there are very many features we have that are created by genes, and yet totally develop their ability only through environmental experience. The gene coding that enables us to have language is a good example of this.

After all, every human beings inherits the same value of genetic coding to have language. There is no variation in the gene coding that influences the development of language in any human being. This is exactly the same for emotion. Just as language, we develop our personal quality of emotion through the experiences of our life. After all, would you think any variation in the gene coding enabling us to have 'curiosity', would make some more curious than others? With the same reasoning, we all inherit the means to develop a personality and to construct a line of thinking, change ideas and thoughts freely, select goals and subgoals as situations change. All these may be totally altered through environmental experiences. The personality of a nasty bully, for example, could be transformed into a loving sincere personality through a defining experience.

None of these feature are limited in their actions by variations in the genes responsible for them. All these features can be completely moved from one extreme to the other through experiences. We also, and more simply, see this free ability in reading a book, writing a letter, completing a mathematical solution, have qualities to love, laugh, cry and hate.

In all our books, we follow this reasoning for the existence and development of intelligence in normal cases, and so not to be confused with, for example, instances of a chromosomal mutation that often creates Down Syndrome.

If we can understand this reasoning so far, it opens up great latitude for us in how we may alter the thinking, and so the physical construction of an individual's brain. In the most simplest sense, if you correct a person's spelling from descussing to discussing, you are actually changing the formation of neural circuits in their brain, which is a physical operation. So, they learn, but only because the brain is *plastic* enough to enable this to occur.

Further in this book, we will see how a whole region of a brain may be caused to change through its ability for *plasticity*. Yet, there are two criteria to be aware of here that must be understood.

First, the brain desires stability in its operations. It gains this by the mind seeking to understand information the way it has learnt to do so. Therefore, a person from one culture may have great difficulty to understand how the mind of the person from a different culture operates. Each thinks as they have learnt to do so. Incidentally, this is why people who come from a different culture to those who devise IQ questions, often score lower than those of that culture.

Second, any physical change of neural networks must first be proceeded by an emotional desire for this change to occur. Thus, if a student does not like their teacher or feels insecure in their class, their mind will try to resist understanding information that does not simply follow the understanding they have so far gained. This is why it is important for a teacher (or a parent) to first gain the emotional confidence of those they will to share their knowledge or understanding with. The saying "he never listens to me", really means "he" does not want to listen, because of some emotional friction.

Accordingly, in this book, we will try to understand how the mind comes to drive changes in the brain to manifest this *Brain Plasticity* by tracing the development of many features of the human being, from the embryo to after birth experiences and so through life. In doing, so we shall attempt to show how the mind is capable of rewiring not only the networks of the brain, but also of repairing aspects of the nervous system. The concept of brain plasticity is far more important than is commonly understood. It actually is intelligence.

Therefore, if we are to truly understand the concept of brain plasticity it is fitting and indeed necessary to understand why we think intelligence is generally an inborn and so a fixed feature of the brain. To begin to understand why we think it so, we need to go back in time to the political circumstances that brought this belief about and so all that followed from them.

Chapter One

As we discussed in "*Intelligence:The Great Lie*", the 19th century was in a continual state of virtual anarchy. The lower classes were increasingly using violence as they demanded better living conditions and more control in the running of their lives. To many people, this demand for equality meant the removal of the ruling class and so an end to the monarch state. Indeed, there were so many attempts on the lives of the ruling class during this time that it became known as the age of assassination. This, we may remember, was only half a century after the French revolution of 1789, and images of the nobility being guillotined were still all too fresh in the minds of many.

In 1848, a very large revolt to the French government came about over the right to vote. This revolutionary fervor spread like wildfire, and almost instantaneously every country in Europe experienced a violent rejection to the government by their people. Every country in Europe, save Great Britain at that time, burst out in revolution. The countries of

France, Belgium, Denmark, Holland, Germany, Poland, Austria, Hungary, Italy, all faced organized revolt by the people.

Fearful of being murdered, as the royal family had been in the French Revolution, which was still in living memory then, many of the European aristocracy fled to Great Britain for safety. By this time in history, Great Britain had weathered very many social storms and in having given her people better living conditions was least in danger of insurrection.

However, within a few short months, those of the establishment used military force to quash all sense of revolution on the continent. Public meetings were forbidden, and executions quick and merciless soon followed. In Paris, 3,000 workers were dragged from their homes and executed in the streets. As the aristocracy returned, a sense of normality and order was resumed. Yet, those in the establishment were ever weary of this social danger reemerging. The problem was, how could it be prevented from rising again?

The solution, it was realized, lay not in suppressing the people by force, because this would only incur resentment and kindle further outbreaks. It lay, as Sir Francis Galton, proposed, in the control of the minds of the people. Words and not swords, were the means to gain the hearts of the people.

Sir Francis Galton. Cut.Dar. S405b.92.1 Cambridge Univ. Library.

These 'words' came from Galton's book *Hereditary Genius*, which was published in 1869. Galton's basic reasoning did not address the problem head on, but did so in a quasi scientific way. Galton outlined in his book an understanding that all aspects of the individual were inherited through their family line. This is to say that as the child inherited the family nose or chin, so did they inherit the brain and so the mental capability of the family. This capability, he reasoned, could be measured by the social success of the family line.

Accordingly, a blacksmith would have a particular nose which he would pass to his son with the same mental capability to be a blacksmith, but not that to be a lawyer. Equally, the lawyer would have a certain chin, which he would pass to his son with the capability to be a lawyer, and serve society no good if he became a blacksmith. This evoked a saying which was to last right up to the 1960s, where children were told.....:

"not to think they are better than they are, and
to respect their elders in age and in society."

Galton argued from this idea of inheritance (which we now know is not valid) that in every population there will always be a small number who have the natural and proven ability to lead the rest. Here was the 'evidence' for royalty and the establishment behind them, that they were to be needed by the common people. So, it was argued that civilization would be seen to suffer and likely collapse, if people of lesser pedigree came to rule.

The great error that too many make in discussing Galton is that they see him as the father of intelligence testing. In one sense this is nearly true, for although he never actually found a way to measure intelligence, he did devise a sort of vague system by which the intelligence of family members could be said to be recognised through the work they did over generations. Thus, family members who were lawyers, were classed to be more intelligent than family members who were merchants. In turn, these were classed to be more intelligent than families of labourers.

Although today, we see intelligence testing to be about individuals, Galton was more interested in the intelligence of the family. The purpose of Galton's work was least to measure individual intelligence and far, far more to show how members of a family could be recognised to have a social level in the scheme of things. He used a particular graph (actually designed by an astronomer) to show how families of higher intelligence, decided by their social role in society, should govern other families.

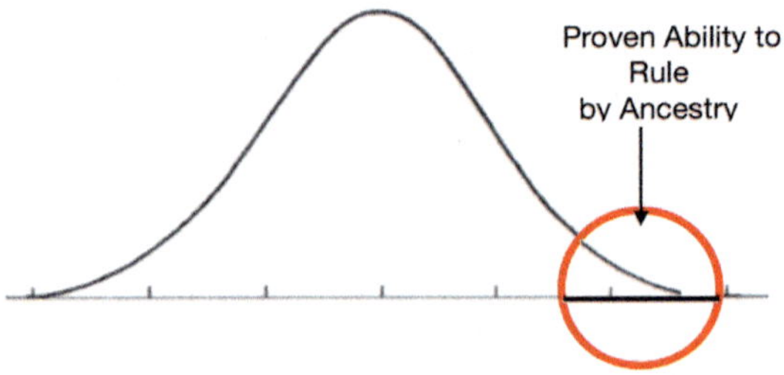

This graph, which we today call The Bell Curve, plays an important part in all our discussions of intelligence. Indeed, in Intelligence: The Great Lie, we saw how it is used to misrepresent what our impression of intelligence is.

Today, we may think this idea of categorizing family intelligence through the work they do is ludicrous, but this is because we have freedom of education and freedom of opportunity. Victorian England was markedly different and operated under a very strict class system.

Galton's aim was very simply to provide evidence that everyone should know their place in the workings of the society and respect those above them to maintain order. His purpose was to quash the rise of socialism, which saw to give all equal opportunity in life and remove the monarch state, which embodied this unfair structure by which the most lived and suffered within.

In time, Galton's real purpose became overshadowed by the rise in intelligence testing, which more subtly and more discreetly saw to obtain the same objective. This was the maintenance of the status quo, by 'proving' through tests that people of a lower social level or of an undesired ethnic or cultural background have such a low intelligence that they should be denied the opportunity to gain better jobs and by this rise within and so disturb the social operation of the society. The book called *"The Bell Curve"* was published in 1994 with exactly this intention.

This idea of creating a mindset to convince everyone to support the order of things was not actually Galtons. Thousands of years earlier, Socrates had been asked how the people could be kept in order. He replied that instead of using force, they would invent a myth that the gods created men of gold to rule, men of silver for guardians and men of iron and bronze to be farmers and craftsmen. Then, a fortune teller would be said to have foretold that if a man of iron or bronze ever came to rule, that the state would collapse.

As Galton based his reasoning upon this, so the establishment built the Science of Cognitive Psychology upon his reasoning. This new science spread rapidly throughout the world seeking to devise methods of measuring human intelligence, so that all people could be kept in their place. However, the problem was that no-one at that time knew what intelligence actually was. In fact, we still do not know what it is today. At least this is to say there is no common agreement to what intelligence is, as people differ in their assumptions of this.

Throughout the 19th century, various suggestions arose that sought to explain the skills or features that make up intelligence. Since intelligence is a social issue, many of these suggestions hinged upon moral concepts, including, for example, religious and criminal tendencies. As we entered the 20th century, and moves desired intelligence to be more definable so that people could be better matched to job tasks, these social attributes hindered any clear definition of what intelligence may be, and so what predictions could be made of an individual's worth.

Charles Spearman overcame this problem by discarding whatever might be thought to constitute intelligence, and saw it simply to be a singular function.

As he wrote in a 1904 paper, "intelligent behavior is generated by a single, unitary quality within the human mind."[1] To Spearman, and to all who were to follow in his wake (which is to say the rest of humanity), intelligence was to be a "black box." No-one was to think how this "black box" might work, or what may be inside it. It was just to be a factor that each individual inherits through their family line, and by the rule of natural variation was to provide different families with different qualities.

We may understand that Spearman looked at the 10, 20, or whatever suggestions that philosophers of his time had made suggesting what creates intelligence, and said it is only important that we have it.

Now, about this time in history, Johannsen in Denmark had discovered the importance of the environment in affecting the gene design. To bring Galton's idea of an inherited intelligence inline with this discovery, Spearman introduced the affect of the environment into intelligence. By doing this, he created the nature/nurture debate we shall return to shortly.

On this basis, Spearman termed Francis Galton's idea of an inherited intelligence, "the reproductive value." To account for how this inborn intelligence could adapt to the needs of the environment, he explained that it had an "eductive value" (or a way of sorting out confusion).

We can see here, by the way he introduces the effect of the environment, that Spearman saw it less to offer a process of development and more that of an inherited quality trying to make sense of opportunity.

In fact, Spearman's reproductive and eductive values were to be decisive in presenting intelligence as a singular and largely heritable feature. In turn, this provided it with a degree of stability that allowed it, in theory, to be measurable. By this means, Spearman brought Galton's theory of inheritance into the 20th century by explaining how it could be affected by the environment, and yet remain a highly predictable feature of the mind deriving from a very stable and naturally organized brain.

The old phrenological idea put forward by Dr. Gall in the late 18th century of the brain being divided into specific zones to serve specific features, gave support to Spearman's idea that intelligence is a singular and dominant feature within the brain. In fact, Spearman was so convinced of this, that he believed science would one day discover a separate section of the brain just responsible for intelligence. As we today have Broca's area for language, so Spearman believed that science would discover, perhaps, Spearman's area.

However, we now know that there is no part of the brain that has a specific area allocated to intelligence. Intelligence is merely a holistic process of innumerable features operating within the mind brain complex at any one moment to process information. Yet, it is important to know of this historical belief, because this underlies how school works today. Let us diverge for a moment.

In general, educationalists do not focus too deeply upon how the minds of their students have evaluated the information they grade them upon. They do not have much time to do this, but more importantly they were trained and live in a work environment that is in such a hurry to process students that there never has been a desire to see intelligence as anything other than being largely inborn, and so a singular feature. School, and so its teachers, work on the principle that the student gets the right answer or a variation of a wrong one through effort and their *natural* ability, which enables them to be graded and so processed. We saw in *"The Illusion of School"* and so other books we have written why this is so.

Feuerstein began to argue against this formal view of a child's intelligence from the 1950s, because he realized how their response could be broken down into definable and modifiable components. However and most regrettably, Feuerstein's efforts, which we discuss in *"For Parent For Teacher: Mediation -Crafting the ability of the child for school",* have largely remained outside public awareness.

In fact, it was not until Gardner published his "Frames of Mind" in 1983, that any disturbance was brought to Spearman's idea of intelligence as a singular operating feature. What struck Gardner was the thought that instead of having a singular intelligence, that we may have a number of them. Gardner suggests nine, which enable the individual to better tune themselves to the specific needs of their environment.

These, as Gardner sees, are:

Linguistic Intelligence: the capacity to use language to understand others and express feelings. Think here of a lawyer, or a writer.

Logical/Mathematical Intelligence: the capacity to understand the underlying principles to manipulate numbers and quantities.

Musical or Rhythmic Intelligence: the capacity to hear and recognize sound patterns.

Kinesthetic Intelligence: the way the parts of the body (fingers etc.) are used to solve a problem or express feelings. Think here of a dancer, or an actor.

Spatial Intelligence: the ability to hold the spatial world internally in the mind. Think of a chess player.

Naturalist Intelligence: the ability to discriminate between inanimate and animate objects, and then plants and animals, etc.

Intrapersonal Intelligence: an understanding of yourself. To know who you are, and how you relate to the world as you see it.

Interpersonal Intelligence: the ability to be sensitive to the feelings and needs of others, and finally,

Existential Intelligence: the ability to pose and ponder questions about life, death, and final goals.

What is strikingly obvious, as we read through these intelligences, is how the opportunity for many of them to develop is not seen to be limited by a genetic factor. They appear to be socially constructed upon values Gardner has determined. In other words, they suggest the mind is actually fluid, but is departmentalized into aspects of intelligence by the definitions of the environment we create. Gardner settled on nine intelligences, but anyone could think of more if they wished to breakdown the environment even further.

Yet, what is missed when anyone thinks to categorise the environment of intelligence, is that in real terms it cannot be defined, because it is far too complex and far too overlapping, as the emotions of each individual struggle to find their own values through their shifting impressions of it.

While we shall come back to this idea of multiple intelligences later, we should return to the model of a singular intelligence Spearman devised, from Galton's idea. The following illustration shows these two parts.

The Spearman Model of Intelligence

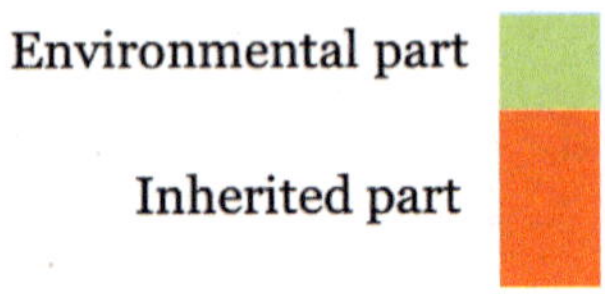

However, it is very important to know that this inherited part has never been proven to exist, because it is impossible to measure human intelligence. All take it to exist, because all have been raised on this mindset that was created for them through Galton's work. Accordingly, psychologists have been arguing for over 120 years as to how much affect this inherited part has on the ability of the individual to develop through the environment. Because of the implications and directions that can be made through the worth of these two parts, they have very political uses.

When right wing psychologists try to prove the inherited part is more determining, excuse is made for more government funds to be sent to schools in richer (right wing) areas. The argument is made that children here are argued to have a higher natural ability, which enables them to make the most out of the opportunities this greater funding will give them. Let us say right wing psychologists try to prove a ratio of 80:20 for inheritance.

On the other hand, left wing psychologists try to prove the environmental part is more determining. This gives excuse for more money to be sent to children in poorer (left wing) areas, since it is said these children need more environmental experience to better develop their intelligence. Let us say they try to prove a ratio of 20:80 for the environment.

In reading this, we should not be naive to think this political play would not happen. Cyril Burt (for instance), as we discuss in *Intelligence: The Great Lie,* was the main psychologist directing government policies in British education for nearly three quarters of a century. His influences spread right throughout the British commonwealth of that time, Canada, South Africa, India, Australia, etc. After his death, it was discovered that Burt had deliberately falsified intelligence test results to cause funding to be diverted away from poorer areas to richer areas through his political interests.[2] Murray and Herrnstein did much the same thing with their publication of *The Bell Curve* in 1994, seeking to divert funding away from Hispanic and African American areas in America. The data they used was also found to be falsified.[3]

However, since this ratio has never been proven and yet all have been caused to think that an inherited quality must play some role in the intelligence of a human being, most psychologists opt for a 50:50 ratio. For this reasoning, the concept of intelligence, as seen through intelligence testings, has been used purely as a political mechanism.

As we can see, the belief that genes vary to create families of different intelligences has long been used by psychologists to determine the use people can be to their society. By their use of IQ tests, psychologists have classified people into levels of intelligence according to their social, cultural and ethnic backgrounds.

Yet, as we saw in *Intelligence: The Great Lie,* and despite strenuous efforts spread over 140 years to determine how variations in D.N.A effect an individual's intelligence, no concrete evidence is available. There certainly is in cases of dysfunctional human beings, such as Down Syndrome, but these variations are not of the norm and are outside the discussions of this book; even though their existence has encouraged the belief that the intelligence of all human beings is so affected by variations in gene quality.

In turn, this belief led to the development of intelligence tests seeking to prove how variations in D.N.A genes affect the individual, but as we have already explained (and do so in depth in the afore mentioned book), it is impossible to measure human intelligence. In a simple sense, this is because the environment is far too expansive to be categorised as psychologists attempt to classify it.

Yet, more significantly IQ test questions do not take into account factors of emotion. In the test, you know or you don't know the answer. There is no consideration as to why the answer is not known. This takes us back, as we discuss in *Intelligence,* to how Terman transformed Binéts one-to-one verbal evaluation to a test paper with boxes to tick so that thousands could have their IQ evaluated in a matter of minutes. However, by ignoring the role of emotion, as psychologists do in these questions (because it does not give the stability their calculations require), they actually fail to acknowledge what it is they are trying to measure. After all, every single act of intelligence is seated in a factor of emotion and so is an integral part of it, as we shall shortly explain.

However, since intelligence tests began to be used to try to evaluate D.N.A genes, and so have created a universal mindset in the validity of this testing, we have more recently discovered the presence of epigenes. Because of the traditional thinking that grew up around the concept of an inherited intelligence, there is a great deal of confusion between genes that form the D.N.A and what epigenes are and the affect they have.

Briefly, we may say that D.N.A. genes are the hereditary instructions for creating the organism, which in our case is the human being. In contrast to this, epigenes are experiences an individual has gained that may or may not entwine themselves to their D.N.A coding, and by this attachment be passed on in procreation.

Let us discuss D.N.A. genes first. These are the genetic instructions that use chemicals from the environment to build cells and so the features of the organism. Thus, we have gene designs for two legs, a heart, two eyes etc. Without this gene coding, we could not have these features. However, having the coding does not make the feature exist. In order to exist, the coding for a feature needs to be fed by the environment.

In the simplest sense, you may think of a seed that contains all the information for a plant to grow. However, if this seed does not receive elements of the environment, such as moisture, warmth, nutrients and later light from the sun, it will never be anything other than a seed. Consequently, different qualities of moisture, warmth, nutrients and degrees of light will cause two identical seeds to produce two very different variations of the plant. In a generalised sense, the same is so with human beings. Let us begin to see how the environment can affect our basic gene designs.

Thus, we have a bone structure, which supports our frame. Such a structure is very dependent upon the qualities of "nutrients" it receives. For instance, after the Second World War, a large number of Japanese people settled in Canada with a diet based on rice. Their grandchildren grew to be twice as tall, because they were raised on a totally different diet. Thus, we see how the inherited gene design for a people, that held them to a certain height for many generations, was changed by the environment in the form of chemicals that fed this design. However, the environment does not just build a gene design, it can totally change the design if it is extreme enough.

In 1957, a drug was administered to pregnant women to alleviate morning sickness. Unfortunately, the chemicals in the drug altered the normal chemicals in the cells of the foetus, causing Thalidomide children to be born with severely deformed limbs. Therefore, even though the gene design was for children to be born with two arms, the chemical in the drug prevented the gene design from correctly developing the arms. Consequently, the arms of these children were often very short or absent, which caused fingers to sprout from the shoulders.[4] We see here an example of how normal gene coding for arms, hands and fingers was completely changed out of recognition by the environment. This leads us to realise how a fixed gene design can be changed totally by the environment, and opens us up to an understanding that some genes may have evolved to allow the environment to decide the efficiency of their feature. After all, from a survival point of view this would seem a necessary evolutionary step.

Thus, we need to be aware that our gene codes have evolved to have different relationships with the environment. Some gene codes naturally vary in their coding through various shuffling stages. This creates natural genetic variations that cause each individual to be unique in their own design. Once these genes experience the environment, so the differences are further accentuated. Accordingly, what we consume (when we eat, drink 'smoke, drink alcohol or take drugs') and move, affects our bodily design.

However, we have gene codes that are inherited equally by all human beings, because genetic shuffling does not affect the quality of their design. For example, our abilities to know language, to dream, to cry, to hate and many more features come from gene designs, which have evolved to allow the environment to completely construct their form. Thus, our ability to read, to speak, to evaluate, to reason and so to think, which we may broadly encompass to be our ability for intelligence, derive from such gene coding.

This is to say that in normal cases, our ability for intelligence is not decided by D.N.A. genetic variation. This goes completely against our traditional understanding of intelligence. However, if we consider how this understanding arose to serve political purposes and not through scientific research, which has ever since tried to prove this political design to be true and has not done so, we may see that, in normal cases, babies are born with equal ability to develop their intelligence. Could it, then, really be true that we are born equal?

Nancy Bayley was able to answer this question, when she and her team made extensive studies on 50,000 infants over 50 years, and found that:

1. Before infants reached 14 months of age, no differences could be found in their intelligence that could be related to the educational or ethnic background of their parents. At this age (*excluding natural defects*) the mental capability of an infant was found to be equal to all others.[5]

2. Black babies performed no better and no worse than white babies in tests of mental ability. They were equal.[6]

3. However, beyond this age of 14 months, evidence began to emerge in how the social and ethnic character the infant was raised in, did condition the ways they interpreted and interacted with the world about them.[7]

4. Thus, of incredible significance to us, Bayley was able to prove that before the first two years of life, none of the factors that may be said to constitute intelligence showed any indication of stability and so genetic limitation.[8]

5. Indeed, virtually all types of other intelligence tests conducted on slightly older children, found the same degree of unreliability in a child's potential for intelligence. Whatever predictions were made upon children of two, three, four, or five years of age, they were all later found to be highly mutable.[9]

So, we have the D.N.A coding that enables us to be human in structure and a part of which allows us to learn to be individually human in our behaviour and intelligence by our life experiences through the environment. If these environmental experiences are deceive enough, they can cause us to completely alter our understanding of life, the part we play in it and so ourselves. This brings us to the concept of epigenes.

Epigenes are not genes in the sense with think of D.N.A. They are experiences the individual has that may or may not transcribe into a chemical substance, which may thereafter attach itself to their D.N.A structure. If epigenes do attach to the D.N.A, they may or may not be passed in procreation to the offspring. By the manner of how genes are selected at conception, an epigene may be attached to a recessive gene and never be available to them, by which it may or may not be passed on to future generations. However, if the epigene is attached to a gene that become dominant, it will be available to the individual through the experiences they engage.. We must remember here that an epigene is not an ability. It is an experience (genetically passed to the offspring) that allows them to better engage a particular environmental experience, depending on their personal emotional state at this time of each experience.

The important difference between inherited D.N.A. genes and inherited epigenes is that the D.N.A. genes have evolved through the historical mixing of family codes, while epigenes come and go through the experiences of individuals. Indeed, what is little appreciated in discussions with epigenes is that their values are not constant. As one epigene is created, so another can be created of opposite value, cancelling out or diminishing the effect. By the same means, other epigenes could be created to increase the effect. None of this can be known in the sibling. However, because of the mindset that has been created by psychology, we too readily believe we witness a natural ability when it is not this. What is witnessed may only be a developed ability that was fashioned through high environmental qualities.

In our book *For Parent For Teacher Mediation: Crafting the Ability of the Child for School,* we introduce and explain the process of imprinting. This is an afterbirth process, where the parent/guardian (by their emotional sensitivity to their child), passes an understanding to them that so assists in their development, but is mistakenly thought to have come through genetic inheritance. Imprinting, as I have discovered, explains how a factor of social inheritance can appear to be a genetic one when it is not.

We must always remember, which the idea of an inherited intelligence nullified, that each individual evaluates the meaning of the environment according to their emotional state. Thus, how each individual engages and takes meaning from every minute experience, of the trillions and trillions they encounter, is based totally on their emotional feeling at the time of each. This is so because their emotional state controls the level of sensitivity by which they evaluate the experience, either vaguely noting it or minutely inspecting it, which in turn decides how this is related to previous experiences in their memories, and so what conclusions and meanings they suggest or imagine from this.

Therefore, it is important to distinguish the difference between an inherited ability and an inherited experience. Epigenes are not an ability. They are an acquired experience of a previous person, which if passed on to the offspring, may endow them not with an ability but with an experience to better adjust themselves to an understanding of the environment. However and as we have just mentioned, their emotional state, when they engage an environmental experience, could cause them to totally negate the value of this epigene.

The problem to all this is that the environment is so complex and so over determining, that it may completely explain the presence of the ability, without epigenes being involved. This is so because everything is decided by the emotion of the individual, as they increase or decrease the level of their sensitivity as they engage the trillions and trillions of minute experiences in their life.

This difference between D.N.A genes and epigenes is vital to understand when psychologists try to state that one family line has better genes than another family line and therefore should be given greater opportunity to make use of their greater potential. This is the thinking that Galton fashioned as he and the establishment created the science of psychology to measure the abilities of individuals (as representatives of their family line) to determine the use they could be the society. All of which, we greatly explored and discussed in *Intelligence: The Great Lie.*

Thus, while the argument for inherited D.N.A. genes was used (quite wrongly) to ascertain the work, social and so political value of a family line, epigenes transcend this boundary and show the importance of education. After all, if an uneducated worker's son may gain a good education, they may go to university and develop epigenes of higher reasoning that could better prepare the family line they will create. However, we must always remember that all interaction with the environment is valued by the individual through their emotional state at the time of every single interaction, because this decides the sensitivity by which the experience is valued.

So, while D.N.A. may have evolved to allow the environment to totally decide factors of behaviour and intelligence, epigenes may convey influences of these through inheritance. However, these are so prone to constant change, as epigenes mix and overlap, that it is not possible to know if the effect we witness in another is created by epigenetic inheritance or solely factors of the environment, as we have suggested with imprinting.

Therefore, and as we found in Intelligence: The Great Lie, since the genes for intelligence cannot be known in the individual and since it is impossible to measure intelligence, we must move away from the political use and purpose of intelligence tests and so SAT scores, which are basically the same, to think of the intelligence of the individual as a description of their past experiences and move to help them psychologically adjust their mindset to develop the potential for interaction that we all hold equally, but show differences by out past experiences, egos and confidences. The purpose of life is to learn. We now move to show how the environment, in its many forms, drives the brain to be plastic and so totally adjustable to meet the experiences of life.

If we now return to Spearman's model of intelligence, we may see how it imposes the belief that when an individual falls below others or struggles too much in their task, that their lesser ability can be said to be caused by some factor they inherited. Yet, in Spearman's view, which became the traditional model for psychology globally, there is in this no real consideration as to how intelligence develops after birth, and so what the child was actually born with to enable this development.

In fact, Spearman made a fundamental mistake in his assumption of the existence of his famous 'g' factor. As a disciple of Galton, he noticed how each child in a school class he visited had gained similar grades in all their subjects. Thus, a child who gained A+ in Maths, was found to have also gained A+ in History and Chemistry. The same being so with a child who scored B or C. Spearman followed Galton's reasoning that ability is essentially inherited and saw in these school children evidence of the inherited ability he was seeking to prove, which he did by terming this the g factor of intelligence.

However, as we explain in *All that is Wrong with School* and other books we have written, explanation for a student gaining similar grades in all their subjects has nothing to do with intelligence. School ability is only based on a student focusing (i.e. not being distracted as most are) upon a rule to be learnt, to be practiced and to be proficient with. All grades in all the subjects are reliant upon this. To which, we must always remember that ability is school is much a projection of competency with language, which is one of our features that is free from genetic variation.

We may so explain here that school works through two languages. These are mathematics and the national language used for communication in the school, be this English or French etc. Competence with these languages and so competence in school learning is based on rules. So, a student who has learnt all the rules of the two languages to explain their thoughts competently and were driven to learn the relevant facts of all the subjects will score highly in all of them.

Conversely, a student who missed the learning of some of these rules of the languages, because they were distracted or bored or did not put the effort into being competent with them, and was only generally interested to learn the facts of each subject, will score lower in all of the subjects. Thus, their general competency is related to their quality of language, which runs through all the subjects. It is this factor that generally determines the competency in each subject and so all subjects as a whole. However, if a student has good language but is generally not interested in all but one subject, they may put less effort into remembering facts of these subjects and score low in them. Yet, in the one subject they love, they would be very interested in all about it and score very high here.

A student's ability through all their subjects, then, has nothing to do with Spearman's creation of the 'g' factor, and everything to do with being sensitive to what is happening in their lessons. It is this sensitivity of the mind, through the strategies the individual has acquired and developed, that drive the ability of the neural networks in their brain to change in their effectiveness. In other words, this is brain plasticity!

1.0 Beginning to understand the core of brain plasticity

If we move away from Spearman's model of the brain as having a singular feature of intelligence, which works as any organ does (a kidney for example), we are placed into the reality of seeing it as a composition of numerous features. It is very important for later that we realize now that these features overlap and that they all develop through a factor of emotion. In other words, how secure the individual feels through the presence of others, will enable them to develop this holistic feature we call intelligence.

Let's consider a very simple but a very important example of the relationship of emotion to the development of intelligence. It has long been reasoned, according to the Gestalt Law of Pragnanz, that once the visual system in the brain has formed, that a child will look upon a circle or a square that is 'almost' complete and see it as complete.

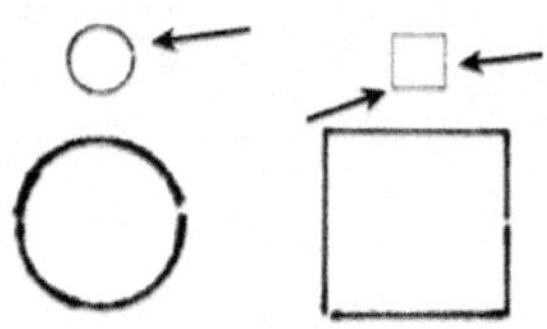

This is a natural ability we are all supposed to have. However, it has been realized that some children who are thought to have a low intelligence do not see the form as complete. They see it for what it actually is, incomplete. Yet, if such children are given emotional love and security their ability for intelligence develops, and at the same time they come to see the broken form as complete. In other words, it was a lack of emotional security that affected both their level of intelligence and their ability to perceive information.

When we think of emotion, we think of feelings such as love and hate, but emotional sensitivity is a fundamental aspect of every act of intelligence. When a child is calm, trusting and fascinated, they are very sensitive and so very accurate in the ways in which they interrogate and process information. On the other hand, when they are distracted by some worry, be this a domestic concern or being threatened in school, their quality of sensitivity is less and so they perform lower.

Remember here that a quality of intelligence evolves through its own history, as information and the way it is understood is cumulative. Therefore, the way information is emotionally evaluated, at the time when it is interrogated and processed, will significantly determine the way it can be associated to at a later stage.

To try to understand what this means, let us move away from the perspective we have of intelligence and behavior as separate functions of the mind. Instead, let us view these simply as interactive strategies the mind uses, as it makes interface and sense of the environment.

By discussing emotion in this way, we recognize that there is a link between behavior and emotion, and also between intelligence and emotion. We have long thought of emotion as only relating to feelings, but emotion works on different levels, as it provides control to intelligence, and to behavior through what we may think of as the intelligence-emotion-behavioral link.

This link is one we do not readily recognize, because intelligence and behavior are perceived as discrete functions served by different sciences. Behavior is placed under the jurisdiction of medicine, psychiatry, psychoanalysis, and clinical psychology. Intelligence is the sole property of psychology served by cognitive psychologists who ignore emotion, when it brings instability into the calculations they need to be stable.

This is not to say there is a direct relationship between the way a person behaves and the intelligence they display. It is, instead, to understand how the emotional security or insecurity of their personality, and the effects of the personality of others upon them, do underlie the strategies they design and the effectiveness of those strategies to operate in acts of intelligence.

In our normal day-to-day activity, we are aware that behavior and intelligence see their worlds differently and respond differently. However, when the behavioral perspective of our world is conditioned to be extremely low, as the effects of stress, anxiety, or depression take hold, we find examples where the relationship between behavior and intelligence is more readily recognizable.

Wolfensberger spent many decades researching into the "mental wounds" that produced inhibiting effects of stress and anxiety on the functioning of intelligence. He saw how the intelligence of a child could be dramatically transformed once they were liberated from the fears that haunted them.[10/11] Goldfarb more precisely measured this relationship between behavior and intelligence, when he demonstrated how institutionalized children performed poorly in IQ tests against those housed in foster homes.

In their normal development, children show us this relationship between emotion and behavior very noticeably. We are, however, less aware of the relationship between emotion and intelligence because it exists on a different level to that which we observe with behavior. With behavior, emotion demands that we notice it as it expresses feelings of love, hope, fear, and anger to purposely seek a reaction. With intelligence, emotion quietly controls the sensitivity of how information is evaluated and what use may be decided for it.

The difficulty with not realizing the effect of the relationship between behavior and intelligence is often because we do not recognize there is one. We have been directed by our sciences to see these features as totally unconnected. When we make easy evaluation of a person's response to an intellectual situation, we are totally ignorant of the long and secret history of their personal problems. Yet, these problems underlie the sensitivity by which they made, and so make interactions with information. Very many, many students I meet, and I refer here to adults, can trace their problems in school and so the grades they obtained and the level of intelligence thought of them to personality problems with other children, and in particular being bullied.

By understanding how intelligence and behavior are linked through emotion, we can better understand why intelligence is not this singular feature we have come to think of it as. In fact, by this understanding it is easier to realize that the word "intelligence" is only a word that describes how the mind and a number of components of the brain work together. We may better understand from this how the mind 'pulls' the brain into operation, as it causes neurons and axons to move freely, and by this construction gives physical shape to the cerebral cortex. This is the part of the brain that does the most thinking.

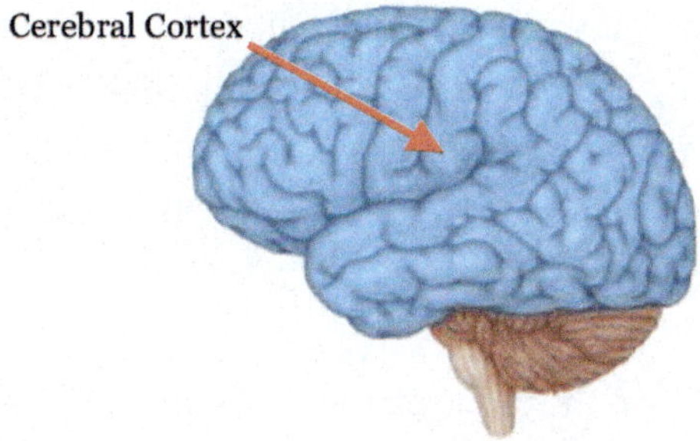

It is very significant to realise, as we have mentioned, that the cerebral cortex in each member of the same family will be totally unique. Each cerebral cortex of family members will be different in shape and so in functioning, since it was brought into construction through their very own personal experiences.

Let us move from this to understand more of how our higher brain forms and gains the ability to operate through the mind's interaction with the environment.

1.1 Beginning to understand the Genetic Factor of Intelligence.

By the way we have been caused to think of intelligence as a singular feature of the brain, and so as a singularly inherited feature, we have come to reason through our knowledge of genetics that quality in inheritance is a factor of genetic diversity.

After all, Mendel's most important Law of Segregation set the basis for our discovery of the process of meiosis and so the understanding that as cells divide they create diversity. It is through this knowledge that we can explain why people have irises of different color (blue eyes, green eyes, grey eyes, etc) and different facial features.

Accordingly, from our discussions in *"Intelligence: The Great Lie,"* we realized that the existence of a genotype (or complete gene instruction for a life form) can only be realized through its presence in the environment. It is easy to understand from this that a particular flower exists because there is a genotype for it, which in being different to the genotype of another flower caused it to be different plant. This is genetic diversity.

However, when we start thinking of the human mind and so features such as compassion, belief, curiosity, and the ability to reason and most significantly language and emotion, which develop in the individual purely and only through environmental experiences, the purpose of the gene coding for these becomes very confused.

In other words, we are caused to realise that every single human being is born without genetic diversity in these features. Yet, without a gene coding for them, we would not have them.

There are, surprisingly to say, many instances where genetic variation has no relevance in the outcome that we witness. This is to say that we are caused to realize that certain gene codes have evolved (let us say through natural selection) to allow the environment to decide how the purpose of their feature will develop. This, as we have just demonstrated, is so with our ability for compassion. Indeed, we shall come to see that many of the physical components of intelligence, such as the visual system to recognize what information is, is brought into construction and given value through an environmental based development.

In later chapters, but more so in our following book *"For Parent For Teacher: Mediation,"* we explain how and why the feature of language can be understood to be the key to understanding what intelligence is. It is very important to realize from this that the feature of language is inherited by every single member of our species without any genetic variation that affects its development. In a sense, we all inherit exactly the same genotype for this feature, and yet we all develop to show incredible diversity in our use of it!

Consider from this that while we inherit the genetic instruction to perceive movement, any genetic variation of this instruction will not weaken or strengthen this ability. This ability to perceive movement is achieved purely through experience. Once we realize our ability to perceive movement is another fundamental part of the intelligence process, because without this we would not notice change and so be unable to know of and compare actions, then we can consider the significance of other features of the intelligence process that are similarly constructed.

Our ability to discard one thinking strategy in favor of an entirely different one, in order to understand the same situation but in a totally different way, is therefore, not decided by the quality of gene coding. Genetic variation makes no difference to this feature. Equally, our ability to freely change our belief at will and so to reason in a different way, is not decided by genetic values. Such is the same for our feelings to laugh, to cry, and, as we shall come to discover, the differences of normally functioning children to think cannot be proven to lie in a quality they inherited.

In fact, as we mentioned earlier, Nancy Bayley proved through extensive tests on the early intelligence of 50,000 babies over a 50 year period, that there is no discernible difference in their intelligences before they are 14 months old.

- From birth to 14 months of age, there is no noticeable genetic differences in the intelligences of babies.

The differences in their intelligences only became apparent once they were old enough to relate to the experiences of those who raised them.

Yet, it was also found that whatever predictions were made on the intelligences of children of four or six, these were found to be totally inaccurate by the time they left school.[12] We shall encounter Bayley's work later in this book.

Accordingly, the insights, relationships, memory strategies, and processing speeds that are used by an individual when they think, can all be shown to be developmental, regardless of their social, cultural or ethnic background. These all rely on two simple factors -- these are language and emotional sensitivity; either of which can create such diversity that each on their own can explain the whole range of intelligence differences that Galton and Spearman saw in a society — without any genetic differences!

We can readily witness this in a foreign language class. All students in such a language class will vary in their competence, but none of their performances can be related to an inborn quality. Mathematics, of course, is also a process of language.

Language is decided purely through experience, and while emotion contains many aspects such as personality, at this moment we may regard a sensitivity with this to be a developmental feature that is indiscriminately inherited. In other words, we develop through our life experiences to be sensitive with information. As emotion brings interest and stability into the child's interaction with information, it is language that brings relevance to this. It is only language that allows one to share their mind with that of others, and so brings both question and gains understanding.

As earlier mentioned, we saw with children who were discovered in Romanian orphanages in the 1990s, how they had almost zero intelligence. These children had no form of genetic disorder and came from genetically normal parents, but they were completely unable to respond either behaviorally or intellectually when they were discovered. Their condition was caused purely and simply because they had been severely deprived of language skills and emotional feedback. There simply was not enough adult supervision for the huge mass of children housed in these underfunded and ill-managed institutions. Yet, once intervention programs were brought about providing these children with love, language, and stimulation, they were displaying normal and above normal intelligence within one year.[13]

Therefore, when we observe how a child speaks or writes their understanding, we have in fact only witnessed the operation of a number of components. It will be significant to grasp here an understanding that each individual will prefer these components in different orders, and develop each to a different level of sensitivity. This, after all, is the meaning of learning, and our genotypes enable us individually to decide how we shall use them. So, it is not correct to think of Learning Styles in education as caused by genetic variations. Each individual gains a preference in how to interact with the environment through the experiences they have had.

While there are many levels to this, both biologically and psychologically, we can understand this in principle by how one individual may prefer to initially recognize information by color, another by outline form, a third by sound, and a fourth by the vibrations they sense. As each begins to process information, each will go about it according to the ways they have acquired and feel most comfortable to do. We will see this in a later account of a man who had been born blind, and lived so for 50 years until he obtained sight following an operation. When he did so, he only ever used vision as a backup process, and preferred to detect and make sense of the world through the senses he had developed security with.

Therefore, we process information as we feel inclined. There is no pre-set order we must follow as we make an act of intelligence. Understanding this will help us to understand why no two individuals recognize or process information the same way, even though intelligence tests rely upon the belief that they do.

Consider what is really behind a child writing their answer or giving the response to a question which their intelligence will be evaluated on. In contrast to Spearman's model of some part inherited and some part developed, try to see an act of intelligence for what it really is, as the child's brain is constructed through experiences unique to them, ...

- by the food based chemicals they consumed that built their brain,
- through the ways the cells of their brain became constructed physically by the visual and audio waves directed to them, as its sensors observed objects and the interactions these made,
- by how their mind imposed levels of sensitivity to these observations, and the processes it engaged to make sense of them,
- while their personality struggled to control distractions caused by what it thinks others think of them,

.... as they create the mark others will judge them by.

To explain how and why we are able to process information differently and thus demonstrate diversity with this, we will consider later in our account the suggestion that the child inherits particular schemas to be aware of and to learn how to interact with the environment.

1.2 Beginning to understand the role of schemas.

- We will begin to see in this section, how schemas develop as skills through language and emotional experiences.

- As we do this, we will come to view intelligence through the relationship of the brain and the environment evolving through an inquiring and querying mind.

- In turn, we will understand that the mind develops security in its interactions through the inheritance of a bonding process.

We inherit a certain gene coding that causes us to develop a bonding process with others. In our early childhood this ties us to our parents or guardian for our safe development. When this process is impaired by a parent, the infant may not talk, be retarded in their movement, and may show no emotion. Later, we will try to explain this bonding through the term of imprinting, and how it can be applied in any later relationship.

In early school it bonds the child to their teacher to facilitate the act of learning. When it is fostered in the later school child by the parent and the teacher working together, that child has the potential to learn anything. Yet, although this process is very little recognized, it plays an integral part in the intelligence process, because it explains exactly why intelligence is reliant upon language, and why language is reliant upon emotional sensitivity.

It is by our failing to understand or to recognize the importance of all we have discussed so far, that lies our error in misunderstanding what intelligence is. Intelligence is not a one thing that just works the way the child is born, as we so often think when we use or hear the phrase: “We are not all born the same.” This far too simple wording hides a tremendous amount of mis-understanding and, as we shall see, ignorance. This will become clearer, once we begin to discover how the fetus develops their intelligence.

When we think about a child's intelligence, and so how well they compare with other children, we fall into the trap of judging them by what we assume they were born with. As we discovered in our two previous books, we have been raised since childhood and conditioned by our social machines to think like this. However, if we can stop comparing children to each other, and instead compare them to the life they have evolved through to this moment in time, then and only then may we begin to understand who they are, and so why they see the world of information the way they do.

As we shall discuss in *"For Parent For Teacher: Mediation"* and more especially in *"All that is Wrong with School"* the different grades that children earn, and so our impression of their intelligences, too often comes down to different yet simple strategies they have developed, as one lesson built upon another. While one child has developed to check each line of a math sum and another has not, while one thinks of how to structure their essay and another drifts through what they hope the teacher wants of them, are not factors they were born with. Yet, these small and many different strategies do make the differences in the grades they obtain, which we see as a reflection of what they were born with.

The greater point here is that when we fall into this trap, we condition our ability to develop their ability. The instant we think of their ability as inherited, that instant we lose the spark of inspiration by which we could offer them new strategies to see things differently, and so infuse within them the adventure of different possibilities.

Without this quality of guidance, they continue to see the world as they always have done, and so continue to conform to our impression of them. May we always remember that the "word" I.Q. is not intelligence.

It is only one idea that intelligence can be measured, but the more we talk about food affecting IQ and how social conditions affect IQ, then the more we lose all sight of what intelligence really, really is.

To bring balance to this I have suggested a new way of looking at intelligence. This "Andersen Model of Intelligence," if it may be so called, focuses upon the process of *"The Brain Environment Complex"* we earlier outlined, rather than that of Spearman's and more so Galton's model of inherited intelligence.

In Andersen's model each individual is seen as developing different skills in a multitude of components over time. Through their early years of life, they develop behavioral skills through those who influence them. As their emotional perspective of the world takes shape, they devise and acquire sensitivity in the handling of intellectual tasks. We see this in the quality by which they select, process and display their understanding of information.

Yet, the proficiency the child gains in this, is greatly dependent upon how their fragile mind is able to navigate its way through the behavioral attitudes of others. It is for this very reason that we explain why the development of the individual's intelligence is not detached from their behavioral experiences. Indeed, we make a great mistake if we think childhood is simply a matter of growing up and learning.

From a very early age, children are placed with other children in kindergartens and primary schools, both of which are emotional minefields. So, when we look at the performance ability (or intelligence) of the older child, what we do not see is the real relevance of how they socially and intellectually evolved to that point in time. The meaning here is that the state of the child's heart reflects the operation of their mind at any stage of their development and so life. If they feel insecure or hurt, as most children do, the techniques they develop to identify, analyse, and process information will reflect their level of personal insecurity and the quality of guidance they were given.

As we may see, once we try to understand how one individual thinks, and therefore what their and so human intelligence is, we immediately enter a matrix of incredibly complex situations. We cannot think of the simple and straightforward relationship between the genotype (the gene design) and the phenotype (how the environment affects the gene design) of a plant, and even suggest there are parallels with this to how human intelligence may be understood. Yet, this is precisely what Spearman's model does.

After all, the phenotype of a plant will change by the more or less water it gets, but the answer the child gives (their phenotype) will change by the more or less they can understand the way information is presented to them, and by their emotional feelings to want to engage this situation. This, of course, is heavily dependent on how well they understood, and desired to engage all that went before this moment. All of these are dependent upon language, first to be able to relate to information and then to satisfy needs and desires.

Therefore, if the child is happy and fascinated, they will be very accurate with the use of the components that create their act of intelligence. For example, they will notice small differences in what appears before them, they will remember past experiences better to fit these differences to, and they will be more eager to present their mind to the mind that is expecting this information. In all senses they will perform highly, and so set the stage for the next act of intelligence when it is desired. However, if they are unhappy and distracted, they will cling to the insecurity they have evolved through and so use the same and poorer qualities to operate these components as they did previously. As they do this, so will they present a sense of stability in the ability they display.

This is to say that the act of intelligence the child makes will be dependent upon the level of skill they have developed in each of the many features of their mind and physical brain. These in the simplest sense, and by far from being complete, could be said to be:

Skills of Perception,
Skills of Association,
Skills of Memory,
Skills of Recognition,
Skills of Presentation,
Emotional Drives,
Behavioral Exposure,
Quality of Guidance, and, of course,
A Sense of Purpose, which gives intention.

The following is a visual representation of two students who have developed their proficiency in some of these components to different levels.

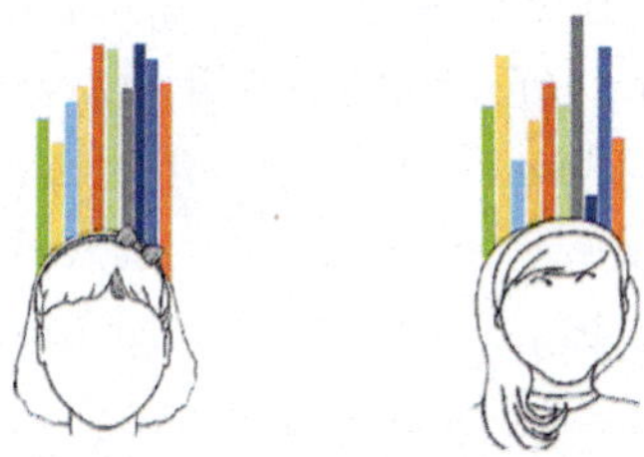

Let's suggest that the girls developed through different experiences to gain different understandings in:

Maths:	5 + 7 = 12	(3 points)	5 + 7 = 13	(0 points)
Spelling:	The bed is large.	(3 points)	The bid is big.	(1 point)
Activity:	I am good at art.	(4 points)	I am great at tennis.	(4 points)
	Grade 10/10		Grade 5/10	

In the world of Spearman's view of intelligence none or too little of the role and value of different features and their skills is known or recognized. We see this when one individual examines the answer of another and makes only a snapshot evaluation of the effort that produced this work, and so assume all too readily that that individual was more or less born to make this level of performance.

Yet, we will show in this book how the smallest abilities of the intelligence system, as by example the visual system to respond to different outline shapes, is decided by after birth development. Without this understanding, the effort that is evaluated is seen to represent the value of all that has passed and so all that the individual is able to produce in the future.

This is the great fallacy with the belief of inherited intelligence. It is an idea that does not accept that any answer or presentation of a mind is only one simple act of numerous acts that have built up through very particular circumstances to the individual, and that if that individual engages very different circumstances in the future, then, their ability to process and present information will be very different. Intelligence is not as static as has been said of it. It is a fluid feature of the human mind, as it ought to be to allow the individual to survive in different environments. We simply do not realize that our social and especially our educational environments purposely create very stabilizing and consistent environments, that so cause the impression that intelligence is a fixed value within the individual.

Before we go further in our explanation of what intelligence is, and so how it develops in the individual, we need to know of and understand the practical applications to the theory I have so far presented. Therefore, let us now move to understand what the human brain is, and how its feature of intelligence can now be understood to develop through the interplay of neurons and brain chemistry.

Chapter Two

The Developing Brain

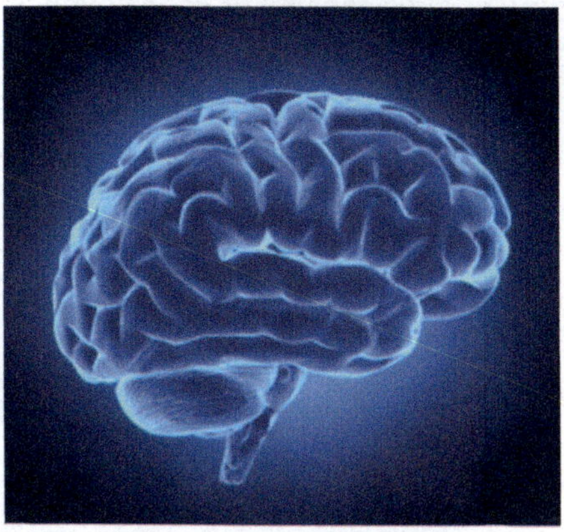

It is said of Einstein that he once said we only use 10% of our brain. We have the general impression from this saying that this is true, and that we only do use 10% of our brain. However, Einstein was a physicist. He knew nothing of neurology, and he lived in a time before brain scanning techniques were invented. The truth and the reality is that today we are only just beginning to understand what the brain may be capable of. The 10% is a myth.

Roy Andersen

2.0 Introduction:

In general terms, we think of behavior as a product of the mind and intelligence that of the brain. So, when we think of "mind over matter" we relate this to overcoming psychological issues. Equally, we think of intelligence as "brain power", so mention of IQ conjures up visual images of the brain working. We have been impressed to think like this by the science that studies intelligence, because such thinking allows the brain to be seen as stable and so intelligence measurable.

The mind, or at least our image of it, is seen to be too free and too unrestricted to have the measurable quality needed to index one human being to another. Setting aside emotional and so mental issues, any mention of the mind evokes aspects of consciousness, if not also psychic and spiritual matters. So, psychologists keep intelligence away from this, and within the confines of mathematical relationships. This is, after all, how the use of each individual can be decided in education and society.

Yet, in this book and beginning with this chapter, we shall learn how and why the mind controls the activity of the brain, and why intelligence is just as much a part of the mind as it is of the brain. We shall also understand why intelligence has a purpose in appearing to be stable, and how the mind can overturn this stability if the desire is strong enough. Intelligence, we shall come to see, is neither limited nor fixed as we have been coached to believe.

As we saw in the beginning of this book, the belief that intelligence is largely inherited arose through a political design in the 19th Century. This was a design that created the belief that the potential of a child's intelligence is related to the social achievements gained by their parents, on the simple basis that they share similar facial features. Evidence was said to be taken by the similarity of the nose, the shape of the chin, and so whatever physical similarity could be noted, that the brain and so its quality to work was similarly inherited.

However, as we have mentioned, there is no defining similarity in the shape of the brain in a family line, because the brain of each individual human being, at least the part responsible for intelligence, is given form by how its neurons are brought into design and given purpose through experience. Accordingly, numerous studies have found how the weight and character of the brains of rats increased and changed directly in accordance with the learning stimulation they were given.[14/15] In this chapter, we shall understand just how astonishingly this can be recognized with the brains of human beings.

As we shall see, the composition of the brain is totally unlike any other feature of our body. The brain is alive, and it learns how to be so. As neurons are continually associating with the visual and audio signals fed to them, the mind of the individual pulls their networks into shape by how they select and prioritize these signals according to the needs they believe they have for them.

To begin this chapter, and so this new book about intelligence, we may begin by understanding that the human brain is not one singular grey mass of tissue. It is, in fact, formed by a number of smaller brains, where the brain of earlier species evolved through phases to create that of our species. While these brains are actually separate, they are so physically close to each other and so interconnected that the impression easily arises that they function together as one whole brain. To think of the human brain in a singular sense, then, suggests that the smaller brains that make it up are all constructed by the same means. Nothing could be further from the truth.

Take the lowest brain, for example, generally referred to as the hindbrain. If we were to inspect the hindbrain in any number of deceased people, we would recognize how very similar they all are in appearance. The hindbrain of each would generally adhere to a common innate design for our species, as it has the purpose to control much of the body's internal functioning.

If, by comparison, we were then to look at the forebrain, the highest situated brain and the most recently evolved, we would find it to be of very different shape among different individuals. This brain is by far the largest of all our brains, and has the responsibility for our interaction with the environment. Here are held the areas of neural functioning responsible for behavior and intelligence, and those that analyse the incoming information received by the body's senses. While the hindbrain very much develops through a standard genetic plan, the forebrain has its form mostly driven to connection by sensory information. We may begin this chapter, then, by understanding that environmental information does change the character and ability of the brain, as it alters the form and the connections of its cells.

Body cells replace themselves at something in the order of 50,000 a second. Our body is continually changing itself as old and damaged cells are replaced with new ones. We seldom take note of these changes, and perhaps only acknowledge them as the decades go by. Yet, if we more often examined a wound or a cut in the skin, we would readily appreciate this changing process as cells multiplied to seal the wound and repair the skin. As each new cell is formed, its characteristics will be largely determined by the chemicals that feed its design, and so cause it to be more sympathetic in its operation to the ever-changing chemical environment of the body.

Before we are born, our genetic design has ensured that we have far more neurons than we would ever need in our lifetime. After birth, we move through certain stages where this neuron excessiveness is trimmed down, so that some remain while others dissolve into the general residue of the brain. The phrase "use them or lose them" ties in with the suicide mechanism that neurons have, and which is activated when they are not used.

It is of no small consideration to realize here that the way the mind and so the brain of the infant is developed by its caregivers, will greatly set in motion the capability of that brain to function and to process information as the child enters school. It is not that children are born differently that counts, and we have yet to discuss how the brain of the fetus develops, but what causes them to appear to think differently after birth. However, in having said this, we have a great deal to understand about the process of neural selection, and how neurons reform their connections to provide a plasticity in operation that ensures a lifetime of learning.

We are led from this to discuss the most important difference in the genetic design between body and brain cells. While body cells are designed to reproduce themselves through a changing environment, so as to continually update their operational effectiveness, brain cells have evolved to be more resistant to biochemical instability, because their purpose is to evaluate chemical signals originating from environmental information. To provide such means of interrogation, brain cells require a very different base of operation. After all, if brain cells were to replace themselves as body cells do, the uniform regulation of this process would cripple their plasticity and cause them to be so disordered as to interrupt the passage of information. Neural circuits, as we shall see, learn to adapt their purpose to information, least as it changes and much more by the drive of the mind to want to recognize and to know how to make use of those changes.

2.1 The Evolution of the Brain:

When life began in our primordial past, features changed as did forms of life as one genetic mutation followed another. Through Darwin's idea of Natural Selection, those organisms, or the features of an organism, that adapted better in an environment survived, while those not so adaptable faded into extinction.

Early life in the sea, such as the ancestors of coral and jellyfish, gained their food as it came to them or as they drifted into it. In time, evolution brought creatures that were bilaterally symmetrical, having front and rear ends to their body, and whose foremost feature was a mouth to obtain food. With this new form came purpose of movement in set directions, and as means of muscular locomotion developed so did the need for an internal co-ordination system. Nerve systems, which once operated independently, began to work together through relay systems. This ability to move in set directions, decided by the need to feed, brought detection sensors. Visual and audio sensors developed about the mouth, and cephalization (the forming of a head) began to occur.

In simple invertebrates, sensors remained about the form of their locomotion. We see this today with grasshoppers who have retained their audio detection system in their legs, so as to more directly mobilize themselves upon the sounds they detect. As invertebrates evolved a spine, so the nerve cords brought the sensors of the organism to one relay centre and "the brain" came into being. The brain, therefore, is the point where all sensors terminate. The information gained through these sensors is used by the brain of the organism to guide it towards food, shelter, and means to reproduce.

As we examine the ability of creatures to relate to the external world, so we see that they are limited in this relationship by the development of their central nervous system, which in turn is related to their physical adaptability. By the greater sophistication of their nervous system, the more a species is aware of their environment.

Paleoanthropologists differ over the evolutionary causes of our highly developed brain. Some believe its origin lay firstly in our unique ability to join thumb and forefinger together, thereby developing greater awareness and sensitivity with information.[16] This is to say that our higher ability to think evolved through a physiology that enabled us to be aware of higher levels of sensitivity, as we interacted with information. Others believe that the development of language was more relevant, and we shall discuss this later. Yet, both support the belief that the brain was caused to develop through interaction with the environment. Leaky gives qualification to this by noting the relationships between steps of evolutionary innovation and brainpower,[17] by which man, in terms of both, is the most evolved. At least, we may add, for the time being.

As we have mentioned, our brain is actually a composition of a number of brains. Each of these brains serve functions that show how the central nervous system of earlier species evolved. Therefore, rather than seeing our brain being different from other species, it is more relevant to see it as the final stage of brain evolution.

The most primitive brain is the one we first discussed, which is the hindbrain. The hindbrain represents the pons and the medulla, and so deals with the internal functioning of the body, where it sets up and regulates operational systems, such as heartbeat regulation and breathing. It also controls an instinctive sensory system. This system does not make analysis of what and why. If pain receptors are triggered, they react immediately causing muscles to contract. This action withdraws the skin surface from whatever is touching it. From an evolutionary perspective, the hindbrain enables an organism to function simply as a machine. It ensures correct operation of bodily systems, and avoidance of external damage.

The next profound brain development was the cerebellum, which is regarded to be a part of the hindbrain. Primarily, the cerebellum is responsible for muscle co-ordination, and in simpler species, such as reptiles, it is their dominant nerve centre. Snakes and lizards, by example, respond instinctively to environmental movement through this brain, and develop from it a means of muscular ability to attack prey quickly or withdraw from predators. In our species, the cerebellum is the small neural sac that lies at the back and underneath the forebrain, and is given form by some 100 billion tiny pin-like cells densely packed together.

The brain that in all senses differs from simple nerve triggers is the forebrain or cerebral cortex. This is divided into four lobes, of which the frontal lobe is really where much of our thought processes are held and conducted. However, it is not quite that the brain works only within sections, as we shall see, the brain works as a whole in a holistic sense.

This evolutionary marvel of the higher species enables them to store experiences, so they can respond to new environmental information with an accuracy and sensitivity that lower species do not have. In other words, they can *learn* with great efficiency. In its form, the forebrain is divided into two hemispheres, each consisting of a white celled inner core encased by a grey celled myelin sheet. The left hemisphere is responsible for the operation of the right side of the body, and visa versa with the right hemisphere.

Fig.1

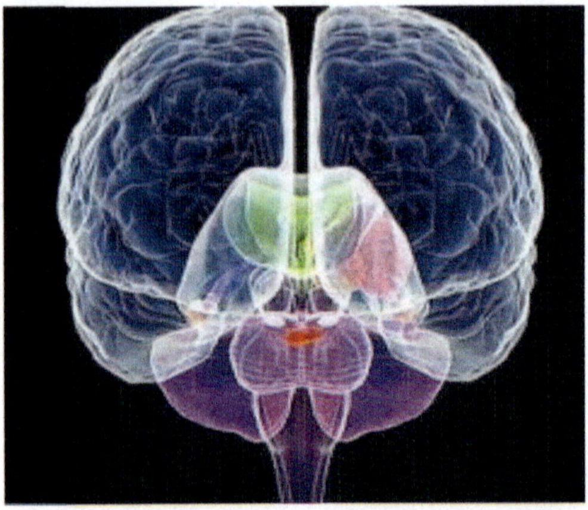

In our species, each hemisphere is described for practical purposes to be sectioned into six horizontal layers. These hemispheres are isolated from each other, yet connected by an estimated 145 million interconnecting nerve fibers. These fibers are referred to as the corpus callosum.

Fig.2

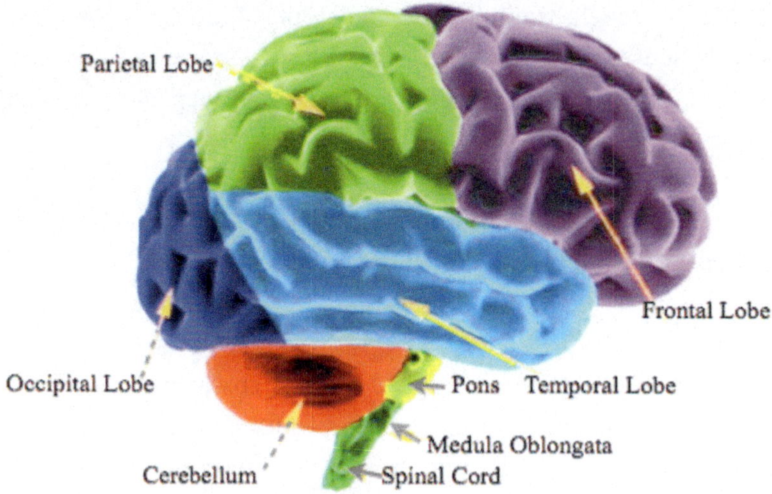

Courtesy of Steve Looi of BrainHealth and Puzzles.

As we can see in the illustration, each hemisphere is regionalized into four lobes, with each lobe having main functions of responsibility.

The frontal lobe is the primary area for personality, attention, concentration, planning, problem solving, memory, decision-making, and the control of our behavior and emotions. This is where we make the choices between good and bad actions, and determine similarities and differences between things and events. Here we store long-term memories, which we have fashioned through the emotional design of the limbic system.

The temporal lobe, marked light blue in the illustration, is the main area for hearing and understanding language. This lobe is responsible for emotions such as fear, isolation, loneliness, delight and joy. Here, visual stimulus is understood and object recognition made. The temporal lobe is also another important area of the brain for the storage of long-term memory.

The parietal lobe is responsible for motor and somatic sensory areas. So our sense of touch, spatial and visual perception, as well as our kinesthetic senses originate here. This lobe is associated mainly with the movement, orientation, recognition, and perception of sensory information.

At the far back of the forebrain we find the occipital lobe. This is the main area for vision. This lobe will play an important part in many of our later discussions.

Beneath the occipital lobe we can see the cerebellum, as we have just mentioned. The cerebellum is responsible for balance, skilled motor activity and coordination. Although, it is also involved with language as we shall see.

The brainstem lying beneath all of these, controls breathing, heart rate, sleep and wake cycles, and arousal and consciousness.

The hindbrain, cerebellum and forebrain, therefore, enable the higher mammalian to control its internal functioning, motor co-ordination, and analyse its higher sensory capabilities. There is, however, one more brain that is quite hidden underneath the forebrain. We refer to this as the midbrain, so termed because it is the halfway stage between the brain that deals with the internal functioning of the body, and the brain that makes analysis of the external world. In essence, the midbrain is composed of three main sections.

The most prominent of these is the thalamus. The thalamus is the routing stage for information coming into and going out from the higher evaluative forebrain. All the information our senses pickup about the external world is fed to the thalamus, and from there it is routed by our awareness to subsequent stages for further analysis and determination of response. All that is, except for the olfactory sense.

Our sense for smell is not interrogated by our thoughts, and is fed directly to control our attraction or repulsion. For this reason we have very little control over perfume or old socks!

Fig.3

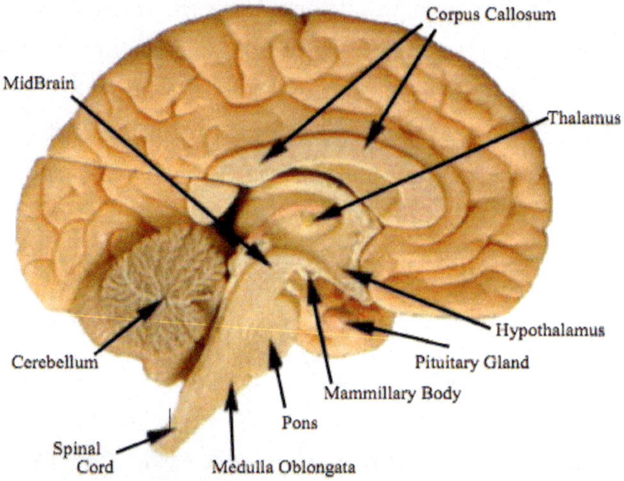

Running around the thalamus is an area known as the hypo-thalamus. The hypothalamus is the main control area for the body's internal stabilization through its awareness of the external world. Here body temperature is stabilized, and energy levels for metabolic processes relating to what we eat and drink are set. Here, the states of sleep and activation are controlled, as is our aggression or timidity. By its control over the hormonal glands, it is the hypothalamus that regulates the state of the nervous system from a para-sympathetic to a sympathetic mode, so that our body is better suited to a flight or fight condition. The activation of the para-sympathetic mode will be determined by the individual from the way they perceive danger, and the evaluation they give to it from their personal experiences. This knowledge will be very important to recall in later chapters when we come to discuss bullying, and the individual's perspective of being inferior to others during the learning process.

The third, and important region of the midbrain is the limbic system. The limbic system contains the hippocampus dealing with short term and long-term memory, and the amygdala, which is deeply involved with memory, predictions, and the emotional flavoring of thoughts. As a whole, it is the limbic system that represents the sensitivity of the brain. It is here that control is given to the hypothalamus for the production of hormones that influence emotions, and for the orchestration of neurotransmitters that chemically link brain cells together. The midbrain, therefore, by its ability to route sensory information and to give sensitivity to that information through its emotional control of chemical regulation, overrides the effectiveness of the whole brain.

Of all the brain parts we have just summarized, it is the forebrain that distinguishes humans from animals by its relative size and construction. This is the part of the human brain that mainly allows us to think. Here are contained the prime areas that deal with memory, and the associated parts that construct our intelligence and personality. The forebrain and midbrain are the most important part of brain evolution for our interests, since these create the sensitivity that enables the individual to adapt precisely and accurately to the continually changing environment.

In its construction, the forebrain is very different from the hindbrain, because it never actually becomes completely constructed. It is only by the continual structural development of the forebrain, that the individual is able to learn to be adaptable to survive in any environment. Once this structuring ceases, the individual will cease to function as a living organism. Here is the heart of all we are to discuss in regard to Brain Plasticity.

It is essential for us to realize that the construction and development of this highly structural and functional brain is greatly dependent upon the information it receives through its senses.

As the brain becomes constructed through the information it receives, so does its senses. Each grow in tandem with the other, each driven in the directions they take by the environmental stimulation that rapidly exerts influence on the mainframe design each inherited.

In *"Intelligence"* we saw how Francis Galton had laid the belief in our understanding that the brain, and so mental competence, is inherited in the same way as any other physical feature. We may see from what we have just discussed that this is not correct. The brain and its sensory systems, and so the intelligence they produce, "learn" how to construct themselves through the information they receive from the environment.

Although Galton wrote about this before our knowledge of the brain had so developed, his contention was never corrected and so still remains one of the cornerstones of our belief that intelligence is limited within the individual, on account, however vaguely this is now taken, of their family's work role and social purpose.

The general idea held by most people is that each function of the brain operates from its own specific area. So the understanding is that we have one specific area for memory, one area for language, one area for emotion, one area for perception, and, as Spearman always hoped, we would have one area for intelligence — although we do not.

Yet, as we are to realize as we become more involved in understanding this chapter, different regions of the forebrain sub-serve each other, so that when a function of this brain comes into action many parts operate in support of it. This will be important for us to understand later, when we discuss the plasticity of the brain's operation. It is therefore relevant to raise the point early, that an impression of brain features operating in isolation of each other is not correct. The impression we have today of intelligence being partly innate, and so having a limiting quality is a legacy from a time when they were thought to do so. The root of this reasoning goes back to a pseudo-science in the 18th century, based on the shape of skulls of criminals in prison, as we shall new discuss.

Accordingly, since we have a lot to understand in this chapter, it would be helpful for us to know how our current understanding of the brain only really began in 1861, a mere eight years before Galton claimed he knew how the brain formed and upon which many psychologists unwittingly still base their understanding of intelligence. Our knowledge of the brain, at the writing of this book, is still very, very far from complete.

2.2 Our Developing Knowledge of the Human Brain:

At the end of the 18th Century, an idea was put forward by Dr. Franz Joseph Gall that the features and functions of the brain could be recognized by the surface design of the skull. Gall's idea, which became known as phrenology, held the opinion that the bumps and depressions on the surface of the skull were a direct consequence of the greater or lesser quality of the brain feature that was supposed to lie beneath them.

The idea that a person's ability or characteristic could be realized by measuring the surface shape of their skull, created a huge fashion for people to have the contours of their head mapped and displayed on charts in their home. Phrenology became very popular, and it survived until the middle of the 19th Century. The illustration here shows the belief that the brain actually had a physical area for moral aptitude, with sub-areas of veneration, benevolence, hope, spirituality, and imitation.

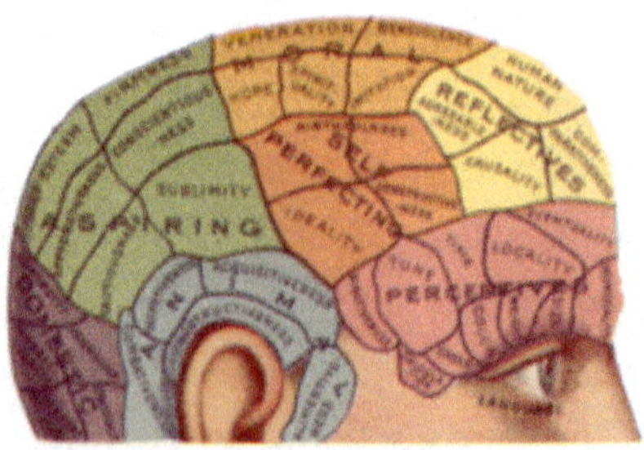

Phrenology

Another area was said to house Reflective ability, with sub-areas of human nature, comparativeness, agreeableness and causality. Eventually, the brain was believed to be divided into 43 areas, which would explain the behavior and intelligence of the individual.

Gall, of course, did not have the technology to be able to observe the living brain. The best he could do was to try to recognize a mental feature, totally guess where it may be in the brain, and then relate this to the shape of the skull. The only way he could do this was by classifying people into different categories according to their known abilities or tendencies, and seek to recognize some particular feature of their skull that was similar to their characteristics. So, Gall would roam prisons seeking to identify some distinguishing features in the skulls of criminals, and then to professions and various vocations trying to find some notable features in the skulls of the people associated with each of these.

This idea of one part of the brain being related to one brain function set the fashion for the idea of localization, which we have just mentioned. However, although medical science subsequently disproved each area and many of the features that Gall had identified, it retained the basic concept that each feature has a specific area in the brain until late in the 20th c entury. Therefore, in the time of Spearman, who started the idea of a singular factor of intelligence in all people, it was not unnatural to think that intelligence was a singular mass of brain cells that would one day be discovered in a specific area of the brain.

Of significance to our account is this legacy that phrenology endeared to us, by the suggestion that the shape of the skull is related to the quality of the brain. After all, when Galton appeared on the scene, with his declaration that the quality of a function to operate was directly related to the physical and especially facial features that could be recognized in a father and son, phrenology still held a lingering respectability within general society. It would not be too much to expect, that with his flair for lecturing, Galton would readily have played upon this in acknowledging the heritable similarity in skull shapes within a family line, and so "his" inevitable link between them.

Within medical science, however, phrenology had already come under suspicion by the 1830s. The idea that one region was responsible for one feature became questionable through the work of Pierre Flourens, who had made a number of studies on the brain of pigeons. Flourens found that if he removed the part of the brain said to be responsible for a specific feature, that after the operation the pigeon would still show an ability for this feature. By gradually removing more and more of a pigeon's brain area, he came to realize that a feature was the responsibility of many parts of the brain and not just one. This knowledge in itself did not seal the fate of phrenology, because it had developed into such a large cult, although it did open the way for a much later discovery made on a human being.

In 1861, Paul Broca, a much noted brain surgeon, was introduced to a patient who was named after the only sound he could utter: "....tan....." Tan had been severely paralyzed on the right side of his body for many years, and apart from this single utterance was quite unable to produce a distinguishable sound. Conveniently as it was for Broca, and as it turned out for medical science, Tan died shortly after this introduction and presented the opportunity for his brain to be examined. As Broca conducted a cortical survey of Tan's forebrain, he discovered a small area that was excessively damaged. Broca concluded from Tan's deficiency that our ability for language originates from this particular area.

The significance of what became known as Broca's area, lay in the fact that phrenologists had long insisted that the function for language was situated behind and beneath the left eye. Once it was realized that this was not so, interest in phrenology rapidly plunged, and a new science of brain anatomy began to develop that sought to understand how the brain actually functioned. At this time, however, very little could be understood with the brain. It basically was an indecipherable mass of soft grey tissue, which a surgeon could only investigate once it was dead and lifeless.

Our first real insight into how the brain may be understood to work arose in 1873, four years after, it is to be noted, that Galton had written: "... if this be the case with stature, then it will be true as regards every other physical feature .. size of brain ... and thence mental capacity."[18]

At this time, Camillo Golgi was working in his laboratory in Italy, when he accidentally knocked a sample of brain tissue into a solution of chromate of silver, and was thereafter able to visibly see brain cells under a microscope for the first time. Once the cells, and the links between them could be recognized, the brain was no longer seen as a body of lifeless tissue as one would look upon a dissected muscle. It was directly from this discovery that appreciation began to develop as to the intricacy of nerve cell relationships.

Golgi's subsequent work with the brain was followed up by Santiago Ramon y Cajal in Spain, who made a detailed study of brain tissue under the light microscope. For 20 years, Cajal systematically investigated the cellular organization of almost every part of the nervous system in all five classes of vertebrate, and laid a broad foundation for the development of neuroscience. Although Cajal did not actually coin the term "neural plasticity," he frequently referred to it, and did much to suggest the adaptability of the brain to the changing environment.[19] In recognition of their contribution to our understanding of brain formation, both Cajal and Golgi were awarded the Nobel Prize in 1906.

Yet, anatomists deal with dead tissue, and despite the interest that Cajal could have sparked, brain scientists instead steered their interests towards an impression of the brain that served the body's physiology, rather than how it interacted with the environment. Interest in how the brain may be affected by environmental interaction was delayed until the 1940s, because of two principle factors.

Although, Wundt had separated interests in philosophy and psychology in his Leipzig laboratory in the 1880s, and so began a trend to understand how the brain related to environmental changes, medical science was too wary to engage itself in what it regarded as activities of a hypothetical nature. The need to deal with precise certainty, and the desire to maintain its authority caused medicine to distance itself from the emerging science of psychology. For their part, psychologists focused too much on how the brain responded to the living world to have any real desire to explore avenues of what they regarded to be, a detached science dealing with a diseased and malfunctioning organ. Change was brought to these attitudes by the number of brain causalities that began to appear during the Second World War, and the development of technology that came through this conflict.

It was through the latter that psychologists began to gain considerable experience in the operational training of service personnel with electronic detection systems. This new knowledge of the adaptability of the brain to environmental information caused medicine to open its doors to psychology, however slowly, and together they began to gain an entirely fresh understanding of what the brain is, how it may be formed, and how it could operate.

These interests brought about the formation of the science of neuropsychology, whose aim is to relate specific environmental instances to individual brain networks. However, because of the incredibly hidden complexity of neural networks, which sometimes share purposes and of the different ways in which environmental experiences overlap each other, this only became possible in very restricted ways with the development of brain scanning techniques in the 1970s.

Barring this, the first attempts to monitor brain activity came about at the turn of the 20th Century, when Carl Jung refined a technique that had previously been designed to measure the electrodermal activity of the human skin. Jung sought to measure the electrical activity of the brain by sensors that were taped to the skull, in an attempt to relate different readings to various mental conditions such as schizophrenia.

As our use of electroencephalographs (literally electrical-brain-measurement) became more proficient, it was realized that individuals suffering from epilepsy generated abnormal surges of current within their brain during a seizure. A reasoning developed from this that a serious seizure could create a level of electricity that could have very serious consequences to the functioning of the brain, and so of the individual's mind. Reasoning followed this that an operation to sever the corpus callosum would isolate the hemispheres from each other, so that any damage caused by a high electrical surge would be contained within one hemisphere. By the mid 1940s, this operation, known as a cerebral commissurotomy, had been performed on a handful of cases in America.

The possible consequences of isolating the hemispheres had long been contemplated, and this had brought forth theories of the effects on the mind of splitting the brain. As the first cerebral commissurotomies began to take place, first on monkeys and cats and then later on humans, Roger Sperry began to investigate how the ability of the brain had been affected by this operation. Sperry was particularly interested to link mental functions to the cerebral hemispheres to seek a higher understanding of their role with environmental experiences.

Following a number of what became known as "split-brain operations," Sperry realized that a patient's personality remained unchanged, despite the operation that had divided their brain. To explain this, suggestions arose that there must either be some secondary route that would allow the hemispheres to retain their interaction, for example through the brainstem, or that one hemisphere had "some" ability to compensate for its loss of influence from the other hemisphere. We shall return to this factor of compensation in the following chapter, when we discuss the observations of Gooch. However, while commissurotomy was found not to affect the personality, it did show very notable effects in how the visual system was then able to relate to the environment.

In the visual system, signals are fed from each eye to both hemispheres, so that signal information from the right eye is passed to the right hemisphere and also to the left. The same being so for the left eye. However, it was discovered that with commissurotomy this crossover effect was prevented, so that visual information from each eye was not shared by both hemispheres.

This meant that information received by the left eye went only to the left hemisphere, just as information from the right eye was restricted to the right hemisphere. Such division of the visual system enabled us to devise observation techniques to better understand the role of each hemisphere, relative to the information that was presented to a particular eye. It was, for example, through this understanding that we were able to realize that the right hemisphere responds better to written words, as the left does to language.

Commissurotomy also helped to enlarge our knowledge of how a hemisphere controlled the opposite side of the body to where it was situated. By example, this enabled us to understand that when an unseen object was placed in the left hand, it could be examined by tactile (touch) experience and recognized easily from the right hemisphere that deals with form. Yet, when the same object was placed in the right hand, it could not be so identified by the left hemisphere, because this has little developed ability to work with form.

Very many of these types of tests have helped us to gain a higher knowledge of the role of each hemisphere, and how one may interact with the other. This has enabled us to understand that the left hemisphere deals with language skills, comprehension, the expression of oral and written language, verbal word recognition, and analytical functioning. In contrast, the right hemisphere is responsible for spatial tasks, recognition of objects and faces, and so non-verbal means of communication.

An extremely important point for us arises from this, in that following a general understanding of split-brain observations the term "brain learning" began to appear in education. The use of this term enables psychologists and educationalists to explain what one hemisphere does, and so what different parts of the brain do. This knowledge has absolutely no relevance to the ability of the student to learn, or in how well they perform. Yet, is has created a movement which believes that it does.

Let me give an example of what I mean here. In vogue with this brain learning philosophy, it was once explained to me by a teacher that: ".....when viewing and drawing are integrated, the combined stimulus effect on the brain is no longer linear, but of logarithmic activation (neurons literally spread out in 3 dimensions!). The neurotransmitter signals from eyes-to-brain, and from the brain-to-hand, come from different parts of the brain. So that when a drawing is made, you can imagine both regions of the brain being activated. The region between the two activated regions could be activated as well, but definitely, there must be a "synaptic correspondence" between the two regions so that the drawing can take place. This "synaptic correspondence," between two brain regions, causes the information formed in the brain to be "more sticky," hence the student is better able to remember the drawing by copying it rather than just looking at it….."

The point, the author of this explanation was seeking to make, is why you better remember a drawing when you copy it, instead of just looking at it. The real purpose of the explanation, however, is what causes the individual to learn, and so what causes one to learn better than another, because this was the whole point of the explanation. Proficiency in relating to information comes through emotional sensitivity, and this has absolutely nothing to do with the author's description of how the generalized brain operates through their liberal description of "synaptic correspondence," "logarithmic activation," or the fact that neurons spread out in three dimensions.

Accordingly, I have attended a number of lectures on the theme of "brain learning," where the lecturer sought to impress their audience with pictures of the brain, and lists of what particular parts do. The left hemisphere, we were told is where language, critical thinking, use of numbers, and reasoning occurs, while an equal list of uses was ascribed to the right hemisphere. Following this, the teachers were encouraged to study their students to find out if they are left-brained or right-brained thinkers.

The lecturer was happy, because the teachers had paid a lot of money to learn this information. The teachers were happy, because they had something new to talk about and do, but none of this made the slightest difference to the children in their classes. Those who did not learn the formula for Ohm's law in physics, still tried to calculate the resistance by dividing the current by the voltage instead of the voltage by the current, and still only got 4 out of 10 in their class mark!

The theory of brain learning sounded very exciting, but nothing changed in education because of it. The performance of students still related to their developed proficiency with the 3 R's of reading, writing and arithmetic, which the teachers still blamed on the genes they had inherited.

- Therefore, while this geographical knowledge of the brain allows psychologists to impress educationalists and parents that they know what different parts of the brain do, this does not allow them in the slightest to explain how the individual brain of the individual student operates, and so why any of this is relevant to education.

What is relevant from studies in neurology, as we shall shortly move to discuss, is how the physical brain becomes constructed through environmental information, and so why sensitivity with this information decides the capability of that construction more than the genetic design it appears to have evolved from. Until we reach this point in our discussion, let us continue our understanding of the historical development of neurology that will bring us to this.

Just as understanding of neurology was brought into being in the West through the injuries service people sustained in the Second World War, interest was likewise stimulated in the Soviet countries. The most notable neurologist who arose in Russia through this conflict was Alexander Luria. As we briefly mentioned in *"The Illusion of School,"* Luria had long harbored interest in Vygotsky's work with thought and language. As a military surgeon now actively involved with brain injuries, Luria was able to combine both these interests and experiences to pioneer what became known as the science of neurolinguistics.

Neurolinguistics has played a very important role in the development of our understanding of how language, as an aspect of conscious thinking, is developed within the brain. By isolating particular areas of the brain with small lesions, the value of those areas could be estimated in the effect they play in language and speech ability.[20] By this means, we have been able to find how temporary disturbance of one area of the brain has affected the ability of a person to encode or decode various phonemic, lexical, and grammatical structures.

Through Luria's observations of how non-damaged areas of the brain could be developed to provide functions that had been lost in a damaged area, he came to realize that one feature was not the consequence of one part of the brain, as Spearman had believed with intelligence. Rather, that any feature was involved in an intricate web of neural structuring with other features in other areas of the brain.[21]

From this understanding, Luria developed a principle of how networks are organized in the brain. He suggested that a feature originated from a primary area, built up through tiers of secondary, and then associative areas before reaching motor circuits to realize the purpose of that function. We may note that virtually all neural circuits conclude in some form of motor function. We raised this in our introduction, where we saw how visual recognition is reliant upon the muscles that control the movement of the eyes and their lens.

While Luria was developing his work in Russia, Wilder Penfield in the Americas, began in the 1950s to use electrical stimulation in open brain surgery. It is possible to conduct brain surgery on a fully conscious patient, because there are no pain sensors in the brain that would cause discomfort. Penfield was largely interested in mapping the motor and somatosensory systems. In such work, Penfield would apply a small electrical stimulus to a part of the motor cortex and note the corresponding muscular movement.

It was while he was using this technique one day that a patient quite suddenly related to an instant from their memory. This caused Penfield to realize that he had found a memory circuit, outside the region traditionally associated with memory. As he proceeded to stimulate other areas of the brain, Penfield realized by the recollections and emotional displays of the patient that memory areas are not localized in one specific place, but spread throughout the entire cortex -- just as Luria had discovered.

It is worthwhile to point out that until it was possible to X-ray the brain and to use PET scanning procedures (which measure the functional activity of different areas of the brain when they metabolize) in the 1970s, the only way it was possible to understand the geography of the brain, its construction, and to gain any insight into how it may function was through the simple techniques we have so far discussed.

So, from the time of Broca in 1861 up until the 1970s, which spanned the entire reign of Galton and the development of psychometric testing, our understanding of how the brain works and so how intelligence forms was restricted to surgeons being able to associate a deficient feature with a damaged area, as we saw with Tan's inability to talk.

However, as scanning procedures did develop, the images they provided began to suggest that the principle of brain organization was more complicated than Luria had suggested. Accordingly, it is now held that very many areas form a network when a function is brought into operation, and that these are activated simultaneously.

We can see in the PET (positron emission tomography) image, on the following page, how different parts of the brain (by the different light intensities created from energy differences) are simultaneously activated when a single feature is brought into operation -- instead of one part triggering off another as Luria had suspected.

Fig.4

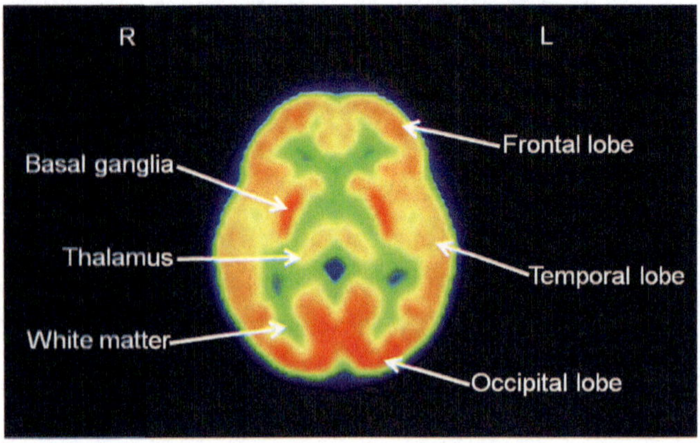

I am very grateful to Prof. Harry Chugani for use of this image.

Therefore, it is due to the advancements in our technology, as we can see by this PET image, that we today view the forebrain not as a number of individual areas, but as a whole singular working complex. The mechanics of this see one part as being as responsible as another, so that a number of areas are seen as working together in a collective sense.

Flourins must have come across this thought over 150 years ago in his work with pigeons, when he found that damage to point X did not necessarily affect function Y. However, tradition has an endearing way of controlling development, and it was not until our advancements in imaging technology that we began to be more wary of the concept of localization, as it was embedded in Gall's phrenology. Take, for instance, the understanding that language derives from the specific area Broca identified in 1861, and that this belief was maintained right up until the 1990s.

In 1993, imaging techniques revealed that the cerebellum, which is believed to be solely responsible for motor co-ordination, showed activation when a person was given cognitive and language tasks even though they had made no bodily movement. Suspicion arose from this that the cerebellum might also play a role in language. This was an idea that went against all understanding of its functioning up to that point in time.[22]

In humans, the lateral part of the cerebellum is enormously greater in size than in other vertebrates, and it was to this area that consideration was first given in seeking a link with the function of language. The output from this area of the cerebellum is referred to as the neo-dentate. It was reasoned that if the passage of signals through this were interrupted, a subject should experience some degree of poor motor co-ordination, such as a tremor.

Yet, in all accounts where small lesions were made in the neo-dentate, no such effect was recognized. As the output from the neo-dentate was subsequently examined, it was found to go to the brainstem. This was logical enough, because a path from this leads to the nerve cord and down to the muscles of the body. However, greater examination of this path subsequently revealed that it went up to the forebrain through the thalamus.

The thalamus we may remember is the routing system into the higher cortical structures. Subsequent investigations showed that numerous paths were identified from the cerebellum up into many parts of the forebrain that deal with cognitive and language capabilities, and where Broca's area can be found. The conclusion gained from this was that in other vertebrates, such as the monkey, the cerebellum is wholly responsible for motor co-ordination, but in our species some area of the cerebellum has evolved to play a not insignificant role in cognitive and language features, as they interact with the environment.[23/24]

This gave profound new insight into the concept we have of the brain's system of organization, and gave further testimony to the insights gained from PET scan imaging in how the brain operates holistically. This enabled us to realize that while different parts of the brain form at different rates, under different conditions, they do "learn" to operate in harmony with each other with the sophistication of a beautifully co-ordinated chemical machine. How then, may we ask, do neurons connect to each other to pass their information, and so give form to our brain?

2.3 The Principles of Brain Cell Operation:

Basically, there are two types of brain cells. There are glial cells, which traditionally are regarded to give the brain its structure and form, and neuron cells, which provide the means of communication within this form. To our interest neurons are the more important of the two types of cells, because it is these that handle information and change through doing so. Having said this, we are now beginning to realize that glial cells also play some part in the transmission of signal information.[25]

While this is not quite clear at the moment exactly how, we should assume that where they do, so will they change in form to allow this possibility. In other words, the structure and so mass of the brain will change according to the information it works with, which is what Howell was talking about when he pointed out that "The brains of idle laboratory mice increase in weight 2 to 3 per cent when they are given interesting, but perplexing tasks to perform, and puzzles to solve."[26]

However, in reference to neurons, it is important for the discussion we will shortly engage that we quite understand why these cells function very differently from other cells in the body. To begin to understand this, let us consider the analogy of a brick wall with a tree growing beside it.

A wall is made up of many singular bricks interlocked together. Tissue cells of the body are just the same as this. They are stationary, and have a structural purpose. The tree has a different purpose. It must learn how to gain information through its sensors. To acquire this, its roots and branches begin to spread themselves as they are directed by sensory information. So, roots push themselves down through the ground as they search for water, ever spreading their tentacles further and further apart. As the roots obtain the water and nitrates they require, so the branches far above them push out their tentacles to maneuver past the shade of the wall and nearby obstacles as they search for sunlight.

If we now take this tree of the garden and place it within our brain, we can see how it becomes "a tree of knowledge," for the roots and branches of the neuron are called dendrites, taken from the Greek for the branch structure of a tree.

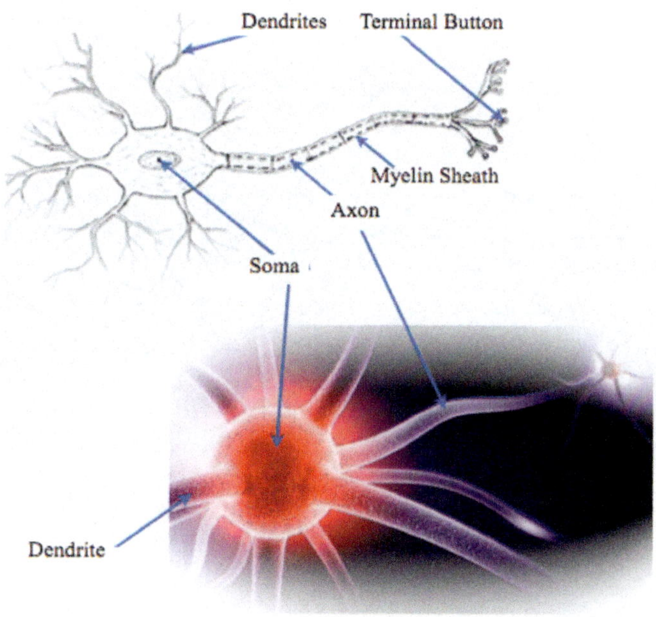

In the same manner as PVC coating protects electrical wiring, neurons are coated with a myelin membrane. This membrane isolates the signal from the electrical effects of other neurons and surrounding ions as it moves through the neuron. Without this myelin coating neurons would indiscriminately radiate their signals, there would be no organized circuitry in the brain, and it would be unable to function.

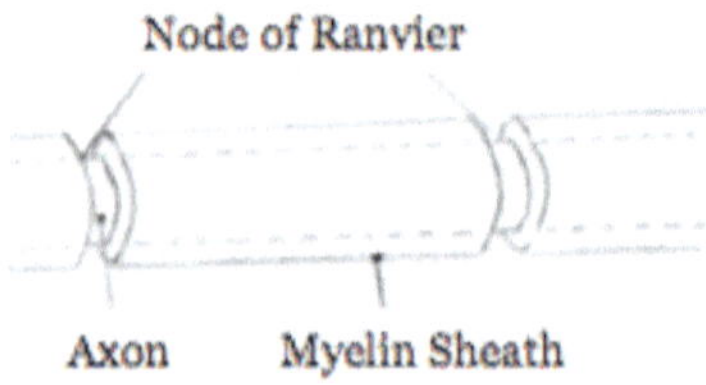

As we have already understood, neurons are not wedged together as body cells are. They lie unattached, close to each other in a medium that allows them free mobility. The part of this medium that separates the connecting points of neurons is referred to as the synapse, or synaptic gap. The signal that moves through a neuron is in the form of an electrical pulse. For this signal to be transferred from one neuron to another, it must move across the synaptic gap.

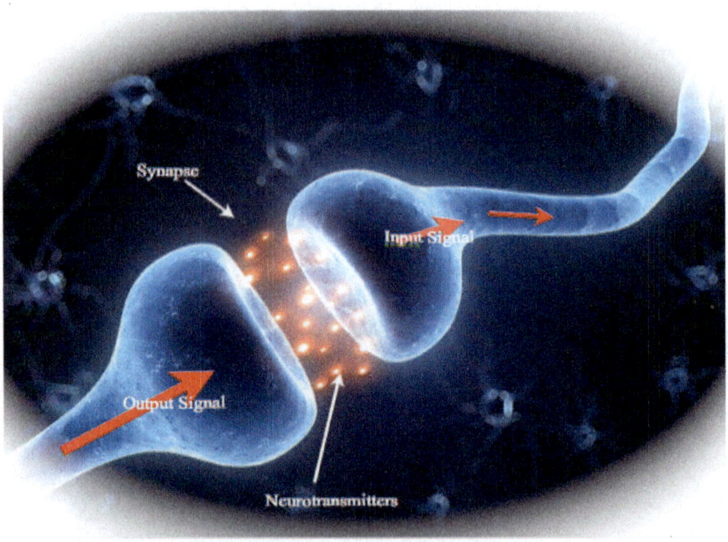

The movement of this signal through neurons and across synapses is made possible by changing its state from an electrical to a chemical base, such that in an electrical form it passes through a neuron, and in a chemical form it can move across a synapse to reach the next neuron. This chemical signal is known as a neurotransmitter, and we have about fifty variations of these in our brain. Serotonin and dopamine are the ones most associated with intelligence.

We may grasp from this illustration an understanding of the sequence of a neural signal, by envisaging its arrival into the brain circuitry from a nerve sensor, be it from an eye or an ear. In the form of an electrical pulse, it will move along the axon of the first neuron in its path, until it reaches the terminal buttons placed at the end of the neuron.

Here, it will be converted into neurotransmitters. These neurotransmitters will then move out into the surrounding synapse, and by various means of attraction and repulsion from surrounding ions will be guided to the next neuron in their path. In this way, a signal moves through a chain of neurons separated by synaptic gaps, alternating in electrical and chemical forms.

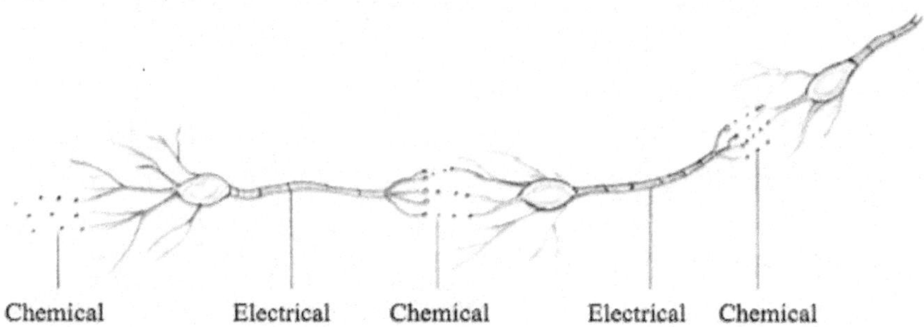

Signals

In simple terms, this is the means by which an electrical signal in a nerve cell is related to information.

When we consider that computers use electrical pulses of "O" and "1" in varying sequences to relay their information, while our brain uses different electrical frequencies with combinations of some 50 chemical neurotransmitters to control its information, we may begin to see how incredibly more complex our processing system is to that of a computer.

This then, is the basic mechanism by which brain cells transfer their information, although how these cells come into contact with each other, how they operate, and what determines the efficiency in that operation is a much longer and far more complicated story. We may begin to unravel this, by envisaging how the brain comes into general formation at the very beginning of life, for here we find true insight into how the role of the environment does explain variations in intelligence, far and beyond the idea of an inherited gene code. This is our introduction into brain plasticity.

2.4 The Formatting of the Brain:

The accepted explanation for the construction of the brain is that it commences about three weeks after the egg has been fertilized, when a tiny cluster of cells first become visible in the upper section of the embryo. Soon after this, the neural groove that runs along the back of the embryo fuses to form a tube. This tube is the forerunner of the central nervous system that makes up the spinal cord and the brain. Cases of spina bifida can occur if membrane substance or nerve roots become trapped in this tube before it is completely formed. However, the tube is normally completed without incident, following which there is a rapid manufacture of brain cells that migrate outwards from the centre of the tube to the tube wall. These form the rudimentary brain cells, some of which become neurons and others glial cells.

As we have discussed, the brain is not isolated within the body but is extremely interactive with it. It is a relationship that is built upon learned experience. By as early as the fourth week following fertilization, a two-way communication process begins to develop in which the brain and the body learn to connect with each other.

This begins when ventral cells in the proto-brainstem grow axons out to the muscles of the body's trunk and limbs. This is followed by axons from the brain searching for and then forming connections with motor and then nerve sensory cells in the muscles of the face, the eyes, and the mouth. As the brain further grows, it begins to receive axons from the nose, eyes, ears, and mouth, and completes this two-way process. The axons that pass through the area of the thalamus in the brain will cause this region to develop as the relay point between the brain and its sensory tentacles, which make up the central nervous system.

As the brain becomes more established, the development of the endocrine system begins to take place. This is responsible for the production of hormones, and the later control of the body's metabolic activities. Centralized neurons then develop inside the now rapidly forming brain, where they send axons up to the forebrain region and down to the spinal cord to lay a path for further development. Along the paths that are laid, certain messenger chemicals are released. These messenger chemicals will later play an important role in the regulation of cell growth and their further development. After eight weeks, the embryonic period ends and the fetal period begins.

The fetal period is marked by the appearance of the beginning of the cerebral hemispheres, and soon after this the brain begins to take the shape we recognize. As brain cells multiply and migrate, their dendrites grow. At the same time, their axons will extend to seek attractive chemical signals that will allow them to link up with distant neurons, and so establish the networks that will allow the body to function as it is designed.

At each step, neural development is either selectively controlled, or allowed to over develop so that it may be trimmed back at a later stage to give the most effective working arrangement.

Guided by environmental signals, as well as unfolding through their own design, neurons are shaped into a basic scaffolding plan. By the thirtieth week, the definite influence of stimuli is recognized. Then, by the fortieth week of gestation the baby will be born, with their brain being a quarter of the weight that it will finally grow to as a mature adult. The distinct shape, the main featuring, and the specific regions will appear remarkably complete. Yet, this is misleading, because many of the circuit connections, especially those in the cortical regions that deal with environmental interaction and so intelligence processes, are very incomplete.

When born, the approximate weight of a male's brain will be 370g. Estimations have suggested that during the first year of life, brain cells grow at the astonishing rate of 250,000 per minute. By the age of three the brain will weigh some 1000g, and by the time it reaches adolescence it will, on average, weigh something in the order of 1350g. Within the first 10 to 12 years of life, the brain will have increased in weight approximately four times.

This weight expansion has largely occurred by the growth of neurons developing into gigantic complex networks, as they are driven in their connections by information from the environment. The images seen, the sounds heard, and the items held all make signals, which do shape the way neurons connect with each other. Thus, the way the infant learns to interpret environmental signals is the way they will form a meaning of the world in which they live. Later, they will use the strategies they devised from this as a means to understand changing environments, and how behavioral and intellectual solutions to problems within those environments may be sought and handled.

- We gain an impression from this simple account that at least one stage of neural configuration is genetically predetermined in its geography. Indeed, we must reason this to be so, because the functional regions of the brain of all humans will be placed in the same location. My thalamus may be found in the same place of the brain as your thalamus, and connected to the various lobes that surround it with the same pathways. How, then, may we begin to understand, do neurons change from relying upon a genetic design to being driven by environmental information?

The first suggestion as to how neurons may actually form a framework of construction came from Cajal in 1893, when he suggested that a distant neuron might radiate chemical signals to draw another neuron to it. By the 1950s, Roger Sperry had discovered that this connecting of neurons was possible through chemical traces, and with some amendment described how it could occur through the theory of chemoaffinity in primary networks.[27]

As the brain is forming, neurons are manufactured and migrate outwards through the membrane tissue. As they do this, they deposit chemical traces that leave trails to their ultimate location. Thus, in the early stages of the brain there are different regions of neurons that will require to link together, in order to establish the geography of the brain. It is the manner by which they do this that has great meaning to us, because these links are not formed by a rigid genetic design.

- In many instances, the design of the gene coding allows for environmental signals to decide how neurons grow, how they link up with each other to create their circuits, and how the efficiency of those circuits to operate is decided.

Let us now examine how neurons form the circuits that give the brain its means of operation.

We may envisage in this a group of neurons in one area of the brain, and another group in a different area, as we have just described. Now, according to the genetic design that is relevant to the purpose these neurons will have, the neurons in one area will be stimulated either by a genetic trigger or by an environmental signal. Once these neurons are stimulated, their axons will grow. It is important that we note that as each axon does this, it does so in a snake like fashion with no clear direction. In other words, a neuron does not have the instruction to know where it is going, or how it is going to take a particular direction. It is just that stimulation has caused it to be active, and it responds by growing its axon.

As this “waving” axon drifts about, it will move through fields of chemical molecules, which will be adverse or sympathetic to the familiarity it is seeking. Situated at the foremost tip of the neuron’s axon will be a growth cone. Molecules that are sympathetic to this cone will attach themselves to it. These chemical adhesion molecules (called CAMs), will then guide the axon head to other sympathetic chemical traces, which, as they attach their CAMs, will direct the axon to zero in on the pre-designed target group.

Once the axon head of each source neuron is within general reach of the target, the CAMs switch the functioning of the growth cone from seeking directional chemicals to seeking actual target recognition chemicals. Once this has occurred, the axon head is then able to detect graded chemicals that have been released from the target neurons, and so will now move specifically towards them.

We may reflect at this point that a number of neurons were stimulated, and the axon of each of these is competing to establish the link between the group they came from and the target group. The deciding factor as to which source neuron will make that link, introduces us into the two phases of neural development. This is where we come to understand how brain plasticity arises.

So far, we have discussed the process of development that is "independent of activity." This is to say that the direction the axon takes is controlled only by chemical similarities and chemical dissimilarities that follow a genetic plan. When neurons link up in this manner, they are said to develop through the process of radial connections.

However, there are other times when neurons are stimulated by environmental based signals, and develop action potentials in the process to regulate the control of this information. When neurons are stimulated and caused to connect with each other through environmental signals, they are said to be tangentially connected.

Therefore, while neurons may be brought into a proto-network through radial connections, the final stage is often completed with tangential connections.

As we shall see, features relating to the intelligence process may have their networks totally designed through tangential connections, and so only by environmental based signals often selected through emotional interest by the mind!.

As we may understand, when environmental signals are used to construct a network, the efficiency of that network must rely upon the quality of those signals. This brings us back to the degree of sensitivity by which environmental information is selected by the brain's sensors to see, hear, and touch, etc.

In normal situations, this sensitivity is rooted in the language that has identified the purpose of that information, and the language which has stimulated a level of emotion to desire it to be engaged. So, children are raised to know the names of objects and how they relate to the world about them, and they are helped or hindered by the personality of others in this.

Therefore, it is important that we understand this difference between radial and tangential connections, because herein lies the difference in intelligence developing through the environment or through a noticeable genetic base.

- Radial Connections are where neurons connect by chemical cues, or triggers that follow a genetic design.

- Tangential Connections do not follow a genetic design, and instead cause neurons to connect by signal information generated from the environment. Learning, and so neural plasticity, relies upon these connections. Let us look at examples where they can be found.

2.5 An Environmental Brain:

The operation of activity dependent neurons, and so the occurrence of tangential connections, does not begin when the newborn opens their eyes and is confronted with their father holding up a book entitled *"How to be a Genius."* It begins in the fetal stage by the stimulation that reaches the unborn child in the form of defused light entering their embryonic sac, the sound of voices they hear, and their own tactile

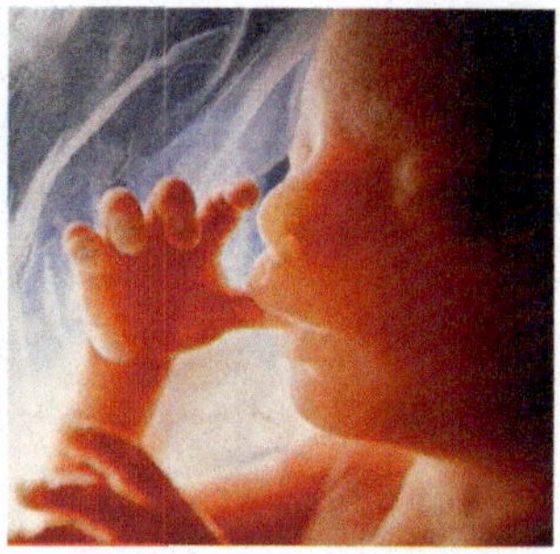

exploration when they hold the umbilical cord, their foot, or touch the lining of their protective world. All this stimuli they acquire is fed to their developing brain to lay down primary networks. As more information is received, association builds up and up, and a basic structuring begins to form preparing the individual for their after birth experiences.

It is important to realize here that the fetus will also receive signals from their mother as and when she experiences happy and stressful incidents, and these will begin to set up the threshold levels for their emotional chemistry and so the platform for their personality.

Since emotion is a vital component of intelligence, as it brings sensitivity to its processes, it is important that we explain at this point that there is a great deal of misunderstanding about how emotion and personality originate, and how they develop.

The term a genetic trait is freely used to explain some feature or particular characteristic that is noticed in the child and their parents. While this term is completely valid with biological features, we shall see in the chapters to come how it is not so with psychological ones, such as a personality manner, a behavioral action or a way of thinking. The latter, of course, is very important to our discussion.

We have already mentioned the process of imprinting, but in the chapters to come we shall better understand how it works and so realize why these psychological characteristics cannot be so easily attributed to a specific gene design, but can be to the actions witnessed and the impressions gained by the infant, especially when they are dependent on their caregiver and so heavily reliant upon the bonding process.

As we examine this, so shall we see how a psychological profile such as schizophrenia can be explained through social inheritance. In this case, the behavior of the parent so disturbs their child that the child alters their neural chemistry to develop similar behavioral characteristics of the parent. In this way, a psychological profile can run through generations. Equally, we shall see that while the personality is also thought to be some part genetic, that recent research has shown how the mother's hormones, heart rate, blood pressure and her emotional states of anxiety, stress, anger, determination, joy, and serenity do have a determinant effect upon her fetus, as these set-up the foundations for their personality.[28]

In 2012, a study found that the personality of the child can be greatly given direction by the feeding process during the first few months of life. Breastfed babies were found to be far more temperamental than those who were bottle-fed. The latter appeared to be more content, but lacked the response searching personality of those who relied more upon sensitive feeding with their mother.[29] As we may see here, the personality much decides the drive of the individual to want to engage information, and to want to learn how to do it their way as they build upon techniques they have developed. This enables them to gain a higher quality from experiences than they would do by merely copying their impression of the techniques of another.

Therefore, we may see that as we develop through this book, we will better come to understand how the bonding process between the infant and the parent works, and so better recognize the holistic process by which intelligence becomes structured. All of this causes us to be ever more wary of the far too simplistic statement that "we are all born differently," as an excuse given to defend poor or inadequate social and educational processes.

It is not, therefore, that the brain is almost complete at birth, and after birth is given some "limited" tuning by the environment, as Galton and Spearman's model of an inherited intelligence suggests. This is quite not the case. The brain of the fetus is constructed through the nutrients it receives from its mother, and its awareness of environmental information, as this is fed to it through its developing senses. So, after birth, just as before it, the brain is a living part of the environment.

As we have discussed that an act of intelligence involves many systems of the brain, such as the regions for visual, audio, memory, language, and emotion, so we may realize that the ways in which each of these systems become constructed must have a similarity. After all, they grow through each other in their development, and serve each other as they function. From this point of view, we may understand that an act of intelligence is dependent upon a quality in sensitivity by which information is first selected, and then processed according to how it is related to similar incidents that have been stored in the memory. It is upon this that meanings are recognized and a potential action decided upon.

The most important sensory system for the development of precision in understanding information is the visual system. Therefore, before we move to consider how intelligence related networks may be constructed, it would be relevant for us to first discuss the extent by which environmental information is designed, by gene coding, to construct this vital system.

The Human Visual System

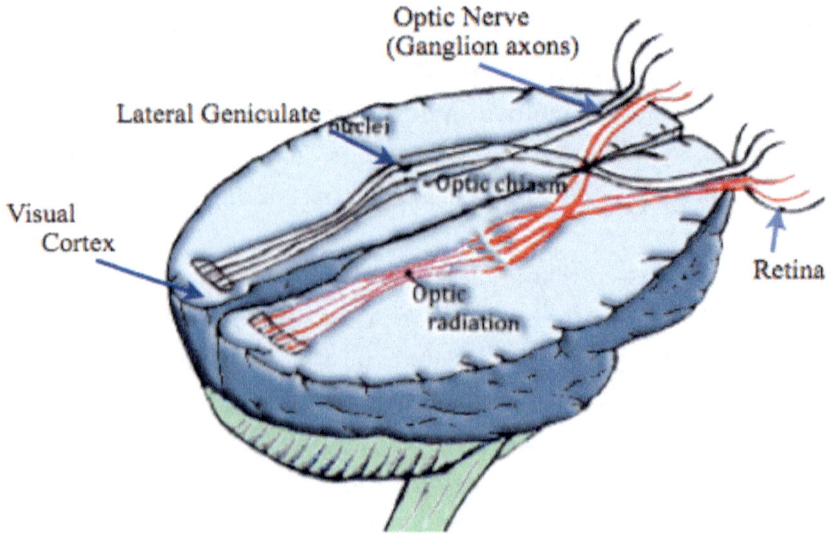

Fig.5

To begin the process of visual identification, we mentally adjust the various muscles that guide the orientation of the eyes so that we can direct them to our interest. Having done this, we then adjust other muscles to focus upon the object selected in that field of vision. As light signals bounce off this object, they enter each eye and are directed by the cornea to the retina behind the eye. The retina is made up of photo receptors, which contain rods for night vision and cones for daytime color vision.

As the light signals hit the photo receptors, a chemical reaction occurs that transforms the frequencies in the light into frequencies of electrical signals. These electrical signals are then transferred on to ganglion cells placed on the back of the retina. The ganglion axons from these cells form the optic nerve. It is the optic nerve that transfers the signals from the retina of the eye into the brain.

Once in the brain, the ganglion axons from each eye divide at the optic chiasm. This allows half of the signals from one eye to remain in their hemisphere, and half to move over into the other. In this way, signals from each eye are available in both hemispheres. Once the signals have passed the optic chiasm, they move to the lateral geniculate nuclei (LGN). The lateral geniculate nuclei are situated in the thalamus, which we may remember is the main routing system of the brain. In turn, these signals are fed to the optic radiation in the visual cortex at the back of the brain. Once here, they are fed to ocular dominance columns (ODC). This stage is very important for what we shall soon come to discuss.

Normally, the ocular dominance columns receive signals from each eye, and according to their signal strength allocate a field of responsibility. This field of responsibility is used to determine the role of each eye in the process of binocular vision. If the signal strength in each eye is equal, both eyes share the detection equally. However, if, as in the following illustration, one eye should generate a stronger signal than the other eye, then, this eye would be allocated greater space in the ocular dominance columns. This greater allocation would enable this eye to make more use of the field of vision.

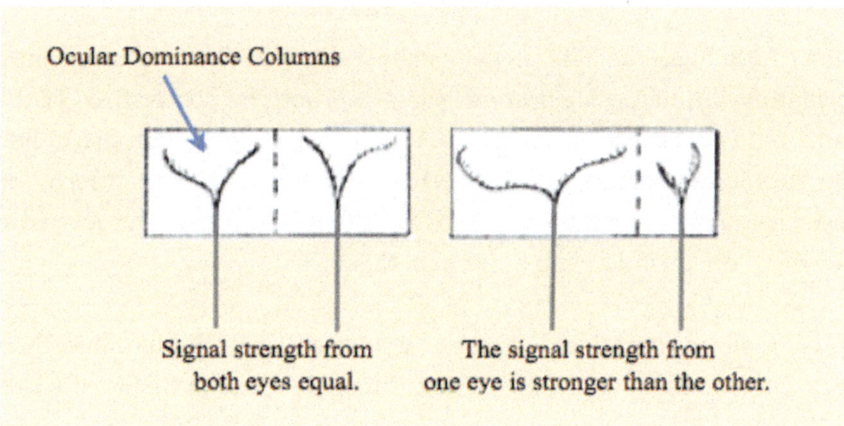

While this system had long been thought to establish itself according to a strict genetic design, Carla Shatz and her colleagues (to whom I am very grateful for this information) have discovered that much of this construction is totally reliant upon information from the environment. We here make a brief summary of their work.[30]

It appears that in a very early stage of the embryonic phase, just weeks after fertilization, the retinas become formed before the eye is fully constructed. As soon as the retina formation is completed, a genetic trigger fires pulses of un-directional signal into the brain to allow them to operate. However, these signals do not provide a recognizable pattern. It is highly significant that they are asynchronous.

This is to say that one retina does not fire until the other has ceased firing. These asynchronous pulses were realized to bring the cells of the lateral geniculate nuclei (LGN) into a system of organization. However, as soon as the eyes had become fully formed, it was found that this "genetic based" firing of the retinas ceased completely. After this time and solely through the use of the defused light available in the embryonic sac, the eyes guided the construction of the visual system from the retina to the lateral geniculate nuclei (LGN). At this juncture, Shatz raised two extremely important points:

First. Although, the lateral geniculate nuclei (LGN) had come into formation through asynchronous signals, if both eyes later fired at the same time (as realized through the use of strobe lighting on fish), then the lateral geniculate nuclei (LGN) cells would reform themselves to this new signal orientation, even though they had already devised a system of organization and built upon this.

It was realized from this that these very decisive cells did not form their arrangement upon a genetic design, but only used the genetic based pulse from the retina as a temporary means to organize themselves in lieu of actual environmental information.

Second. We may recall that under the principle of chemoaffinity, the axon growing out from a source neuron was described as being given its direction by chemical cues, which had been deposited according to a genetic design. However, in her work with the visual system, Shatz found that in the case of the ganglion axon, which develops from the eye retina to the lateral geniculate nuclei (LGN), this did not occur.

When a neural deactivation drug called tetrodotoxin (TTX) was applied to the ganglion axon, as to prevent signal information moving through it, it became un-directional. Therefore, instead of the axon ever extending itself in a purposeful direction, it began to grow numerous side branches seeking information it was unable to locate. This, again, showed that the all-important crossover at the optic chiasm was totally governed by neurons operating through and directly controlled by environmental information.

Once this environmentally complex first stage of the visual system was completed, it was realized that the second stage (from the LGN to the Visual Cortex) unfolded its development through radial connections as guided by chemical cues. At least, that is, during the remainder of the pre-birth construction. However, the axons from the lateral geniculate nuclei (LGN) that went to the visual cortex did not form any type of segregation in this area. This meant that prior to birth there were no ocular dominance columns (ODC), by which the signals from each eye could be compared.

It was realized that it was only after birth, when direct environmental signals entered both eyes, that a segregation of this area was brought into existence. This segregation created the ocular dominance columns(ODC). In other words, as long as the eyes were presented with only indifferent light intensities, the signals they transferred to the visual cortex (at the back of the brain) were not distinguishable enough to contest each other. Without this distinguishing quality the brain could not create areas of allocation, and so construct the ocular dominance columns. Environmentally derived information was found to be essential for the entire development of this process.

This understanding provides clear insight into the extremely important value of environmental signals in the design of a vital brain system. This is a system that previously had been thought to develop strictly and only according to a genetic plan. It is also a system that plays a fundamental role in intelligence.

Another study I would like to introduce the reader to highlights this point even more. I am extremely grateful to Martha Constantine-Paton for her time, kind guidance and illustrations to the following.

As we have mentioned, in our species and other mammals the signals from each eye are compared in the ocular dominance columns to provide the feature of binocular vision. However, this is not so with lower vertebrates such as the frog, for the signals from each of their eyes are not compared. In their case the entire visual information from one eye is transferred to an optic tectum on the opposite side of the head, and kept isolated from the visual information received by the other eye. Frogs have monocular vision.

Fig.6

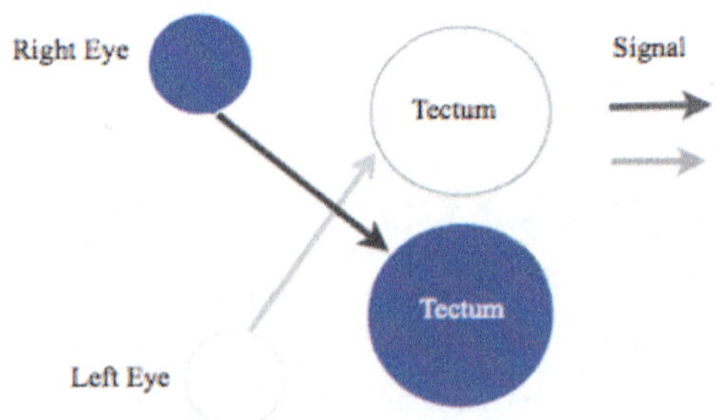

As we know, the brain of the frog has a genetic design to accommodate signals from two eyes. To investigate how environmental signals could override the genetic design, a number of experiments were conducted early in the 1980s on frog embryos. These experiments are no longer fashionable, but at the time a third eye was grafted on to the head of an embryo. The researchers discovered that an axon developed from this third eye, and grew within the brain to connect with one of the tectums that a normal eye had connected to.

Fig.7

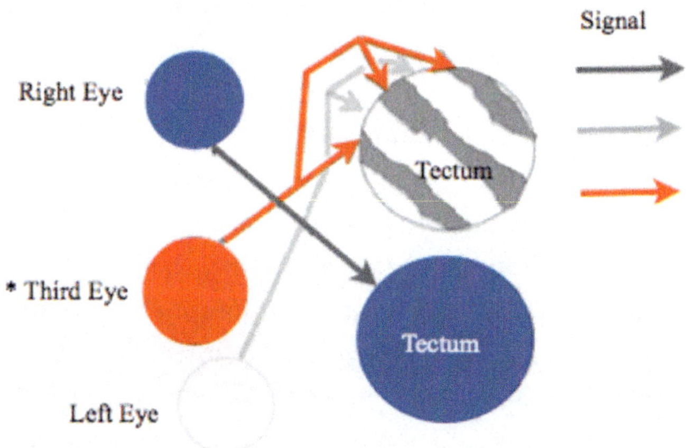

We are shown here a demonstration that without a genetic coding to know of a third eye, the brain of the frog accepted this, and developed it as normally as the two eyes it was genetically designed to handle. However, something else happened here that was even more astonishing.

As we can see from the illustration in Fig.6, the frog does not have the genetic design for ocular dominance columns. There is simply no DNA coding to allow the higher level of visual detection that we have. Yet, as we can see in Fig.7, when the third eye connected with one of the tectums of the frog it did create Ocular Dominance Columns. The presence of these enabled the signal strength received from the two eyes to contest for allocation. When they did this, they created the ability for binocular vision in a species that has no genetic design for this.[31]

The example of how environmental information can drive a foreign eye to adapt as well as any of the normal eyes is remarkable enough, but by the realization that this environmental information also changed the genetic design, we are woken to how the brain gains its adaptability in functioning even at a very primitive level.

As we saw in our chapter on genetics in the previous book, and as we have just seen here in the examples of visual development, the characteristics of the phenotype can be totally decided by the environment when the genotype desires this to occur.

So, in the cases we have just examined, it is not a case of a limited gene design developing through the environment (as is said of intelligence), but of an adaptable gene design enabling the environment to decide the operation and capability of its feature. How, then, may we come to understand, are neural circuits created to allow intelligence to occur?

In *"Intelligence,"* we discussed that an act of intelligence does not give any recognition of an innate ability. Rather, that an act of intelligence can only ever be seen to be a snapshot of the effectiveness of very many different systems within the brain, as they were formed through experience. We discussed that these systems are, amongst other things, products of language skills, perceptual skills, and memory strategies, all of which are set about emotional drives as these direct interest, sensitivity, and attention.

As we can see, and this is precisely why intelligence cannot be measured, the environment outside and inside the brain is far too complex to explain this process simply. All we may do here is to generalize how neural circuits of intelligence can occur, and yet realize as we do this how and why it is sensitivity with the environment that drives ability, and not an inherited factor recognizable by the social standing of the family line, or we might add color of skin.

2.6 Neural Plasticity:

To understand the difference between radial networks formed independently of stimuli and tangential networks that are formed though a consequence of it, it is necessary to understand the purposes of each. While it is obvious that neurons may not connect in a haphazard way, we may now know that this does not imply that they must first be laid upon an inflexible genetic design.

So, while the rule of chemoaffinity may suggest that radial connections form the skeleton of a complex framework and that tangential connections build upon this to provide an operational efficiency, it must be seen only as a general rule. May we now realize that some neural circuitry may be formed entirely on a genetic plan without modification through signal movement. We see this with brainstem connections as they form vital functions. In contrast to this, some neural circuitry will rely upon a genetic design (by chemical cues) that is later given modifiability by signal design, while other neural circuitry may be formed totally and only through signals from the environment.

- As we can see, the developing brain may cause primary pathways to be created either through chemical cues or through the artificial generation of signals. In such ways, a basic circuit design will be created and be able to function, but once it is functioning it may then be totally reformed as it becomes more able to relate to external signals.

- This means that as networks grow, they will arrange themselves in association to each other based upon the value of the signals they receive. As the information increases, so the complexity of the circuitry increases to enable clearer distinction to be gained with information. However, if the information decreases the circuitry will deteriorate, and this will affect the value of the distinction that may be made with further information.

We can recognize this more by the intention rather than the simple effort that a child puts into the learning of a task, and so why they become more familiar with the content of information by the sensitivity they apply to understand it. This is related to the quality of guidance they receive, and how happy they are with themselves.

As we observe the different performances that different children make, we overlook the actual desire of the child to want to be sensitive with information, and even more so how they have been sensitive with information in the past that led to this. After all, children are forced to go to school. We demand of them that they learn facets of information that has no interest to them, and we ignore the distractions their mind struggles against that disturbs their value of attention and so the intention each can make.

While we may understand from this how each child builds up networks of different levels of efficiency, we can never-the-less see in this a basic model of how the child learns (for example, the basic rules for algebra) to develop proficiency through many worked examples. The more they understand what they are doing with each example they work through, the more elaborate their neural circuits are caused to be, and the more extensive become the networks associated with these.

It is very relevant to note here that because learning is associative, that proficiency in one particular skill (algebra, for instance) does not just relate to experiences with this, but with experiences in other areas, factors, or aspects of life that can be related to it, because the student can pull these experiences into "algebra" to recognize what to do and how to proceed.

However, if they stop working with algebra, and try to do a complex problem after a long space of time, what was once easy and automatic may now seem very difficult. The links between the networks that were once secure by the movement of information have deteriorated, and with this the ready means to associate to the knowledge and reservoir of experiences they once were very familiar with.

Let us look at how these networks of association are created in the first place.

Way back in 1949, Donald Hebb realized that some neuronal circuits are entirely dependent upon signal activity to became constructed, and use this activity to maintain their operation. As he put it:

"The physical wiring of the brain changes according to the thoughts moving through it. Neurons that fire together wire together."

Through many observations, Hebb noted how individual neurons built up a circuit.

First: He noted that most cell assemblies that support functions interactive with the environment, have motor components that require training to interact with the signals they receive. (So, with intelligence we write, draw, or operate our body to engage and interact.)

Second: He observed how certain networks are constructed in infancy if, and when they receive repeated and similarly identifiable signals.

Third: He experienced that such a network will relate to even a very basic sensory input signal, and

Fourth: Cells that are repeatedly active at the same time will tend to associate themselves together.[32]

Hebb suggested that neurons which are unrelated to each other, could be brought together to form a common circuit by the idea of very special synapses.[33] Accordingly, he reasoned that if a neuron should release a signal into the synaptic gap, without having a target neuron to go to, the synapse will over activate this signal to raise its strength. Hebb synapses do this by feeding neurotransmitters from the synapse back to the pre-synaptic neuron. This increases the flow of neurotransmitters out of the neuron and into the synapse. This higher volume of signal movement across the synapse now allows the post-synaptic neuron time to adapt itself to the characteristics of the new signal. Once its receptors have been so modified, the signal is accepted and a link is created between two neurons in the continual formation of a circuit.

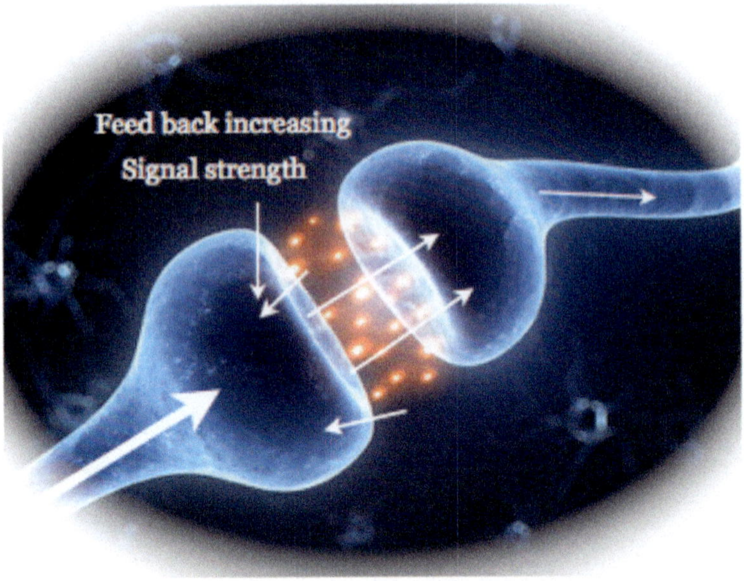

This ability for over activation is termed Long Term Potentiation (LTP), and Hebb synapses that create this can remain active from hours up until a number of days once they are triggered.

If no further signals are received within this time, then the activation simply ceases and the link is lost. However, if further signals, similar to those that began the process are received, and become more repetitively so, then the receiving neuron will construct further receptors to be able to handle these new signals. When this physical change of state occurs a new neural path for information is established, as one neuron drives another in the construction of a circuit.

- Memory and working circuits, such as those used in analysis, are built-up by neurons linking together as we have described here. The more we re-encounter a mental task, the more changes occur within the related neural circuits to enable a greater proficiency. This is essentially brought about by the stable and frequent movement of information through the synapses that link the neurons together.

- As the signal information flows with more regularity, the number of receptors on the post-synaptic neuron increase. As competency builds up through this synapse, signal flow through other synapses that are dissimilar to this decrease. This improves the overall tuning of the circuit. When the signal activity is sufficiently strong to drive the post-synaptic cell well enough, other synapses with a similar firing pattern can also be maintained on that neuron. This, in principle, is how neurons develop their circuit organization, and how we may view the child's brain operating as it learns information and seeks to respond to a question.

It has to be remembered, as we discuss this, that we learn through association. So, while we may think we are learning something new, the truth is that this "new thing" has associated itself to some information we have previously stored in our memory. Once this association has been made, new circuits of information will be built up from this so that eventually this information may be recognized in its own right.

- The determining factor in the effectiveness of how this information is stored, and so how circuits are created that will enable future information to access it and so make use of it, will lie in how it was identified, and so to what information it was compared to and then associated with.

- Therefore, the more interest we have with new information, so the more elaborate are the circuits created through it. It also means, of course, that children who are bullied or insecure are very likely to have constructed circuits of information, and developed means of selecting and processing information that are as insecure as is their sense of knowing who they are.

This brings us back again to the role of emotional sensitivity in learning, and this we discuss again in *"Preparing A New-World Education"* when we will look at the child in the classroom. After all, it is the classroom environment and so the structure of education that moulds the intelligence of the child. Indeed, we may recall from our previous book how Goldfarb demonstrated the importance of emotion in intelligence, when he compared the low intelligence scores of institutionalized children against the much higher scores of children raised in foster homes where they received personal love, more security, and greater attention.[34]

- Therefore, how well we interrogate information, how well we analyse it, how well we check for errors in the progression of that information, and how often we recall it in different ways especially if we can include some emotional content, decides how effective an association memory circuit is to produce information accurately with speed. In the world of school, such strategies mean a problem is recognized faster and means to deal with it are more easily found.

We may add to this, that it is such factors and the circumstances in the life of the primary school child that allows them to earn a gold star. As the child develops through the same framework, they later obtain 10/10 on a regular basis, and later in life a high IQ score if they should be so interested in the facts and issues of life.

It is only within the past 35 or so years, that we have truly been able to grasp the extent to which the brain is able to form through the emotional and instructional world in which it develops. We have long witnessed how this is possible in animals, and many experiments on rats and monkeys have shown how their brains developed when they were given learning tasks. One experiment showed how the brain of rats developed when they were encouraged to learn a new balancing task, such as walking up a sloping wire. The area of the brain known as the vestibular nuclei controls balance. In the case of these rats, their vestibular nuclei were found not only to contain a substantial increase in the amount of RNA through the learning of this task, but also a dramatic change in its composition.[35]

Therefore, when we talk about the effect of the environment on intelligence, we are really discussing the way the brain becomes designed, and how adaptable this design is to the interrogation and analysis of information.

This was clearly pointed out from studies that demonstrated how the brain size of mammals living in the wild was found to be considerably larger than that of their cousins living in a domesticated or laboratory environment. The wild Norway rat, for instance, has a brain size 7 to 15 per cent larger than the laboratory white rat,[36] which would be understandable if the brain were shaped by environmental stimuli. After all, a creature living in the wild would by necessity to survive have to be more inventive to overcome the far more varied challenges than those found in such an ordered and sterile world. Howell, we have just discussed and may be reminded of, explained how "The brains of idle laboratory mice increase in weight 2 to 3 per cent when they are given interesting, but perplexing tasks to perform, and puzzles to solve."[37] Therefore, we can see from this that it is stimuli that drives the shape and the functioning of neurons, the circuits and networks they create, and the physical form of the higher brain itself.

It is not, for instance, that a neuron has just one terminal button from which to pass its signal to the next neuron, but something in the order of between 10,000 to 200,000 that are selected, used, or discarded on the effectiveness of the role they play in the circuit that is developed.

Schreckenberg and Bird further demonstrated how the brain is given order and quality of operation by the quality of the information it receives, when they discovered how different kinds of music caused different kinds of structural changes in the brain of rats.

When disharmonic sounds, in the form of incessant drumbeats, were played to a group of rats, they displayed significant decreases in memory retention, as well as hyperactivity, aggression, and inattentiveness. Later examination of their brains showed excess branching of neuron dendrites with significant increases in messengerRNA. On the other hand, when Strauss waltzes were played to rats, they showed improved ability in maze training.[38]

Within humans, Shaw found that listening to the music of Mozart caused neural circuits to alter their arrangements to improve the ability of spatial temporal reasoning skills, such as those used in mathematics and logical thinking.[39/40] While we tend to think of how neural development can be related to increased stimulus, it is also worthwhile to remember how those networks break down in elderly folk directly due to their decreased mental activity.

So far, we have only considered how neurons can develop themselves through activity or lose their connections through lack of it, but it is now realized that the brain is capable of growing entirely new cells through signal activity. It is, for instance now realized that the hippocampus in rats creates between 5,000 to 10,000 new neurons each day. From this, we may understand that the traditional idea that we are born with X amount of neurons and do not create new neurons after birth, and so in adulthood, is wrong. It is now understood that the adult human brain does create totally new neurons in certain areas, which makes sense when we realize that the brain has to learn to adapt to a continually changing environment.

- For all the reasons we shall shortly examine the most necessary means for this adaption is language. It is of no small significance to now know that songbirds do grow new nerve cells when they sing, and also increase the physical size of the area of their brain that is related to singing.[41] The significance of this is that the way in which songbirds learn their song, is very similar to the way in which we learn the sounds of speech. Speech, of course, is a component of language, and language as we are brought back to realize is an underlying component of intelligence.

- All we have just mentioned concerning the arrangement of neural circuits by environmental signals comes down to language, because it is by a sensitivity with language that information and the uses it may have are known. It is also by sensitivity with language that we can understand each other's feelings to overcome insecurities and distractions, and provide greater sensitivity in the selection and processing of information.

In summary of all we have discussed so far, we can realize that the brain's ability to design itself through environmental information which is associative, and by the psychology of the mind to seek continually and test for stability, are strong arguments against the idea that intelligence is stable because it is limited by an inherited worth.

It is then highly significant that we really grasp, that in regard to the inheritance of intelligence, the onus is not how much an inherited gene code can relate to an environment, which we use to explain differences in intelligence, but what is the real purpose is of that coding, is it to accommodate the environment, or is it to adapt to it?

If it is the latter, then, this adaptation must lie in the psychology involved that drives the skill of language, which underlies the articulation in skills of reasoning.

As we have examined how a vital component of the intelligence system can be virtually designed by environmental information, it will be of no small significance for us now to examine an incredible example of how adaptable the human brain can be. I am, in being able to share this, indebted to Mr Ewen Mackinnon the Consultant Pediatric Surgeon to the Children's Hospital in Sheffield for providing me with the following information from the late Dr. Lorber's file.

In 1980, John Lorber, who at that time held the chair in pediatrics at Sheffield University, lectured at a conference to fellow pediatricians. The title of his lecture was "*Is Your Brain Really Necessary.*"[42]

The focal point of Lorber's lecture centered around one male student. Lorber had noticed that during a class, the size of the head of one his students was larger than normal. Intrigued to understand why, he arranged to take a number of CT scans. Although Lorber was expecting hydrocephalus, he was astonished to see that the scans revealed that some 90 to 95% of this young man's brain was missing. Yet, despite this, the student appeared normal in his physical functioning, and social life. Indeed, he had just acquired a 1st class honors degree in mathematics, and had scored 126 in an IQ test.

Fig.8

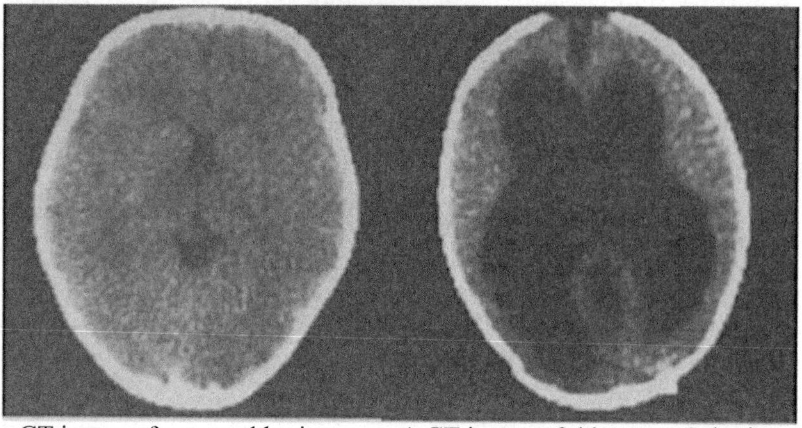

CT image of a normal brain. A CT image of this person's brain.

It would help us to understand this case if we examine how this damage occurred.

The brain is a huge convoluted sheet of very fine neural tissue. This soft tissue is isolated and protected from the hard surfaces of the skull by what is known as cerebrospinal fluid. This CSF is manufactured within ventricles or hollow chambers of the brain, and flows through channels to spread itself around the brain matter. Due to a number of conditions the flow of CSF can become obstructed, and this will lead to a build-up of fluid. If this build-up of fluid occurs very early in infancy, the skull will be pliable enough to grow in support of both the brain and this excessive fluid. It is for this reason that people who incur this condition are known to have exceptionally large heads.

However, if this build-up of CSF develops later in life, when the boned skull no longer has such pliability, the pressure created by it may bring about a far more life-threatening situation. In either case, brain tissue is likely to be progressively destroyed. This condition is referred to as hydrocephalus. Because CSF has the same density as water, hydrocephalus is more commonly termed “water on the brain.”

The normal brain is a well structured and compacted organ containing many millions of cells. Through the basic organization of these cells, the brain functions to enable the individual to interact with the environment. Yet, all the discrete brain areas that we individually associate with motor and visual functions, personality, and memory, etc., simply were not to be seen in the scans of this young man. It is not that a number of regions relating to particular functions had been displaced or even destroyed, but that devastation seemed virtually complete. We can see this from the dark area in the centre of the cortex, which represents the extent of the CSF occupation. Despite this incredibly extensive damage, the young man displayed a normal personality, normal movement, and had demonstrated above normal academic achievement.

The second image is very suggestive of a great deal of neural damage. However, since it is normal under this condition for the tissue to be pushed towards the inside of the skull by the CSF, the real extent of the damage cannot be known.

Therefore, we cannot know how much of the tissue has been destroyed, and how much has been simply moved from its normal position and compressed into a very dense mass at the skull’s inner surface.

Yet, what is obvious is that the brain has demonstrated a great deal of adaptability by enabling this young man to display such normal functioning. To understand this readily, consider how the visual system would be normally arranged, as we show in the following illustration, and how it appears to be totally absent in this young man who displayed normal visual performance.

Fig.9

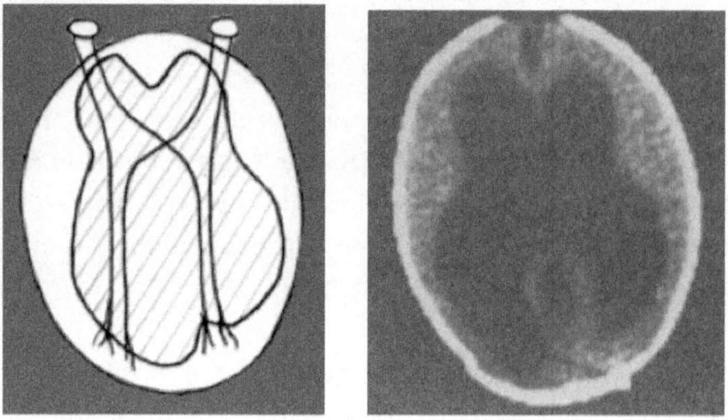

When we think of how highly intricate the circuitry of the brain is, with neurons criss-crossing each other in multiple directions and depths and with one circuit operating through the complexity of many others, we have to wonder how this functionality could have been maintained in this young man.

How could axons have been stretched and somehow maintain their multidirectional connections under the enormous pressure of the CSF? Of equal consideration is how could the synaptic gaps maintain their vital distances under this pressure? For if a synaptic gap is unable to conduct the normal flow of neurotransmitters, the whole circuit to which it belongs will break down.

If it were said that the neural structuring of the brain had arisen through the unfolding of a genetic plan, it would be difficult to conceive how that plan could have given such compensation for the devastating effect of the CSF as its sophisticated wiring experienced such disturbance. Yet, if that structuring were largely a product of environmental information, it would necessarily contain a degree of plasticity that could account for the high adaptability we witness here. In fact, it may be wondered if the existence of the brain's highly sophisticated systems could have been maintained if they were not driven and so constructed through environmentally based signals.

Not all hydrocephalics, it should be said, rise to Lorber's example, and many exhibit signs of mental difficulty. There lies in this case then, and in others that provide evidence similar to it,[43] a cause to recognize that the difference between degeneration and adaptability, if not some degree of regeneration, may lie in intention.

This is the factor of psychology, and while we often think of how the mind can drive the physiology of the body, we may see from the examples we have discussed in this chapter how it is equally capable of rewiring the brain.

I have experienced the extent this can occur with deaf and blind children. With no means of seeing or hearing, their brain had developed to operate at a very low level of interaction. Yet, when people like Roman Gouzman set about to develop their tactile skills, a new avenue was given to raise their level of language. As information built up, so did suggestion of newly developed brain circuitry, for this would have needed to occur for the very different level of intellectual performances that became witnessed.[44]

The brain, then, does not develop before the child experiences the environment, and thereafter makes use of it. From the earliest stage of its construction, cells of the brain send out their axons to connect with proto-sensory detectors about the body. As soon as these are able to detect environmental signals in the form of light, sound, and touch, they build up the structure and operation of the brain's circuitry, so that when the child is born their brain is already "of" the environment, and "living" as a part of it. We never do stop interacting with the environment, and so neurons never stop making new circuits and strengthening old ones they use.

As we may have understood so far, our knowledge of how the brain works, and even what it is in a holistic sense, is continually changing. Without a true understanding of the effect of the environment, our knowledge that the new born has inherited the mixed genetic codes of their parents, has always supported the belief that they will be limited in their mental capacity by that of their mother and father. However, when we do this, we forget that in the process of meiosis (where the parent's genes are mixed) that mutations arise.

It is important to understand this, because it means that the DNA of the child is not just unique to them by the one only way their parent's genes were mixed at the moment they were created, but also because these genes incurred mutations in this time. The idea of a genetic mutation brings to mind a great shift in some feature. We may think of the creation of a new form of species. Although, more likely we will think of the Thalidomide children who were born without normal arms in the 1960s, because their mothers were prescribed a drug to alleviate morning sickness that interfered with their genetic design. So, we think of a mutation as creating some immediate and very noticeable change. The reality is that small mutations are a normal part of the genetic process. Cancer is caused by a gene mutation.

I did not fully understand, as I know many readers will not, what cancer really is. We know many people die of this and we hear of huge amounts of funding that have gone into researching into this condition. It may be, then, of very great interest to many to follow the explanation of Professor Thomas Seyfried of Boston College.U.S.A.[45]

Mitochondria in cells creates the energy for a cell to work. Mitochondria derives its energy from oxygen. Should a cell or a tissue incur some chronic insult, this may lead to a loss of oxygen to the mitochondria and so not enough energy for its operation. In this condition, there is an ancient pathway by which cells obtain their energy through the fermentation of glucose and glutamine. Deprived of the necessary oxygen it needs, mitochondria will draw in glucose for its operation. The high level energy that glucose contains, essentially causes the cell to move into rapid reproduction. In other words, cell production goes out of control. This is what cancer is.

- Prof. Seyfried (I take no responsibility to this) makes a very clear explanation that cancer can be halted and stopped by cutting out glucose and the amino acid glutamine from the diet, rather than the normal radiation treatment this is now conducted. You may watch Prof Seyfried discuss this on the Youtube "Can We Stave Cancer? What You Need to Know| Dr. Thomas Seyfried."

What is often not realized is that the nucleus of the cell carries the historical data for that species and beyond. This is to say that each of us carries the DNA coding in our cells that goes back to the very first Homo sapiens sapiens. This historical DNA is referred to as transposons. Since their discovery in the 1940s,[46] transposons were always regard to be dormant in the cell, and so not to interact with the active DNA. While this understanding has not changed in regard to body cells, it has more recently been discovered that this is not so with brain cells.[47]

It is now understood that while the DNA in the cells of the body has developed a means of isolating transposons, so that they cannot attach themselves to it and thereby alter the coding, this is not so with neurons. In an evolutionary sense, neurons have not evolved a means to prevent transposons from attaching themselves to the DNA, which they appear to do with great ease, and once connected they alter that coding. Neurons do not divide through the process of mitosis as other cells of the body, but one buds another into existence. It is now understood that because of the interference of transposons, each new neuron will be genetically different to the mother neuron that produced it. This phenomenon is known as genetic mosaicism.

In short, we are caused to realize that we have evolved to have great genetic stability in the physical organization of our body, and great genetic instability in the design of neurons, as oppose to glial cells which form the general structure of the brain. It is by the shifting genetic design of neurons that their efficiency is caused to be heavily reliant upon the neurotransmitters that connect them, and by the environmental signals that pass through them. More directly, this knowledge brings two meanings to us

First, while our bodies, and essentially the color of their skin, can be genetically defined into a particular race, such as Caucasian and Negroid, etc, our brains cannot be. Neurologically, we cannot be classified by the outward appearance of our body. The ability of the brain of any human being is as different as any other human being on the planet. With the knowledge of transposons, it can no longer be thought that one race is more superior or inferior to another, anymore than can be said of their social divisions, because the brain cells of every human being contain the original and active coding of "Adam and Eve"!

Second, Galton's idea that the brain of the child can be identified with the facial features of their family line, and so operate with the same efficiency as that family by the social success they have achieved, is completely destroyed. By the knowledge that transposons freely change the DNA of neurons, we are caused to realize that there is no direct genetic link in the ability of the child's neurons to function with those of their parents. There is no more of a simple way to say that the genetic factor of a child's intelligence cannot be based on that of their parent's. The historical nature/nurture debate now has no foundation.

With this understanding, we must only consider how the normal child's intelligence is nurtured. In other words, the child's intelligence is now greatly determined by how they are caused to be sensitive to the world in which they live far, far more than we have ever realized before. This will have very great meaning to all we shall move to discuss. In fact, at the very end of this book, I give a short "hands-on" understanding to what I mean when I refer to the Art of Sensitivity in Awareness, which is a vital factor in the development of anyones intelligence.

*

In our next chapter, we shall look closely at the theories behind the general idea that brain development is limited to time frames. As we shall come to see, open-ended learning is entirely possible,. However, it requires a degree of consciousness to alter networks that the brain regards to be stable and so reliable.

To conclude this chapter, we may say that there is no evidence that there is one specific place within the brain that is responsible for intelligence. Rather, that the act of intelligence appears to arise from very many separate places within the brain at the same time.

As a thought is triggered....

sometimes by a visionary impulse sometimes by random

association ....

it connects with different memory banks stored in different areas. ...

A memory evokes an emotion.....

Emotion pulls in a behavioral response. .....

Behavior outlines preferences,.....

preferences choose features for intelligent appraisal, ...

and so on and so forth.

Since the physical shape of the forebrain is largely determined by interaction with the environment, we may reason from this that so is the capability of its operations similarly determined. After all, we have just examined how neurons are driven to create networks and how the effectiveness of these networks rely upon emotional sensitivity, just as we have begun to understand how the psychology of the mind can overturn the biological stability of these networks.

Therefore, as we have seen how functions that serve intelligence, such as the visual system, are caused by their genetic design to be created by environmental information, it is reasonable to consider that similar patterning takes place for the nervous system in general.[48]

We know that features such as language, reasoning, desires, intentions, and awareness of possibilities are purposely not restricted genetically. So may we reason that there is no evidence that the genetic base for the act of intelligence of one can be compared to the genetic base of the act of intelligence of another, providing there is no evidence of a malfunctioning nervous system of genetic origin. Even if we know there is some genetic difference by the apparent behavior of one, we can never really know how this is responsible for the differences we see in them.

To apply what we have discussed in this chapter into the realms of education, it is to realize the practical applications of what the term "neural plasticity" can actually mean. The least it can mean is that we stop judging the performance of a child as a factor of "something" they were born with. The most is that when we are teaching a child some aspect of our world, that we pause more often to consider how their brain cells are trying to decipher what to us is clear and obvious by the extent of our experiences, but what to them may require greater points of reference.

There is, however, one more scientific chapter to discuss, which is vital to close completely the case on the belief that intelligence is limited by inheritance. To engage this, as we will now do, allows us to understand why motivation guided by emotional sensitivity is the means by which any child can dramatically improve what others think of their intelligence. As this becomes more accepted, it will cause the teacher to seek new means by which they can explain what they mean to a class of minds who live in different worlds.

* *

Chapter Three

The Living Brain

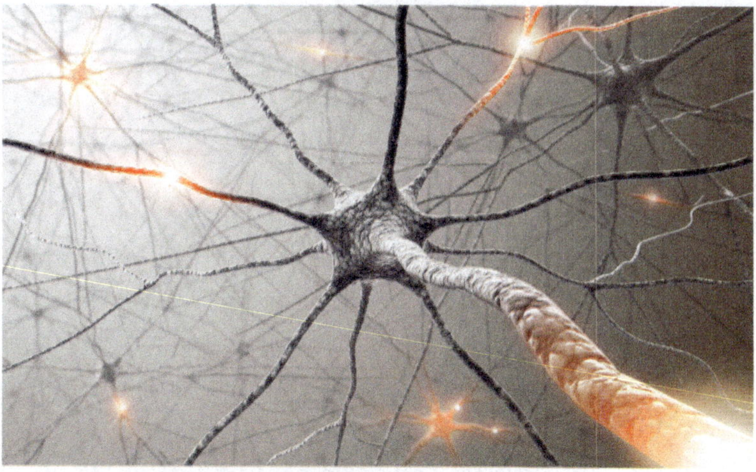

"Any man, be he so inclined,
could be the sculptor of his own brain."
Santiago Ramón y Cajal

3.0 Introduction:

The impression we have of the brain being created and developing through a biological time plan, encourages the belief that its entire operational development is essentially pre-designed. Through this belief, and to account for the learning stages of childhood, a reasoning has developed that we are given a limited number of years following birth when we can more readily learn than at any other time in our life. Once those years are past, further development is considered to be highly restricted.

This limited timeframe of early learning is referred to as the critical period.[49] Although, in general terms and in education, it tends to be called “a window of opportunity”, to describe a number of years following birth when the child can maximize in developing or learning something. Every feature that we use to interact with the environment is said to have its own critical period. This is so for vision, as it is with motor development, musical development, and language, etc.

While the theory of critical periods gives great latitude for the young child to design their skills with the environment within this timeframe, it offers very little consideration to ways they may be able to alter those skills once it has finished, because after this cessation their ability is more or less believed to be signed, sealed, and delivered.

In this chapter, we will discuss exactly why the concept of critical periods is wrong when it is applied to human learning. When this term is misunderstood, as it generally is, it places great stress on young children to maximize on their skills in a limited timeframe, and diverts money from later stages in education to fund this early learning.

This lack of finance deprives older students of the resources to understand better what they are learning, and hinders them from correcting or improving upon aspects of their earlier education they had difficulty with. Without the opportunity to correct earlier mistakes and misunderstandings, their opportunity to develop will be restricted by the impressions and understandings they had earlier gained. Understanding why this concept of critical periods is scientifically wrong will also help us to understand the true nature of brain plasticity and open-ended learning.

The introduction of critical periods will also enable us to begin to discuss more fully the process of imprinting. Imprinting is a very important feature we genetically inherit that again is not affected by variations in genetic codes and is left to environmental circumstances to full develop. As we saw earlier, imprinting creates a bonding process. In the infantile state, it enables the infant to copy and so learn some feature from a parent for their survival. Yet, should this bonding breakdown due to the ill behavior of a parent, the infant will reject copying or learning from them. So, we discussed how a baby may not smile if deprived of love, or a toddler not walk or talk until far beyond their normal age if they are badly treated by a parent.

As we saw earlier, imprinting develops a relationship between two individuals, more generally a parent and their child but it can also arise between a teacher and a student, whereby the weaker of the two brings into their perception of who they are, some characteristic of the one who is influencing them.

We may, for example, hear the comment "He is just like his father", see a girl brushing her hair in the same way her mother does or, more significantly to our interest, recognize some action or thought process, which, in being displayed, seems remarkably similar to that of a parent or a teacher. This copying can be viewed as a means of mimicking some feature of a person one admires, so as to see themselves as similar to that person in some manner.

By discussing the process of imprinting in this and the following chapter, we will come to realize the very important difference between an actual genetic trait (such as a child having the same color irises as a parent) and a socially inherited trait (such as an intelligent action or thought displayed, that by being identical to a parent, is mistakingly thought to be a genetic trait — when it is not). In fact, this aspect of an adult was simply consciously or unconsciously mimicked into the body language or way of thinking of the child. From an evolutionary point of view this might be thought to be a survival tactic.

Understanding the principle and process of imprinting, therefore, will help us to see the role of genetics in intelligence in a very more informed light.

3.1 Critical Periods: A Concept of Limitation:

The idea of development having a termination point arose through the studies of Spalding in the 1870s, as he sought to distinguish between altrical and precocial species. Altrical species are those such as man, who are born helpless and dependent upon a long period of maturation. Precocial species, as by example the domestic chicken, are born with the ready ability for mobilization, and are capable of surviving independently of their mother from a very early age.

Although, precocial species have the mobility for independence very early in life, Spalding observed that they rely upon a short but intensive period of association with a parent, from whom they can directly copy or imprint the characteristics necessary for their survival.[50]

Spalding's work was followed up in the 1930s by Konrad Lorenz. It was Lorenz who, working with precocial species and geese in particular, suggested that while there was no evidence of trial and error learning during this imprinting stage,[51] that it could set the basis for learning development after it. The imprinting stage was therefore a critical time or rather a specific period in development.[52]

- In other words, Lorenz was saying that the quality of development after the critical period, was much determined by how closely the sibling had mimicked the actions of their mother during the imprinting phase.

By the 1950s, interest had arisen if critical periods occurred in altrical as well as precocial species. This led to the suggestion that human beings may undergo some kind of imprinting experience.[53] Consideration that this may be applied to our species, probably gained direction from Hebb's 1946 discussion of how we customize ourselves to initial fears by repetitive exposure.[54]

However, a decade was to pass before Gray suggested that infantile smiling was an act of imprinting, and thereby forged a direct link with the human infant and the act of imprinting as an early learning experience.[55]

When the educationalist Piaget put forth his theory of phases in child development, as we discussed in *"The Illusion of School,"* he so merged concepts of motor and intellectual development that they became seen as welded together.[56] This created the impression that when a stage of motor development was said to be completed, so could the same be said of its accompanying intellectual stage. These time periods of development brought the concept of critical periods into human development.

However, as Piaget's phases were reliant upon trial and error experiences, they conflicted with the idea of imprinting. It was through this discord that a mood developed that, given substance by experiments in the visual system of kittens, brought about a general disassociation between the idea of critical periods and that of imprinting, at least within our species.

As the rift between critical periods and imprinting grew, the perspective of the former changed to explain the absence of the latter. While the term "a critical period" initially arose to describe the duration of an imprinting phase, which once completed was then ready for trial and error development, it now became descriptive of a trial and error phase that when completed suggested a restriction in development.

Thus, while ethologists described:

- Imprinting to be the mimicking by an offspring of the behavioral and intellectual strategies of its parent.
- The critical period is the length of time the imprinting period lasts. After the critical period had ceased, the organism adapts to its environment through trial and error learning.

Educational psychologists transformed these to mean:

- Imprinting is either taken to be a mimicking process of the infantile baby, or the effect that is witnessed is otherwise explained as a genetic trait and ignored. In the case of the latter, when a child displays a mannerism of a parent, a facial muscle movement, a hand mannerism, or employs a thinking strategy similar to that of a genetic relative, their knowledge of this act is said to be biologically inherited.
- The critical period, with the concept of imprinting now removed, explains a biological time period of unrestricted trial and error learning within, that is, the capability of the individual's genetic quality. After this period had expired, further development is said to be much restricted to the development that was achieved during the critical period.

At this point, we leave further understanding of imprinting until we engage the subject again in great depth in our following book "For Parent For Teacher: Mediation", where we explain how intellectual and thinking mannerisms are copied and not of a genetic trait. However, before we are ready to do this, we first need to focus upon the meaning of a critical period, and if it really does limit the development of the child.

It may have been Piaget's theory of biological steps of development that paved the way for critical periods in human ability, but it was an experiment made by Hubel and Wiesel on the visual system of kittens in the 1960s[57] that decisively established the idea of imprinting within humans.

By closing one eyelid of a kitten at birth and opening the eye three weeks later, it was found that the visual system associated with this eye did not operate. Hubel and Wiesel believed from this that a critical period for visual development existed for a period of three weeks from birth. While their work was primarily made on kittens, it opened up consideration to similar developmental systems in humans.

The contention that human beings do have critical periods was said to be confirmed by Lenneburg in 1967, with an explanation that lateralization (the completed development of the cerebral hemispheres) is completed by approximately 11 years of age.[58]

Subsequently, Hubel and Wiesel extended their work into the human visual system, and confirmed that man, as other animals, was dependent in his visual development upon a critical period.

With factual information that a feature of the human brain was shown to be dependent upon the type of experience it encountered, within a specific period of time following birth, the concept of critical periods in humans took hold. Explanations readily came forward after this to suggest how all features of the nervous system develop through an early, but limited period of flexibility.

With the belief that each ability was controlled by a specific period of development, psychologists waded into social and educational planning with the intention that infants and children receive the fullest opportunities possible for the development of their intelligence. As the media hit on this new idea, anxious parents brought in political support and suddenly a whole new industry appeared within education of time-frames of learning.

This prompted Bateson to suggest that social behavior was determined by childhood experiences.[59] In turn, further suggestions arose from different psychologists that other features of the mind and the body were limited in their development by specific years. So we find that emotional control is said to be decided by the experiences of the first three years of life, motor development by the ages of five or six, and the human visual system by the age of three, as is the ability for hearing and language learning.[60] Such "authorized" views brought influences into educational design and home education in how children should be taught music and a second language as early as possible, to maximize on their opportunity before the cut-off period for these abilities was reached.

While the concept of critical periods brought support and finance into early learning programs, it unfortunately distracted interest from developmental programs that extended beyond their timeframe, because after the completion of a critical period learning was now said to be severely restricted. However, it was while psychologists and educationalists were examining the structure of early learning that evidence began to arise from other areas that not all human features, including aspects of intelligence, could be determined by a critical period.

3.2 A Nervous System with an Open Development:

While it should be noted that Lorenz's observations of critical periods cannot be recognized in all precocial species, their presence in altrical species to which we belong is much disputed.

To begin to put critical periods into perspective, we should discuss that Lenneberg had examined a number of case studies of children who had incurred aphasia. Aphasia is a condition of loss of language. In these cases, it appeared that when aphasia had occurred before the age of 11, children were able to fully recover from it. However, in cases where this condition arose after the age of 11, recovery was less than complete. Believing that this difference between complete and partial recovery at about this age was caused by the hemispheres having reached full specification, Lenneberg reasoned that this stage of final brain development would suggest the existence of a critical period in language development.

However, studies made in the early 1970s suggested that lateralization occurs between the ages of 2 and 5,[61] well below Lenneberg's estimation. Anderson remarked upon this when he discussed Lenneberg's theory, and pointed out that since some children over five years of age accomplished full recovery from aphasia, then lateralization could not be the cause of the cases that Lenneberg had examined. Further discussion upon this concluded that recovery from aphasia was reliant upon the quality of language the child had experienced before neural damage occurred, and to the corresponding period of development after it. This meant that recovery was not prevented by a critical period.[62]

Anderson offers an example to this, suggesting that if a child was not introduced to the skill of language until they were 10 years old and aphasia developed after this, then recovery would be expected to take some four or five years after it had occurred.[63] He backed this up with reference to the case of Genie. Genie had been locked in an attic and deprived of all human language skills from infancy to the age of 13. When she was discovered and released, it was found that she could later learn and develop near normal language skills.[64] We can see from this that the restrictions in language development, which Lenneberg had identified in cases of aphasia, could not be explained with the idea of a critical period.

However, fueled by the greatly publicized work of Hubel and Wiesel on kittens, a whole industry was now in motion expounding upon the dangers in ignoring critical periods in child development. A mass of literature emanated from psychologists to direct educational policies to develop early learning teaching practices, and create developmental opportunities for very young children. These gave fuel to newspapers and magazines to warn parents of the danger of not placing their children on intensive courses to maximize on the time of each critical period. Few wanted to consider the implications that a critical period did not account for Lenneberg's loss of language. Too many had too much to lose, despite the stress that young children began to incur as progressively minded or worried parents enrolled them into intensive evening programs, where they could learn to play the violin, learn formal dancing, or have early education in English and mathematics, instead of learning to play, developing their imagination, and just having fun.

Having said this, it now falls upon us to re-examine what really happened when Hubel and Wiesel temporarily closed off one eye of an experimental mammal that set this whole enterprise in motion.

Hubel and Wiesel based their work on the belief that the strength of signal from each eye drives the cells of the visual cortex into specification. (We may recall our earlier discussion on how the allocations of the ocular dominance columns or ODC are determined.) Hubel and Wiesel reasoned from this, and sought to demonstrate with experiments, that when one eye was shut off for a period of time, its associated neural circuitry would close down and cause an irreparable loss of function. However, while it is generally accepted that the act of sewing an eyelid closed created this amblyopic situation, this is not evidence of an irreparable loss of function.

In fact, Duffy proved that sufficient light was still able to get through a sutured eyelid to drive cells in the visual cortex.[65] By doing this, Duffy was able to demonstrate that the observations made by Hubel and Wiesel did not confirm that any neural system had closed down. Rather, that what was witnessed was the normal mechanism of cellular allocation responding to imbalances in signal strength.

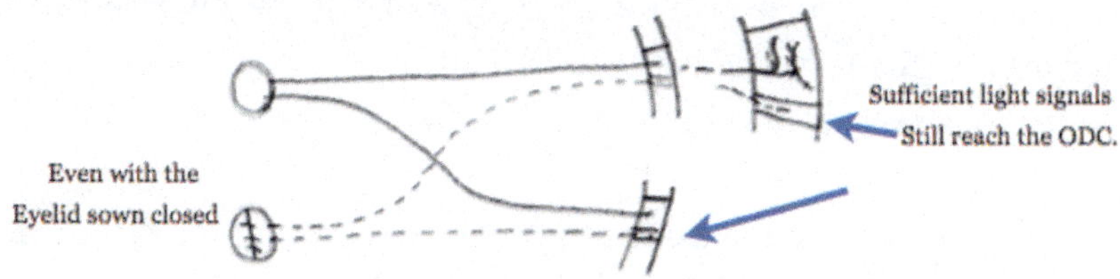

Despite the work by Hein in 1976,[66] and Kasamatatsu in 1979,[67] who had proven that cells of the binocular system were found intact after sutures had been removed from an eyelid sewn shut for the length of a critical period, Hubel and Wiesel were still awarded a Nobel Prize in 1981, due to the otherwise universal acceptance of their work.

I am deeply indebted to Paul Harris for helping me to realize that if Hubel and Wiesel had subsequently stimulated the visionary systems they examined, with the full spectrum of spatial frequencies that would drive the appropriate cells for a sufficient length of time, the condition of amblyopia would have disappeared and with it the phenomenon of their critical period.[68]

This has been confirmed through the earlier work of Van Sluyters, who proved that the effect of a critical period was completely reversible,[69] and of Cynader who showed that there was a direct relationship between recovery from monocular deprivation and the application of stimulus.[70]

There are also very many recorded instances of adults who were born blind and were first able to see following a successful operation after their middle age had passed. Latta for instance, as early as 1904, recorded the successful operation for the removal of a congenital cataract in an adult.[71] Von Noorden since remarked upon a number of similar cases, and in the 1970s Valvo even described how sight was gained in eyes that had never formed completely by insertion of an artificial lens. Sometimes, the lens had to be inserted inside a tooth nerve that had been placed in the eye to overcome tissue rejection.[72]

However, very many of the cases of people being able to see for the first time in later adulthood showed two particular factors, which partly explain why the visionary systems examined by Hubel and Wiesel did not correct themselves immediately after the conditioned eye had been opened to light.

In all the cases that have been put forward of adults being able to see for the first time following an operation to remove congenital blindness, it has been noted that they were too psychologically dependent upon their other senses to interrogate the environment, and that they tended to use this new visionary sense only as a backup support.

Thus, and with very great significance, we may note how a physiological structuring seems to be dependent upon a psychological one. This is of great interest to what will shortly follow.

Of equal interest, and one that supports the point just raised, is that a very long time does occur between the gaining of the ability for sight after an operation, and the actual development of vision. In other words, neural circuits "need time and appropriate training" to restructure themselves after an operation to provide a normal level of competency.

So deep is the belief in genetic responsibility to unfold a biological plan, that we all too readily fail to understand the value of the environment. Von Monakow spoke of this at the beginning of the 20th Century, when he brought awareness to the difference between initial and residual symptoms following brain operations,[73] as he explained how the unpredictability of what could be developed always seemed to be over shadowed by what was seen to develop. Any kind of neural reconfiguration is a very protracted process, and cannot be evaluated in the short term.

The insight which Von Monakow offers, shows that in regard to damage to or operation of the brain, the reforming of broken circuits is much dependent upon the manner in which subsequent experiences draw the disassociated circuits into reconstruction. Such a process of re-construction is heavily dependent upon a psychological presence, both in the manner of the evaluation of new experiences, and in the desire to want to identify with them. This echoes the achievement of the hydrocephalic to whom Lorber referred.

More importantly it also echoes the suggestion we raised in our previous book *"Intelligence"*. When we notice significant improvements in a person's development, which occurs only because the gene has "somehow" allowed the environment to make this improvement. As we expressed the point in *"Intelligence,"* psychologists still do not understand the role of the genes in intelligence.

- We may so far summarize that visual circuits, just as language, become settled in their functioning following a period of adjustment to experiences after birth, but that this is not to imply a permanent limitation in development.

- In point of fact, in the late 1970s a number of researchers, including Hubel and Wiesel themselves, found evidence of a repression/de-repression facility in the visual system. This gave evidence that the development of the visual system can be triggered to provide periods of "increasing" as well as decreasing structuring and operational formatting!

Through experimenting with the visual system of mammals, Hubel and Wiesel pioneered important knowledge in the principles of neural circuitry according to vision. Their work in the construction of the visual cortex enabled further research to begin to understand how the human brain processes the information it receives from the eyes, and so how it builds up an understanding of the world through this sense.

The popularity achieved by their work has, however, led too easily to the acceptance of their conclusion in the existence of a critical period in vision. In direct consequence of this the applications of a critical period remain an accepted theory for all features of human development, despite the scientific evidence that stands against them.

So we find that in building upon the popularity of a critical period in vision, Held reasoned that eye-hand co-ordination experiences early in life determine the motor-sensory skills of the adult.[74] Accordingly, mainframe human motor development is seen to be determined within the first six years of life. Indeed, the process known as polyneuronal innervation seems to support this.

Prior to birth, each muscle fibre is innervated by two or more motor axons connecting it to the brain. After birth, this multiple connection is trimmed back to a singular motor axon through the ways in which the muscle has been moved, and by the desire of the individual to control those movements.[75] However, even though suggestion comes from this that the motor connection between a muscle and the brain is irreversible after such trimming back has occurred, it has been clearly demonstrated that with the correct mediation motor actions can be redesigned.

Andras Petö has been so successful with his method of conductive education, that children with severe motor dysfunctions have been able to achieve remarkable development. The underlying reason for the success of his procedure lies partly in teaching children how to learn how to use their muscles, but much more in creating a belief of what is possible through levels of mediation. Petö and his staff in Budapest have consistently proven for over half a century, that a motor dysfunctional child can develop to achieve what others thought was impossible for them.[76]

A remarkable example of motor relearning came from an experiment conducted on a monkey well after its supposed critical period had passed. As a means to examine its spatial co-ordination, the nerve roots of the spinal cord were severed so that it could not visually co-ordinate the direction of one of its arms. However, it was found that the monkey could later be taught to operate the direction of this arm with such sensitivity that motor learning and hence axon remodeling must have occurred.[77] There is some evidence, therefore, that a freedom to reform connections, which we refer to as plasticity, is not limited to the brain, but may be an inherent property of the nervous system as a whole.

It would be logical to assume that if an adult incurred the surgical removal of one of their cerebral hemispheres, a procedure known as lobotomy, their ability to function would be limited by the absence of the networks that had become established in the hemisphere that had been removed. Yet, Gooch has presented a number of cases that challenge this assumption. Following lobotomy, some patients were found to be able to rewire the remaining hemisphere to the extent that they could gain the full set of functions that were previously provided by both hemispheres.[78]

While Gardner discussed this plasticity in regard to the success of adults to recover from strokes,[79] it is both interesting and significant to note, as Gooch suggested, that this ability for reconstruction may at times appear more readily when a hemisphere has been removed. It seems that a brain that is damaged is reluctant to modify the networks it has stability with, for the reasons that are now obvious to us. However, when that damage is so extremely extensive, then some condition arises that allows great redesigning to be possible.

To consider this, see how the brain is built up through association. As a circuit increases its operation, so the more other circuits become built into it, with each being reliant upon the other.[80] Should damage occur, these networks cannot simply rearrange themselves, because to do so would be to ignore the relationships of damaged circuits upon which the operation of the whole is reliant. Any remodeling of the operational circuitry is therefore dependent upon psychological drives, which provide the necessary stability for the interaction of the physiological arrangement of the neurons to function smoothly.

- It may now be said that neural circuits develop a psychological stability, which makes their physiological arrangement resistive to open design. It is this resistivity, without consideration to the psychological drive to overcome it, that has given credence to the theory of critical periods. And, may we add, recognition to the stability in intelligence that is too easily said to be limited by the value of a genetic coding.

At this point, I would like to introduce a man I met recently, because the work he does brings new light to our perception that a child's poor performance in school is a factor of their inherited ability. Peter Griffen in England is a new breed of neuro-motor therapists[81] who have had amazing success treating children of all ages with poor physical and sensory conditions, such as dyspraxia, ASD, ADD, dyslexia and general learning difficulties (problems with reading, writing and mathematics, the 3'Rs, upon which their whole performance in education rests) by correcting their infantile development.

We are born with many primitive reflexes to learn to survive, but these can be inhibited in the first year of life through poor posture and restriction in voluntary control. It is now understood that such poor motor development in infancy can restrict the way the later child perceives their world, and so how they develop to interact with it.

Through a short period of exercises the child is taken back, "neuro-physiologically" as it were, to a very early stage in their life. These exercises allow their sensory system to release the physical inhibitions incurred in infancy. This correction of their "motor physiology" encourages their "mental psychology" to reform the "physiology of their brain wiring." In turn, this enables the child to reconstruct the way they process information, and so develop to perform better in the world of school.

One support for the theory of critical periods arises from the knowledge that we shed a massive amount of neurons in childhood, and never stop the process of neural decay.[82] The reasoning behind this assumes that we can learn better earlier in life, when we have such a higher abundance of brain cells than later in life when we have much fewer. However, the reduction of neuron population does not necessarily imply limitation in development, because the brain naturally creates far more neurons than it would ever need, and neural decay is more often a means of utilizing energy for those cells that were for whatever reason selected in the structuring process.

Indeed, such early proliferation of neurons, followed by an extensive period of elimination, appears to be an evolutionary advantage to one of a pre-designed linkage system.[83] This enables stronger links to develop over weaker ones, and ensures the necessary degree of adaptability in brain organization. Thus, while neural structuring is associative, it has to be developmental, and need not be inhibited by the loss of unnecessary neurons. Indeed, great flexibility in design can easily be gained by the changing of existing links, aided by minor additions of surplus neurons.

3.3 The Plasticity of Intelligence:

When Cajal made our first study of brain cell organization in the 1880s, he was struck by the plasticity of the brain, which, as we have just mentioned, is the ready ability of neurons to reorganize themselves. More recently we became aware of neural decay, and as we have seen this helped to prompt the belief in critical periods. However, we are now beginning to understand that Cajal may have had more insight than has been realized, for as our technology ever increases so are we beginning to realize the ability of neurons to regenerate themselves.

Accordingly, it has become realized that neurons can re-grow an axon that has been removed,[84] and there is increasing evidence that the central nervous system does have an inherent capacity to regenerate myelinating cells. Instances have been discovered where certain types of neural damage have been repaired by spontaneous remyelination.[85] Myelin, we may recall, is the fatty sheath that insulates a nerve cell and enables it to conduct a signal. When this sheath breaks down, as it does through hereditary metabolic disorders such as adrenoleukolystrophy (as was the case with the child in the film Lorenzo's Oil), or through acquired diseases such as multiple sclerosis, nerve cells fail to conduct their signals to each other and a break down of the nervous system arises.

It was in seeking to combat this excessive demyelination, that research in the nervous system showed the possibility of reversing this process by transplanting myelin producing cells from the Peripheral to the Central Nervous System. Such Schwann cells have been found to reproduce themselves when placed in the CNS with the ability to migrate to the defective myelin cells and repair them.[86]/[87] Knowledge such as this, aided with reports that the drug metformin used by diabetics has the capability to cause new neurons to form,[88] helps us to understand how neurons may repair themselves and grow to repair existing circuitry or create new circuitry if the conditions allow. When we discuss this sense of flexibility, which again emphasizes the unknown property of the gene, we find ourselves returning to the image of brain plasticity that Cajal so strongly advocated.

- It is not then, that the brain is fixed in its orientation, or that critical periods exist as Hubel and Wiesel claimed for vision, and as Lenneberg believed for language. In consequence, there are no critical periods for music, mathematics, or any aspect of intelligence.

In their innocence the child mimics without analyzing the skills they observe in their parents. These adopted strategies provide them with a means of survival, until they can build upon these through their greater awareness of the environment. It is not, therefore, that at the cessation of a period the feature associated with it is thereafter limited. Not at all. It merely means that the individual has their own means of self-reliance, by which they have a means of adapting. As the environment alters, so may their ability with the skills they have and can develop.

In school and in society our environment changes only slightly, and without necessity for change or knowledge of the possibility for this, the individual relies upon those skills they first acquired. Yet, should the environment so desire it, or the individual desires to completely redesign those skills (as by example through adult education), then they are totally able to do so. To do this only requires their awareness that this is possible, and their determination to overcome the stability that questions the need for this change.

- So, it is by the desire, the need, the effort, and the want to cause the change that it occurs.

Indeed, a strong support for critical periods has always been the native-like accent young children can acquire in learning a second language, which is not normally observed with adolescents and adults. However, study on this topic has shown that adults can gain such native-like accent if the identification and the motivation for them to do this are present.[89]

This psychological profile necessary to drive a change was not realized in the study of animals, for while we and animals do have basic analogous structures in our nervous system, which is the basis for our use of studying them in how we may learn, our levels of comprehension are not compatible. Therefore, the failure to recognize the necessity of a higher level in reasoning (as through explanation, understanding and commitment, not to mention our features of imagination, planning, admiration, honor, integrity, morality, etc.) that allows humans to be more adaptable than animals was not recognized in studies of critical periods. It was in the failure of this, that the concept of a period of ready development became misunderstood.

In consequence to this, critical periods are not caused by proliferation, migration, differentiation, synaptogenesis, and apoptosis of the brain as it is argued.[90] It is simply that the brain requires of the mind that it creates a psychological stability for its operations as the child moves into and past adolescence.

- After the childhood phase, the development of the normal physiology of the brain (the construction, development and reconstruction of its neural wiring) is at the disposal of the psychology of the mind.

As Freud so clearly described way back in 1924, as an organism interacts with its environment, it does so by adjusting its psychological (alloplastic) state, to engineer changes in its neuro-muscular (autoplastic) state.[91]

By this stage of our discussion, it may now be better accepted that the operation of the nervous system is reliant upon a purpose of motivation. While this has been recognized to affect the performance of even young children,[92] failure to understand this and what it implies creates an impression of the brain being restricted in its adaptability by a rigid architecture. When this line of thought is followed, distraction is gained from realizing how our consciousness directs the chemical operations that govern the development of our neural physiology.

While it may be said that the final testimony to the existence of critical periods occurs at about the age of 11, this also is about the time of the onset of adolescence. While different features of the nervous system develop at different rates for the purposes they serve, it is not coincidental that they all come into some final stage of stability, but not permanence, at this time of life when the human being seeks to find great psychological stability. After all, this is the time in their life when the individual begins to resist the opinions of others, whom they see as smothering the perceptions they are trying to flower as they develop their identity.

It can be said from this that our personality guards the neural arrangements we have built-up, which allow us to understand our world through the identity by which we perceive ourselves and all that we engage. Accordingly, the older we become, and so the more established our neural networks are, the more difficult it is for us to want to achieve such neural restructuring. We recognize this with the difficulties adults demonstrate in re-educational programs, where they refuse to acknowledge errors they have developed in their skills. It is, after all, by these "errors" that they identify with themselves in their environment, and so know who they are.

- It is, then, by the striving of the consciousness to understand the world through that which it has met before, that creates resistance to new strategies that offer new potential, and not the conclusion of an innate design. All our features of interaction with the environment are set to a stability, which we have determined through our psychological perceptions of the experiences we have engaged.

As we move deeper into adulthood, we hold to the systems we have developed, because we have learnt to trust these as our identity grew through them. Therefore, any brain "plasticity" will require the desire of the full commitment of the personality and a guidance of how to transform one understanding into another, for we may only know the world by how we see it through others. The basis for all understanding and all change, as we shall come to see, is language.

- When the change in one fails in the eyes of another, it is, we shall see, because they did not understand what was actually meant -- the language that was used to them.

So, we move now into our following chapter to begin to discuss how intelligence really does come about. As we move through this book, and so through the others which follow, this idea that the psychology drives the physiology will shadow us through all the chapters ahead – as we come more and more to understand what determines the ability of the human child to learn.

* *

Chapter Four

The Origins of Intelligence

Voltaire once wrote, "Doctors are men who prescribe medicines of which they know little, to cure diseases of which they know less, to human beings of whom they know nothing." A quarter of a millennium later, we are still trying to understand how the mind of the individual works."

Roy Andersen

4.0 Introduction:

We have long been raised on the belief that intelligence is one part inherited, and one part a product of the environment. Beyond this, and save some understanding that the Organism is affected by Stimulus to give its Response (S-O-R), intelligence is just a feature to be noticed in one individual and graded against the quality of some other.

In our book *"Intelligence"*, we saw that the inherited aspect of intelligence is explained as a mysterious black box, with little if any distinction between the brain and the mind. It is simply that genes go in one side, and come out as intelligence the other. How the individual's own genetic quality is then shaped by the environment is as much a mystery.

We saw how psychologists have attempted to measure intelligence as soon after birth as they could, in attempts to limit the complexity of the environment and so try to estimate what the genetic factor could be. However, as we found, all such attempts were in vain, for in the early years of life the characteristics of intelligence were found to be too inconsistent to compare one infant to another.

Subsequently, it was realized that children do not demonstrate a reliable character in their intelligence until after they had entered the world of school. We have previously discussed how and why school is a conditioning environment, and over the following two chapters we shall discuss why children produce a constant stability in their intelligence on account of this.

To move away from this concept of a black box and to try to understand how intelligence comes about, we discussed a great deal about how the brain is physically shaped in its formation through environmental signals. As we have come to see, the environment of intelligence has a far deeper meaning than to be simply explained as the variation of information encountered. So, in this chapter we finally enter into the brain environment complex, and finally begin to consider how the mind of intelligence comes into formation.

To begin, it would be to say that if we could open this black box between the genes and the act of intelligence we observe, we would likely recognize four prominent features within it:

Diet.

Emotion.

Language, and

Strategy.

We have discussed the significance of the chemicals we put into our body, which create the body and so the brain. Eating fish, we saw, increased the level of the neurotransmitters dopamine and norepinephrine, because fish is normally high in tyrosine. This, in turn, enables a higher levels of neural response. Equally, we saw how caffeine increases the speed of thinking, of concentration, and of accuracy in mental performance.[93] However, as important as diet is, it is not the most significant factor in the development of intelligence.

Strategy defines the actions of all the interactive skills we develop through experience that enable us to make an act of intelligence. The way we perceive information, which is to know of its existence and to recognize what it may be, is determined by our senses. As we shall find, the very basic and fundamental setting up of this recognition procedure is determined not by the efficiency of a genetic code, but from a genetic code allowing the environment to design that efficiency. Strategy, then, is not just the choices made in the numerous mental processes that give efficiency to a protracted thought process. It will be amongst other things, the means by which the biological components are brought into design through the evolving design of the mind.

Another content of the box will be emotion. As we have discussed, emotion gives quality to all these strategies by the level of sensitivity it generates. Yet, it is also emotion that can destroy this sensitivity when it is distracted by a behavioral concern, such as a threat from a bully, some other insecurity in school, or a concern from the child's home life.

We shall see in this chapter precisely how a victim of bullying can create a surge of chemicals that so floods the sophisticated wiring of their neural circuits that their effectiveness in thinking is diminished, and their performance in lessons is lowered. Emotion, we shall come to see, is after language, the most important part of intelligence. Yet, this is little known for the decisive role it plays, and seldom understood by teachers who confuse it with motivation or lack of it. More importantly, emotion is allied to personality, and this we are to see greatly determines how the individual desires or struggles to engage the information of another as they express it through their personality.

Finally, we should recognize language in the box. This plays many parts. We may, for instance, recognize information and we may play with its usefulness in our mind, but it is only through others that we can know what it is, the purpose it has, and to know of something greater in the world we have not discovered ourselves.

Language is this medium of intelligence. Language is the means by which intelligence exists, and so ties it to the social and cultural worlds it evolves through. Language, however, is not just the means by which we share understandings. It is the most indispensable medium by which a baby gains the attention it needs to learn, and for which nature has provided an essential tool for this necessary bonding. The concept of imprinting, as we have mentioned, is very neglected. When it is not, it is very misunderstood, as little recognition is given to how it changes form and effect as the child matures and moves through adulthood. It is therefore, only by language that emotion can be tempered, and so sensitivity in the intelligence process is brought under control.

The word language, then, has different meanings. In one sense it is the behavioral codes, the gestures, mannerisms, and indications by which one demonstrates to another their personality and their desire to engage with them. In another, it is a spoken and written medium of communication, shaped by the work, social, and cultural codes of a group of people. In another, it is a national language, or a regionalized or social variation of it. Language is also the means by which school defines its information, and it is the means by which it evaluates its students through the rules and codes of interaction it teaches them.

These three vital components of intelligence, all derive from genetic schemas. We all inherit them. They are the essential gene designs that enable us to have intelligence, and yet the ability for language, for emotion, and to devise strategies are not dependent upon how gene codes may have varied from family to family. The operational worth of these components is not effected by genetic diversity.

The theory of natural variation, which Galton used to explain similarities in social and work ability, does not occur here. All human beings will inherit these three features equally, but it will be the experiences each encounters that will give shape, quality, and meaning to them.

Watson, we saw, desired to explain intelligence through his SR formula, which avoided the involvement of a genetic base. This was overtaken by Skinner's recognition of the organism that did incorporate a genetic, and so a hereditary base. Our interest in this chapter will be to discuss how the inheritance of schemas for strategy, emotion, and language can cause the concept of genetic variation to take on a whole new meaning.

To grasp the essence of this, is to consider again how the role of the gene in these instances is to allow the environment to make the variation. This is to say that when a child enters the world with normal sensory skills, they should be regarded to have the same potential for intelligence as any other child, irrespective of their color, the financial standing of their parents, or their cultural origin. We have, after all, no means now to prove otherwise.

To begin this chapter, we may be aware that nature has provided us with a number of schemas that:

- enable the sensory systems of the brain to design efficiency through physical interaction with the environment.
- enable the brain to devise cognitive strategies to make use of the information its sensors relay to it.
- provide a means of natural bonding to ensure the existence of a teaching/learning process.
- provide a sensitivity to cognitive processes that are related to behavioral experiences.
- provide a language, which allows intelligence to exist through the continual exchange of thoughts and experiences.

Through behavioral experiences, children, adolescents, and adults develop proficiency with these schemas, by which they display variations in their intellectual performance. Let us move now to understand how.

4.1 A Schema to Learn to Perceive:

To begin this section, we may note that incidents of mental retardation, which are attributed to lack of oxygen during the birth process, have greatly impressed upon us a belief that complications arising in the fetal period have an effect that is irreversible. There is, however, much evidence that impaired brain development in the fetus does not necessarily affect their after birth intelligence. Indeed, most infants who did incur some prenatal neural problem have been found to overcome this by after birth experiences, and develop to function normally.[94]

It is to understand this plasticity of the brain that we now move to understand how we learn to perceive the outside world. Once we can understand that the visual system, as a part of how the brain functions, does not just work, but that it learns how to work, then, we can better acknowledge the plasticity of other brain systems and so that of the overall brain itself. By this understanding we will see why the intelligence of the individual is not as fixed as we have been led to believe.

Within the first three months of life, the fetus will already have activated a schema that enables them to learn how to be aware of differences in environmental information. As we saw in the fetal development of vision, and as we may understand of our audio and tactile senses, these are all brought into a proto-construction by information that, although deriving from the environment, is non-specific.

The purpose of this information is merely to initiate a general awareness in the brain that information has different levels, and so structure it to relate this to understanding. To know that one level is different from another, the fetus must have some means of storing information and be able to relate to this. Therefore, to compare one difference with another they must have some means to learn how to categorize information.

Thus, as the fetus contained within the embryonic sac becomes sensitive to light information, they develop an awareness of how to compare different light intensities. By the same reasoning as their audio system develops, they will learn to respond to different sound intensities. This will be the differences in the noise they hear, such as the language of their parents, the laughter, the shouts, the crying, the sounds of motorcars and of television. The unborn child is aware of all this information. Most of it, of course, is meaningless, save for the emotions transmitted to them from their mother, and the words they hear that set the codes for the language they will come to understand from their parents after birth.

Consider, now, that the intelligence process begins by the fetus developing simple categorization schemas to distinguish between vague differences, and that after birth the knowledge of the existence of differences enables further development. In the example of vision, the lighter and darker intensities experienced by the fetus help to create a scaffolding for the more definable shapes the newborn will experience.

However, the quality of detection, and the means they employ to analyse what they see after birth will be determined by their emotional state. When they are calm and happy they can be fascinated and precise. When they are worried or unhappy their detection can be casual and vague. This relationship with perception and emotion has an obvious meaning in understanding how the foundation stones for a child's intelligence are laid. As we shall see, when a new born is deprived of immediate facial contact with their mother, they can be deprived of adequate facial processing experience, and through this lack of human rapport later develop attention disorders such as ADHD.[95]

Feuerstein acknowledged the effect of emotion in perception, and so its consequences when he wrote: "There is much evidence that a determining quality of attention is reflected in the evaluation of a perception."[96]

- So we find that a quality of attention guides the quality of perception, which in turn guides the qualities of all the cognitive processes that build upon this to exhibit a quality of intelligence.[97]

Evidence in how a quality of perception is related to a quality of academic performance, rather than intelligence, can be found in studies with myopic children.

There is a general awareness that myopic children tend to be academically attuned. This has led to the impression that myopia is related to high intelligence, and since this visual impairment often has a genetic base so the impression is gained that high intelligence can be equally explained.[98]

However, it needs to be understood that the genetic base to myopia can be of very little consequence. An ophthalmologist suggested to me it may be about 20% responsible for this visual defect with diet and stress accounting for the difference. However, as we can understand from our discussion of genetics, the known presence of a gene in an individual gives absolutely no knowledge if it is responsible for the performance that is witnessed, and so if that gene has anything to do with the impression gained of this individual.

In fact, far from having a genetic cause, Gallop sees myopia to be psychologically driven. As he wrote of this condition, it is "the tendency to shrink visual and perceptual space and to restrict the musculature (and often the emotions) while attempting to solve the problem of responding to visual stress."[99]

From this, we may understand that even should the gene component have a high responsibility for poor vision, the human being would have many tools available to make compensation for their inferior sight. After all, although there are 56 classifications of myopia,[100] they generally relate to a refractive inability, and the muscles supporting the eye and its lens can be taught to make compensation for this to create a new focusing ability.

This is exactly what Orlin Sorenson has demonstrated, and so explains how near-sightedness can be completely corrected through exercising the muscles of the eyes, such that a person of any reasonable age having a 20:80 vision has the potential to correct this to 20:20 to give themselves perfect vision.[101] The ability for this, as Freud informed us, hangs entirely upon the psychology of the matter, which again echoes Gallop, and refers us back to the means to overcome critical periods as we have discussed.

Yet, the plasticity of vision is as little discussed as is the plasticity of intelligence for the same reason. Optometrists, like psychologists who sell IQ tests, make their bread and butter through convincing people that they need them to dispense artificial lenses, which compensate for their weak muscles. They seldom teach people how they could build up their eye muscle strength, so they would not need artificial lenses.

As we can see the discussion of myopia and intelligence needs to be brought into balance, because myopic children do not operate with the same confidence and quality of interaction as non-myopic children, when they are operating in an outside environment that is unstable and rapidly changing.[102] In "real life," therefore, it could be said that myopia creates a low intelligence, were it not for the fact that we associate the word "intelligence" only with the pen and paper world, and so fail to recognize a balance with what is happening inside and outside the classroom.

So, it is not that myopia is related to high intelligence, but that myopia is related to the academic world. This is an important distinction, because it opens us up to why a myopic child performs so well in school. Fuchs realized the answer to this, when he found the condition of near-sightedness to be easily associated with high intelligence (albeit academic studies) purely because of the techniques habitually developed in visual exploration.[103] This brings us back to understanding that intelligence relies upon sensitivity firstly to recognize or associate with information, and then to the stages with which it is processed and presented. These, as we have just seen, hang upon a psychological and so an emotional base.

The ability to perceive is, of course, only one part of the visual system, but when we think of the visual system it is far more than being able to see. There is not, for instance, the ability for vision and a different ability to think, and so to have intelligence, because the process of thinking relies upon the information the brain receives from its external sensors. The understanding that the ability for vision and so the ability to think is unrelated, creates the impression that we naturally "know" the value of information we see.

So, it is thought that we see a tree and learn this to be a tree, by the name we are taught for it. It follows with this thinking that how well a child defines a tree (or more to the point $4x-7z/x = 4.2$) relates to their ability for intelligence. This is not the case. The brain "learns" how a tree can be recognized, just as it learns how to recognize a letter or a number and so how they can relate to each other. The brain learns through experience patterns of basic stimuli, so that it can build up the ability to recognize trees, buildings, people, etc. May we see, therefore, that this neural ability to learn how to decode the environment plays a key role in the elementary development of intelligence.[104] Let us understand just how decisive this biological learning process is to ability.

In the 1970s and 80s, research was made on the visual system of kittens that related to how experiences after birth could affect their perceptual ability. The results obtained through this research demonstrated that this vital feature of intelligence, which allows the ability to know of and so interact with the world, is totally constructed and determined through after birth experiences. This is to say that the ability of the brain to be able to know of basic visual information is not an inherited feature.

Blakemore and Cooper proved this by keeping kittens in the dark two weeks after birth, except for five hours a day when they were placed in a large vertical tube. The tube was arranged in such a manner that it could let in either horizontal or vertical strips of light, but not both at the same time. After five months, it was found that the kittens that had been raised under horizontal light were blind to vertical light patterns projected to them. Equally, those that had been raised under vertical light were blind to horizontal light patterns.[105]

Daw and Wyatt observed the same thing. They reared kittens in the dark from birth except for a period of two hours each weekday, when they were subjected to strips of vertical light. After nine months the kittens were released into a normal environment, and found to be blind to horizontal structures. This was realized when they started to walk off the edge of a stool they had been placed on, because they could not see its horizontal edge.[106] Pasternak and Merigan raised kittens under stroboscopic illumination, which prevented them from moving their retina in the same way a normal kitten would, and discovered they were totally deficit in motion perception.[107]

In conclusion of such experiments, Rhawn reasoned that if either a kitten or a human being were reared in an environment exposing them to only vertical or horizontal lines for five hours a day, their limbic system nuclei will atrophy, random interconnections will be maintained, or neural pathways will develop abnormally.[108]

Prior to this knowledge, a belief had evolved through a number of psychologists in the 1930s that we individually inherit the ability to recognize visual objects. Since at this time in the 20th century intelligence and so all its components were believed to be valued through inheritance, this would have been a natural assumption.

Accordingly, the Gestalt School of Perception put forward theories that we naturally perceive the whole of an object, and in doing so recognize the parts that make it up. Explanation grew from this to describe how the brain relates to information by building up profiles of smaller patterned parts. In order to do this, it was reasoned that the brain naturally recognizes basic information such as lines and circles, which it could join to decipher the visual images it is presented with. This meant, of course, that different individuals inherited different qualities of this ability.

The Gestalt theory is explained through the many Laws of Pragnaz. To our interest here, these are "The Law of Organization" and "The Law of Good Continuation." The former deals with how we define the break down or build-up of stimuli, to explain why we understand information in terms of figures to backgrounds. The latter, based on the "Principles of Closure and Good Form," reasons that we naturally connect incomplete information to make sense of what it represents.

The Gestalt theory rapidly gained universal acceptance, and so became the approved explanation of how we perceive information on a genetically defined base. However, despite the ready agreement to this theory, which persists to this day and so influences our perception of an individual's intelligence, there is now much to be said against the viability of its arguments.

Polanyi, for instance, drew wariness to exact applications of its principle of closure, where he saw this only as providing clues to coherence and not precise definition. As he explained, when we view two opposing profiles, we shift from one to another as we seek to determine our understanding. Since the quality by which we establish that understanding can be changed at will, the application of Gestalt reasoning does not establish a true coherence.[109]

In Chapter One, we discussed how Feuerstein had shown how children can be taught to recognise correct form through guidance in their emotional sensitivity.

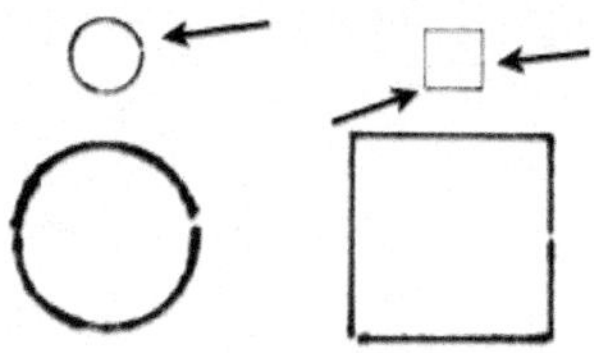

Building upon the work of Rev, Feuerstein found that this ability does not lie in an inherited quality. Rather, that an inability to perceive an open circle as closed is suggestive of some level of psychological disturbance, which has impaired this ability. Therefore, to develop the intellectual feature is first to rectify the behavioral problem. As he points out, "The projection of a virtual relationship ... does not occur as a spontaneous response to the pressure of stimuli."[110]

In other words, the change comes not simply from the application of information, but from the change within the child to desire it and to know how to achieve this change. This, of course, comes down to the quality of language by which they are so inspired and guided.

Equally, Hochberg explained that for the eye to perceive an image, it must direct the fovea of the retina with pin-point precision to different places in the visual field. This would mean that different parts of the overall image would be seen in succession, by the same part of the eye at a rate of about four discrete glances per second. If this happened, it would mean that fragmented parts of the image would be superimposed with rapid succession over a neural field that was hypothetically tuned only to precise recognition! While this operation would then not be feasible, it is also to be noted that since all the Laws of Gestalt must be realized to make the perception of an image possible, these laws and the principles upon which they are composed must not conflict.[111] Yet, this is precisely what does happen. They do conflict!

The reality of this is that the theories of Gestalt give nothing by which a prediction can be worked upon. They are only theoretical, and therefore give no valid understanding of how a vital part of the intelligence process is created.

We can sum this up, as did Hochberg, by saying that we perceive whatever most probably produces the stimulation we receive. In other words, a "learning" psychological structure generally reflects the physiological arrangement of how we perceive.[112] This is a key to understanding the whole concept of brain plasticity, and so any and all aspects of learning and whatever we may think intelligence is. As Freud reminds us:

> "Any physiological change must first be preceded by a more dynamic psychological one."

Despite the lingering influence of Gestalt theories in psychology, there is much evidence that the brain designs its ability for perception through the environment, instead of merely unfolding it through a genetic plan.

This was particularly highlighted by a notable study by Annis and Frost in 1973, on Cree Indians in Canada. These researchers found that Indians raised in a city were able to readily detect horizontal and vertical lines presented to them in a perceptual maize, but could not so easily recognize diagonal lines. On the other hand, their genetic relatives raised within tents could easily recognize diagonal lines, but not so vertical or horizontal ones.

Explanation arose from this that the visual impressions to the infant raised in a tent were of leaning poles and structures overlaid with animal skins, and that these tuned their perceptual world to a variety of natural lines. This also explained why vertical and horizontal lines were more apparent to those raised in an artificial environment of rooms, walls and windows. Research such as this has proven that our basic ability to perceive lines, and from this angles and so all visual perception is not restricted by inheritance.[113] They are abilities we learn, as we can see from the following illustration, and they do play a decisive role in the development of intelligence.

Views an infant sees.

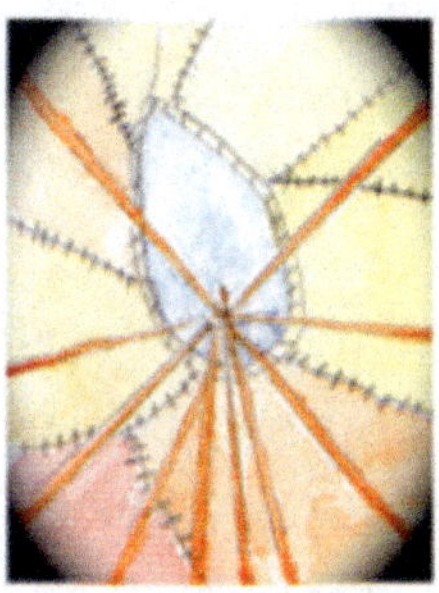

Inside their teepee.

In their bedroom.

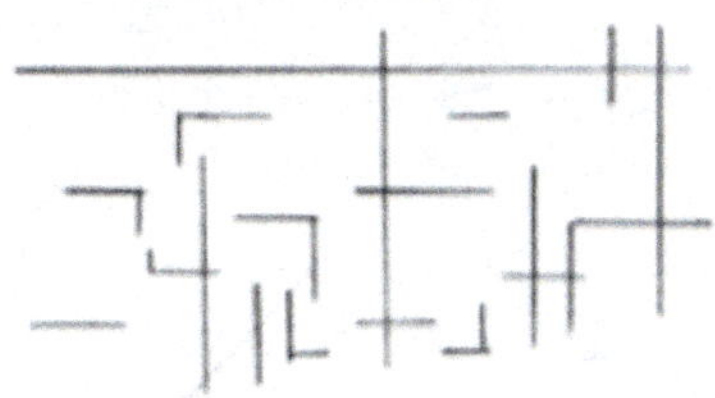

Equally, children who have an episodic grasp of reality perceive objects and events in isolation.[114] This does not just mean that they see information separately, but most importantly that they think of information as disjointed, and so build up all of their intellectual processes upon this. When such children are compared to children who do not have this condition, they demonstrate a much lower value of intelligence.

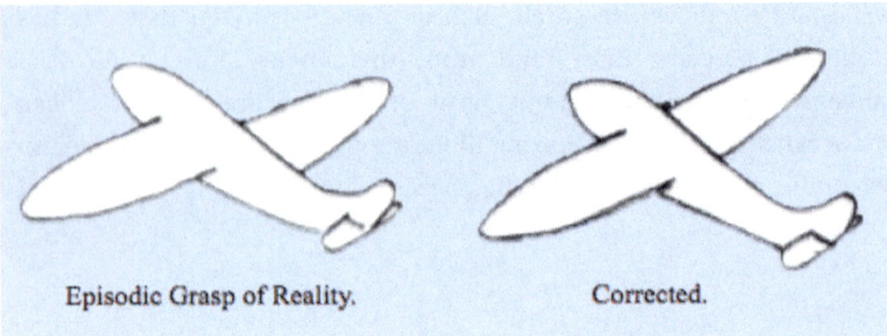

Such condition of an episodic grasp of reality is believed to be genetic, and so beyond correction. Yet, Feuerstein has repeatedly proven that it is correctable, that it is not a limited genetic feature, and that its occurrence lies in a behavioral problem, which can be addressed to greatly improve the said intelligence of the individual.[115]

As we can see, the principles of Gestalt, as these relate to the ability of the individual to perceive based on the quality of their genetic codes, are not correct. These theories arose in the time when IQ testing was at its height, and so when the belief in innate ability was very strong. However, such perceptual abilities as we have examined are totally developmental. This emphasizes again that the basic means by which we can recognize information, in order for it to be processed and projected as an act of intelligence, is designed by the gene coding to be decided through the environment.

How much perception is a learned process was exemplified by Gregory when he discussed the case of a man who had been born congenitally blind, and was able to see for the first time following the removal of his cataracts at the age of 54. It is very significant for us to realize that following this operation, the man did not immediately gain normal vision. In the beginning, he could only perceive objects standing out against a background in the figure/ground phenomenon, and his ability for normal vision was found to develop through stages of learning.[116]

- There is no reason, from what has been considered here, to believe that the functions relating to how we perceive information vary between individuals because of variations in their normal gene codes. Therefore, any neural construction before birth of the ability of the brain to make perception, is only to create a temporary scaffolding for after birth experiences when information has an intelligible meaning. The development of the child's perceptual skills after birth relies upon the clarity of information, they emotional desire to know of it, and most importantly their desire to respond to it.

- It is not, then, that our biological means of perception, which is a most elementary feature of intelligence, is decided by normal genetic variation where one child has a different innate value to that of another child. Our gene coding allows the environment to build up our perceptual skills, as Annis and Frost discovered with Cree babies.

Consider this development with the eye movement of a newborn. They stare intently at one thing, hold their stare and then drift to find another thing to stare at. As the young infant is doing this, they are setting up templates for their understanding of visual data. It is only later as their body becomes more mobile, and their perception has been shaped to recognize complete forms, that their eye movement will begin to dart more fluidly as does ours. I recall, as I write this, watching a baby stare towards a corner of a room and hold that stare for many minutes.

I looked at the same corner, and saw only a corner. However, as I watched the baby, I realized they were examining the way the two walls met to form that corner. As I studied the baby, I began to wonder if they were studying the differences in lines and shades that helped them to define the junction of those two walls. The baby held this observation for many minutes, and seemed fascinated by this experience. Then, something happened that really helped me to understand what they were doing.

Suddenly, the infant revolved their head in what seemed like a meaningless intention, until that is I realized that they had turned to focus upon a window recess, high in a wall near the ceiling. As before, the baby held their gaze for many minutes and then, when they had gained all they could from this, they returned their gaze to examine again the corner they were observing when I had first noticed them. As I watched this baby stare intently at this corner again, it struck me how they may be comparing the information they had gained from the window and what this must mean to their neural structuring. This baby was developing a system of recognizing surfaces that are adjacent to each other. They were learning the meaning of their environment, in just the same way that you or I would make study of a new feature that interests us.

As I watched this baby, I wondered how old they would be before they noticed the difference between the window in the wall being open and bringing a cold draft, and the window being closed with no draft. How long would it be before they contemplated their first thought of "What if .... ?"

Then, however, the baby's adventure was suddenly interrupted by the sound of their mother's voice, as she picked them up, kissed them, and carried them off for more things to see, to watch, and so build up their own understanding of how all things interact in the world they move through.

4.2 Defining the Start of Intelligence:

More as a way of substantiating that we are born with a quality of intelligence, than trying to estimate how intelligence comes to be, numerous attempts have been made to assess differences in the reaction ability of new-borns. Behavior, babbling, responses to audio-visual information, and language related skills have all been monitored in an attempt to recognize innate characteristics, so that they could be differentiated from developmental influences.

Throughout the long history of this research, which has spanned over 80 years, the differences that have been noted in babies have been shown not to be consistent. Furthermore, whatever levels have been agreed upon, these have been found to have very little relation to the level of academic performance later realized by the child as they progressed through their education. There is not, and there never has been, the base to evaluate the intelligence of a child on the similarity of how they look with a genetic relative, as Galton always believed there was.

Most of these types of infantile tests were centered upon the two systems of assessment that arose in the 1930s, which grew in response to the wave of intelligence testing at that time. One, devised by Gesell, sought to identify infantile characteristics by measurement techniques in line with the methodology of IQ testing, while the other, designed by Bayley sought to evaluate characteristics through behavioral studies.[117]

It is interesting to note that when Bayley first introduced her scaling system in 1933, she had been very much influenced by the psychometric movement and originally devised her tests to define potential ability. However, as she came to realize that infants do not give reliable responses, and Bayley personally used her system for over 50 years, she adapted it to recognize what she termed "significant criteria in development," and sought to identify the stability of these features in performance. Upon this theme, she produced the most respected and widely applied means of infantile intelligence assessment.[118]

What struck Bayley, very early in her career, was that within the first two years of life, none of the factors that may be said to constitute intelligence showed any indication of stability.[119] Indeed, virtually all types of tests conducted on slightly older children found the same degree of unreliability in the estimation of their intellectual potential. Whatever predictions were made upon children of two, three, four, or five years of age, they were all later found to be highly mutable.[120]

We may understand from this that in all the ages prior to a child starting school, there is no clear indication of a stability in their intelligence by which they can be reliably compared to that of another child.

This stability of intelligence only seems to begin once the child has entered the school system, where they are constantly challenged by other children. From that moment onwards, the child will be formally introduced to a collectivized ideal of language. They will be taught the alphabet, and the formal recognition of words and word usage. They will be taught rules to understand information, and rules to use that information. As each child struggles to make their own sense of these rules, they will repeat their sense of understanding with each interaction they progress through.

As lesson follows lesson, a pattern will begin to appear in how the child interacts with the information of their lessons. This can be recognized in how well they understand and make use of the rules of school, and how by their personality they decide to incorporate these rules into the manner of interaction they have devised to that moment in time. As the teacher has too little time, and often too little inclination to perfect each task each of the children in their class develop through, each child devises their own understanding of what the lesson means to them. As each believes they are making the perfect action, they never understand why others gain more stars or higher marks. In this way, each child develops their stability in handling information, and so demonstrates their patterns of competence.

So we find that the later student who has not learnt to check for errors, as they progress through a mathematical equation, continues to fail to do this; just as the student who has not learnt to use the rule that i comes before e except after c (with some exceptions) continues to make the same spelling mistakes. It is much because of the self-limiting and conditioning world of education that children demon-strate a stability in their intelligence.

This cognitive ability of infants and young children is unbound. Their thinking is a personal action. They, and others, do not demand a quality of control with it. Their sense of reality, just as their fantasy has no boundaries. Inanimate objects take on a personality, and interact with animate objects with no restriction. The mind of young children is a delightful fantasy. Such thinking that they make is a pleasant activity of the individual's mind. It is a personal adventure that may or may not be shared. The harsh and cruel reality of civilization has not yet given it form. However, this will begin when the child enters the school world.

If intelligence only becomes stable enough to compare children once they are in school, then it means that before school they do not have a quality of stability that justifies the use of the term intelligence. By its definition, intelligence only exists when the cognitive ability of any number of human beings is stable enough for them to be compared to each other. Therefore, we may say that infants and small children think, but we cannot talk about their intelligence, because this has not yet developed within them.

When we use the word intelligence, we do so as a means to compare the ability of one to that of another. She has a high intelligence. He has a low intelligence, etc., etc. As we have seen, education just as psychology has spent over a century trying to put specific numbers to these different qualities, so that the potential of its students could be known to the working world. It might therefore be said that education creates a factor of stability in the human being by how it operates, which sets the base for the intelligence of the individual.

Consider now that from the moment the child enters through the school gates, their indifference to information will be forced to change. From that moment onwards, and for the rest of their life, they are taught to classify and interact with information through strict codes and rules of how, what, and when to think. This is intelligence! The transformation of the innocent thinking child of nature to the student who must survive in a defining and calculating world is not a natural one, although it is regarded to be so for the reasons we discussed in our previous books.

In the weeks prior to birth, and from the moment of their birth, the child will develop to understand what their world means, and how they should interact with it through language. Before the infant can talk, the imprinting process provides them with the necessary attachment to their parents to learn communication skills. As the baby/infant/child grows this imprinting process becomes more complex, and as it does so their means of language become more sophisticated. As each step of the child's development unfolds, they learn more of the world and more of how to safely interact with it through language.

Such attention that the parent gives does not only shape the thinking skills of their child, but it sets up emotional strategies, which, in turn, give regulation to a whole host of bodily activities. When the parent gives love, their infant develops their thinking interface with the world with a happy confidence. If the parent neglects, or is cruel to their child (and this does happen), the child becomes emotionally withdrawn and fumbles through their interactions with the world, never sure of what they should do and if it is safe to do so. It is necessary to accept that this is seldom a one or the other situation, for if we can acknowledge the vast degree of influences that can affect a child, so may we better understand what variation in ability means before the child enters school. Once in school, such factors take on very decisive meanings as the child struggles through the personality of other children to learn and to demonstrate their competence in this.

The only medium that transforms this carefree and unassuming mind of the child to the rational conscious decision making mind it must become in school, is language. By their failure to keep up with the rules of language in school (be it English or French etc., and that of the language of mathematics), students misunderstand and devise ineffective strategies that become translated into the grades they are given. This transition of the child's mind from before school to the effect of school has another affect that George Land discovered.

Starting in 1968 and working on a NASA example, Land and his team found that before stating school, 98% of the children tested displayed a genius level in their creativity. However, after five years of schooling, this level had dropped to 30%. After ten years in school, only 12% still showed a genius level. After they all had finished their education, only 2% still showed a genius level in tests.[121]

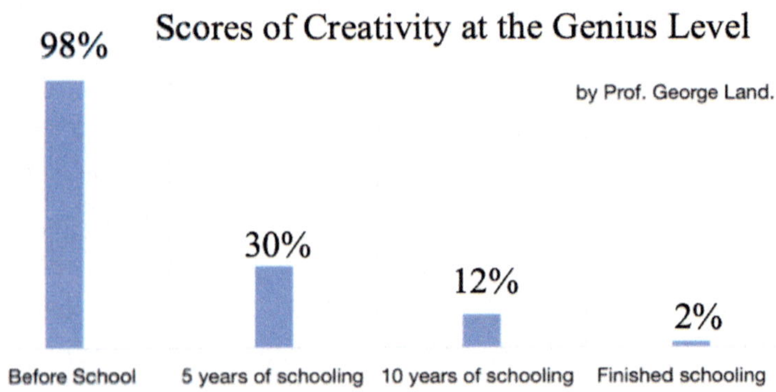

Land's work shows the effect of school to dampen the creative drives of a child and so how they change through the way the school works.

As we explain in other books (for example "All that is Wrong with School"), this lowering in creative ability is a result of students losing confidence to explore in their thinking, because they have not kept up with the progressive rules and learning required of them as their school years progressed.

Before we move to discuss finally and examine what language is, it would serve us well to understand again why Galton's theory of continuous variation does not give any evidence at all to support the idea that an individual's ability is limited by the genes they inherit. As we do this, we shall now lay to rest the long and disputed nature vs nurture argument, or as we have often described it "the genetic to environmental ratio.

Chapter Five

Everything Hangs on Language

The Great Debaters. Wiley College. Texas.

Intelligence, I came to realize, is life.
It has to be fought for to survive,
and its sword is language.

Roy Andersen

5.0 Introduction:

In *"Intelligence"* we saw how Quetelet had devised his Law of Errors about the way arrows fell. We discussed, at that time, how he only focused upon that which was witnessed and used this to make predictions. He did not focus upon the causes that created or manufactured what he witnessed. So, for example, Quetelet observed the degree of drunkenness in his society, and having obtained a variation of how much people drank in excess, used this to suggest how people may similarly drink in some future time in any society.

However, the real importance and so the significance to anything that is witnessed, is why it is so. Therefore, the significance lies not in how people vary in their drunkenness, but what are all the factors that so cause them to behave in this manner. So, for example, Quetelet did not discuss in any depth why people drank, nor if a new tax was levied on alcohol how this could affect how much people would drink. It was, we realized, only by ignoring or excessively limiting this factor of .... cause .... that Quetelet could actually produce the stability he needed in the predictions he made.

It is very important that we clearly understand how this "ignoring of the causes" distort the effect that is being projected, because this is exactly what Galton made use of. Galton used Quetelet's idea of all things varying above and below the average to explain, through his "The Law of Deviation from the Average", how values of intelligence vary.

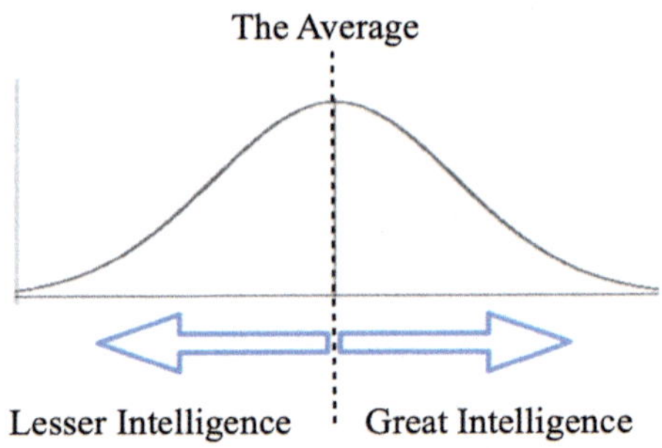

Today, the general belief is that any act of intelligence an individual makes is partly due to the quality of the genes they inherited and partly due to the experiences they have had. However, when Galton first entered upon the scene with his declaration that intelligence was inherited, none of this was known. Neither our knowledge of genes nor the role of the environment on genetic design had by then been discovered. Therefore, Galton, at least for most of his life, saw intelligence to be wholly inherited.

He would certainly have understood the affect of environmental influences, in the sense of social contacts influencing the position a man could attain and by this position what may be said of his intelligence. So, a judge would be said to be more intelligent than a merchant and a merchant more intelligent than a laborer, as we discussed in Chapter One.

Yet, by his need for intelligence to be used as such a social tool, Galton saw to explain away all factors that could affect the sense of permanence in intelligence that he needed. To this aim, he referred to the line of popes, explaining how they were elected purely on merit with no social influence. So, just as Quetelet ignored the causes that gave the effect he was focusing upon, Galton happily promoted only inheritance as the cause to explain how intelligence varies in a population.

However, in contrast to this, we know that intelligence is not the singular feature Galton thought it was, and is, in fact, a product of many features coming together. Most significantly, we have identified how these features develop their after birth competency, completely without any regard to a genetic diversity in their inheritance.

In other words, the gene coding does not predetermine the level of competency of a feature that makes up the intelligence of a normally born individual. Of course, the features of language and emotion are very good examples of this. Although, there are many other features, such as the ability to perceive movement, to observe change, to devise ways to make association, and to evolve strategies for memory, etc., etc. All these develop their competency only through experience.

All this we have well discussed, and so it falls upon us now to consider how each of these environmental factors of intelligence can vary. If we can understand how each feature of intelligence has developed to vary, so we may have greater understanding of each can be improved and so how the whole intelligence of the individual can be developed. How much they may do this, relies upon the quality of the guidance they receive and the emotional drive they have within themselves for this.

As we have seen how school begins the formalization of an individual's intelligence, we may realise that children vary in how easily they are distracted in their learning development. Some children will be more distracted as they seek other stimulation and others less so, because they are more interested in what is happening. Equally, children will suffer from the effects of being bullied in different ways according to the experiences they have and the form this bullying takes.

The same must be said for the security that children feel in school. How much they are liked or disliked by others, will affect the ways they interact in their lessons and thus the performance they give. There again, how secure do they feel in their home? Do their parents fight a lot? Do their parents watch too much television, and so ignore sharing mind adventures with them? To what degree are their parents responsible for them? What type of education have their parents had, and so how sensitively do they teach them things?

When we think of the quality a child is raised in at home, so must we also consider the influence of school upon their development. After all, not all teachers are great teachers and so we must consider the effect that different teachers have upon the performance of their students. So, the quality of teachers will vary about "The Law of Deviation from the Average", just as will the quality of the school, the quality of the educational material used and all the many, many factors affecting the student's mind.

Therefore, we should not think of each feature, and they will far more than we could count or imagine, that contributes to the intelligent ability of the individual as a one thing they simply have. Each feature within each individual will vary from low to high and set about the average. As may see in the following illustration, any group of children will vary from being very unhappy to very happy by degrees, just as some will have no confidence to explore while others will be over confident.

A small sample of some of the "many" factors behind performance

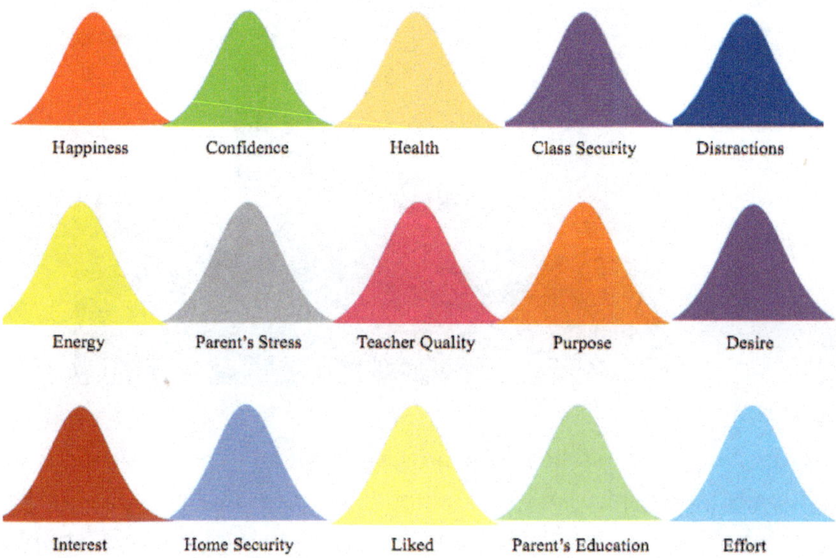

If we collect all these variations together to create a single collective value for any one individual, we may see how their place in the Bell Curve will vary with others, without any relation to genetic differences.

Yet, all these variations are hidden within the individual when they make an act of intelligence. Johannsen made this point, as we discuss in *Intelligence.* A combination of variations gives no explanation for why any one of the variations occurred.

Therefore, any understanding of how such factors can vary upon an individual's intelligence and so dramatically cause them to vary in the scheme of things is completely ignored by psychologists. They simply can not identify them individually. All they may do is broadly label their effect as environmental. This is one reason, why human intelligence can not be measured and so why the role of the gene can not be known through psychometric testing.

Yet, if we do consider these factors that construct intelligence (from Happiness to Teacher Quality - which is only a very, very small sample of such possible factors), there is only one cause to the variations they make and this is language.

By the quality of the language of the adult and how sensitive they are in this to the needs of those they are influencing, unhappiness can be turned to happiness, insecurity to security, disinterest to fascination, and a fear turned to inner harmony. After all, how much a child is disliked or liked by others, is nothing more than a discussion with them into how they see others and how they can change the projection they make.

All the factors that we can imagine of the environment ride upon the sensitivity by which language is shared. This is why language is the root to intelligence. We saw this when children in Romanian orphanages were deprived of it. Jamie Escalante proved this again when he coached his class of Hispanic dropouts to perform very highly in their final examination. We discuss this in other books, but a movie was made on Jamie's remarkable achievement called "Stand and Deliver".

Let us move then to understand more of what language means in the intelligence process, for this will bring us closer to discussing the real advantages of mediation in the learning and the teaching process, as this prepares the child to maintain a democratic society better in a world of so many conflicting pressures.

5.1 The Base of Variation:

When we hear the word language, we automatically think of the language of a people, be it English, Spanish, Russian, or Turkish, but when we talk about language in regard to intelligence we mean it in a deeper sense. Here we regard language as how information moves, how one describes their mind to another, and how well they interpret that other mind. Language in the context of intelligence, merely refers to the efficiency by which information is recognized, interpreted, and related to experiences. This is as it is for the language of mathematics.

We can easily see why intelligence is dependent upon language when we make an inquiry. How well we can explain what we want or how well we define our problem, and so how well another explains how they can assist us, enables information to flow smoothly and efficiently or to bring about delays, misunderstandings and mistakes.

In a group context, the language of a people is the means by which they share thoughts of what things are and the meanings these have to them. These meanings, but much more importantly the thought processes they create, will change with the jobs and lives that people have, because groups of people find different relevances with the flow of information.

In this way different groups of people, as we may define them by their culture and work-social levels, will have developed particular strategies to deal with their world that will be different from those of another group. For example, the meaning of rain will be different to people living in Norway to those living in Northern Africa, and each will have their own terms and feelings to describe different forms of rain.

We must always be aware when we discuss language, that words do bring emotional relationships and so do inspire a level of interest or disinterest to the individual as they see their world. This, in turn, drives levels of recognition and association, and so qualities of understanding that are all part of the intelligence process. Poetry has always tried to encourage or educate an awareness to and of this. Wordsworth demonstrated this when he conjured up imagination and inspiration to the common daffodil, writing as he did of "ten thousand dancing in the breeze."

Thus, within a culture, people will see different values to information according to the jobs and lives they lead, and so develop to handle them in different ways. The mind of an accountant will become trained differently to that of an artist, as an artist will to that of a farmer. Yet, there again, different work levels within one group may have greater language similarity with those of the same work level in a different cultural group, than they would with a different work level in their own group. So, a teacher in Spain will have a language (or a developed way of thinking) more similar with a teacher in Thailand, than they would with a bank manager in Spain. May we see that language is relevant to the needs people have when they share the information of the world they live in.

It is of further significance to realize that people develop different levels of sensitivity with information through their jobs, and so create different levels of understanding (we may call this intelligence) to what is taken to be the same information. So, an accountant will be trained to check the flow of information far more carefully, than, say, a forester, for while information in the world of the forester moves slower and changes less, the information an accountant works with can change instantly with dramatic results.

As we will finally come to conclude our long account in *"The Real Dangers of Artificial Intelligence"*, this awareness that people learn different values of information through their jobs will take on a serious consideration. As artificial intelligence will change the jobs that people have, so will it change their ways of thinking. As we have recently explained, the brain of the individual is shaped and functions by the work tasks that it does through the language the individual knows of. In an evolutionary sense, this could mean that our brain will diminish in size and function as artificial intelligence takes over much of the thinking we now do.

Language, then, is the means by which one human being can express their mind to that of another, and the success they have in this will lie in the clarity and the sensitivity they employ to recognize that the mind of the other is different from their own.

The common failing with language arises when one assumes the mind of the other is the same as theirs, and they broadcast their meaning with little consideration to the difficulty the other has to translate what they receive to what they already know, and at the same time fail to realize how they emotionally desire to want to do this. This is the principle of language, but how does it really work?

5.2 The Relationship of Language and Thought:

We shall now discuss how the ability of a student to develop in any subject will greatly lie in their language capability.

In a formal sense, language has three components. These are phonology, vocabulary and grammar. The ability to know of these derives from gene codes, but the proficiency displayed in each of these is a pure consequence of experience. Yet, all performance in education that is evaluated, and so taken to represent some factor of innate ability, will have this language as its foundation.

When Spearman recognized, in the beginning of the 20th Century, that students score similar grades in the different subjects of their curriculum, he saw this as evidence of an inherited general factor of intelligence. This general factor of intelligence is the basis for the impression we have today of what intelligence is, where it comes from, and how the child's grades in school can be explained through this.

The language the teacher uses to explain a lesson to each individual in the class, will largely determine how well each can relate to the progression of this subject. The language by which each student shares their feelings with others, in their class, will give them a quality of attention or distraction to its information. The language and sense of identity each has developed through their home life will have prepared them for the first lesson in this subject, and so play some role in their development through this. The desire of each to want to excel in this subject, and so their motivation, will lie in the goals that others have helped them to realize through the ideas, hopes and dreams they shared with them through language.

Therefore, the proficiency the child has with English (or their national language) will not only determine how successful they are with this subject but with all the subjects of the curriculum, because all of these, including mathematics, operate upon a language directly related to this. Therefore, if language is the key to grades, and so to understanding intelligence, how do we acquire it?

As we have mentioned, the fetus is aware of the language of their mother and will have encoded their brain with the basic phonics to understand this language by the time of their birth. After birth, all children indiscriminately develop their ability for language in set stages. Chomsky noted, that by the first six weeks of life all babies coo, by six months they babble, by 12 months they can speak their first word, by two years they can construct two word sentences, and by their fifth year of life they have acquired the basic and yet complex grammatical structures of their language. Through this understanding, Chomsky put forward his theory of universal grammar ability, which is to say that the child natural inherits the ability to know of language, and does so indiscriminately.[122]

Thus, we may realize that Chomsky was saying that each human being inherits the ability to know of language, but that its development is steered within that human being through the emotional and stimulative world they are raised in. Bates developed upon this to explain how language develops through the general development of brain mechanisms, as they relate to the complex social environment of the child.[123]

Therefore, while some have taken Chomsky's use of the word "ability", as they interpreted the meaning of this word through Galton's legacy, they have much misunderstood what Chomsky was saying. Chomsky merely stated that man must have some innate means to demonstrate his unique ability of language, and that this must be different from the lower capabilities of animals. The ability to do this, he reasons, must be acquired through some genetic means, a means he believes is gained through a schema. He calls this schema the Language Acquisition Device or LAD.[124/125]

- The Language Acquisition Device, then, gives explanation for how we actually acquire the ability for language, and how we do this without any genetic diversity.

The relationship between language and our ability to think was recognized by Sapir and Whorf in the 1930s, when they brought understanding to how cultural and social differences cause people to think differently through their different perspectives of this. As they pointed out, since no two languages are sufficiently similar, then, the peoples of those languages must live in distinct worlds of thought.[126] However, it was not until Gordon brought relevance to all this, when he examined the language of the isolated Amazonian Piraha tribe in 2004, that we truly understood how and why we devise language through the functions we do, and so how our language can construct our thinking capability.

Gordon found that the Piraha people had developed a culture that had not necessitated the use of past or future verbs, and so caused them virtually no understanding of past or future times. They lived in, and so only thought in the present time. In addition to this, they were found to count only with one, two, or many, so they could neither relate to nor imagine any higher numerical situation. They could, for example, understand one fish and two fish, but they could not understand the meaning of four fish. The concept of four fish was totally beyond their comprehension.[127] As Gordon pointed out, "A people without terms for numbers, do not develop the ability to determine exact numbers."[128] We may reason from this that the skill of these people to think, or if you wish to say how they demonstrate their IQ, is shown to be determined by their language, with their language being a direct consequence of their culture and so the job tasks they do. In other words:

- Gordon's findings prove that we learn to think, through the language we have evolved, through the tasks that we do.

In a simple sense, this is very evident in our normal day-to-day life, when we hear people verbally express the actions of their mind through the training of their job. A politician, for example, can be seen to weigh-up the meaning of a situation, before they express their mind. Their job task requires, for their survival, that they consider many aspects of information, and formulate it in very specific terms when they relate their mind to another. A trained soldier will explain their thoughts in very categorizing terms, not necessarily a "yes" or "no", but very close to such meaning as they were trained to listen and respond to condensed and salient information. Similarly, a police officer will explain their mind with clear and unmistakable actions, just as a sales person will use their language to define the needs of their mind. All these people have been trained by their jobs to recognize and to process information in different ways, and this reflects the world as they are caused to see it.

These skills in language and thinking, which relate to a job skill, usually develop in the individual in adulthood, such that the degree by which the individual conforms to this identity relies on many personal factors. However, when such language and mind training occurs from birth, as through a cultural design, the individual is much more absorbed into and becomes a living part of this process. A very great example of this can be found with a people who have retained one of the most sophisticated language experiences through their social tasks.

The European and Ashkenazi Jews are a people who have an unparalleled history of cultural and social rejection, and a level of persecution that saw them discriminated against en masse, mercilessly tortured, and murdered. Their means of worship, as this provides an identity for them, has been severely restricted. Wherever they went in Europe and Russia they were treated as social outcasts, often confined to ghettos and restricted to ownership of land. As a direct consequence of this, these people developed a strict sense of sectarian identification that was propagated within their communities through a special language.

This was a language of evaluation that emphasized knowledge of not only valuable commodities, but more significantly the worth of information, for it was only through the precise understanding of information that these people could gain the security to survive. To teach their children how to understand information precisely and how to share their thoughts with precise accuracy, was the lifeline for the continuation of their culture. As Feuerstein points out:

"Many Jewish communities were subject to abject poverty, political oppression and social discrimination, but mediation (the art of explaining the value of information) persisted at the informal and formal levels of Jewish communal life ..... So that the wisest scholar in a community was awarded the highest status, with the intention to inspire parents in the social significance of raising their children in cognitive excellence." [129]

For this reason, we find that the European and Askenzasi Jewish cultures evolved a social habit of raising each subsequent generation in very high language skills. This social "transmission of intelligence" was clearly impressed upon me, when, in visiting Jerusalem, I was invited to take dinner with a Jewish family. During the course of the meal, a child asked their mother a particular question. The mother's reply was most illustrative of the point we raise here.

"Tell me...," she said, ".....what do you say? Can I read your mind?"

In response to this, the child then redefined their question with specific point and clarity. It was only after the mother was satisfied that her son had explained precisely his meaning that she consented to his request, and did so with an expression of deep affection.

While I could only imagine the average parent of another culture replying "yes" or "no" in such an incident, if they gave any type of a verbal response, this Jewish mother had used a very small and normal incident to transmit the interactive skills of her culture. She taught her child exemplary skills in defining and moving with information, which shows how language guides intelligence.

Accordingly, it was most illustrative to see how she "naturally" ended the whole learning experience by instilling into her child a feeling of security and success. It is upon these very two factors that the base for intelligence is set, and this is mainly the responsibility of parental skills and affection. With certain Jewish sects, this is a cultural tradition.

As we would find over and over again in any culture, and at any level of society, it is the loving devotion of a parent to seed the secrets of inquiry and endear the confidence to pursue this that is the cause of higher intelligence. The genius of Mendeleev, who designed the Periodic Table lay, as Bronowski saw it, in the singular efforts of his devoted mother, who zealously indulged his childhood passion for games of relationships. It was a "hobby" that finally that bore fruit, when Mendeleev realized how the properties of elements relate to each other as do cards in the Game of Patience.[130]

From this, we see that the intellectual origins of many of our geniuses such as Einstein, Von Neumann, Leo Szilard, Leonard Bernstein, George Gershwin to name but a few, can be attributed not to a genetic inheritance, but to a cultural one. Theirs was a bathing from birth in clearly defined rules of interactive strategy that stimulated imagination, and were germinated through love with a strong sense of identity.

Heinrich Graetz gave definition to this "Jewish" intelligence in the 19th Century, when he wrote: "When Jewish superior intelligence is assumed to be positive" he wrote, "it is rarely seen as biological. Rather, it is understood as a quality that can be attained by any group if only the "right" rules are followed. If Jewish superior intelligence is seen as a negative quality, as a hair-splitting judgement or narrowness of imagination, it is deserving a love of twisting, distorting, ingenuous quibbling."[131]

However, such quibbling as Graetz mentions, and which Shakespeare made issue of, has a greater purpose than is apparent to the Gentile. It is my understanding that the purpose that underlies such quibbling is a desire to know the real value of a person, for it is through the force of argument that the true identity of a person is revealed. This is a need that may be most understood in a people so long deprived of roots, and whose greatest desire is to share understanding through trust.

Yet, such paternal instruction for the acquisition and respect of knowledge, as we have discussed here, is only witnessed in branches of European and Ashkenazi Jews. Other Jewish branches do not share the same quality of intellectual standard, or (and this is an important point) that of paternal devotion. In fact, a major problem to Israeli authorities is the very low level of intellectual performance that Ethiopian and Chinese Jews display once they settle in Israel, and the subsequent difficulties in educating them to reliable roles in their new society.[132]

It is not, then, that Jews as a distinct people can be thought to have a genetically superior intelligence to other people. It is merely that two branches of Jewish people evolved a high cultural level of intelligence through the unique circumstances of their very particular history.

Accordingly, intelligence is not here regarded as a gift, but as the continuation of a practice. "Amongst Jews" wrote the philosopher Wittgenstein "genius is found only in the holy man. Even the greatest of Jewish thinkers is no more than talented. (Myself for instance). I think there is some truth in my idea that I really only think reproductively. I don't believe I have ever invented a line of thinking. I have always taken one over from someone."[133]

How this Jewish intelligence is socially transmitted, was brought to my awareness when I became involved with a group of such intellectuals. To an outsider, impression could easily have been gained that the intense arguing that soon erupted within them lay in some bitter feud. In fact, I thought they were going to kill each other. It was only after the point of the discussion had been agreed upon by all, and everyone started laughing and sharing love with each other, that I came to understand how each had been fighting to understand the meaning of the other, and so how much real value was placed upon information by these people. To these people information was not to be flaunted lightly. The people that I had seen arguing were, in fact, only living with their thoughts. Each thought was desperate to survive, and each thought sought the means to adapt itself to do so. It was through closely observing the behavior of these academics, that I came to realize that ...

Intelligence is life.
It has to be fought for to survive, and its sword is language.

This means of evaluating information, as demonstrated by these Israeli professors although in a tempered version, is much of what is lacking in education. In fact, the child in education is not encouraged to fight for their understanding of something, and is likely to be penalized if they interrupt the teacher too much as they try to orchestrate 30 minds in rhythm with their own. The natural desire of the child to test the value of information will have been quashed within the first few years of school, as Land showed us. Thus, by the circumstances of their learning environment the child will be conditioned to elicit the all too familiar "I don't know" response, when asked a question. All this we shall come to in good time.

It may be, then, as Leaky postulated, that over millions of years the human brain evolved in size because of our unique interaction between thumb and index finger.[134] This mechanism allowed our ancestors fine control over the tools they developed and therefore, how they could shape the environment.

By how they shaped their environment through the work tasks they evolved, so they brought design to their language, and through language they, as we today, brought shape to their thinking. We have seen examples of this in the very low intelligence levels of Romanian children who were deprived of language, how the language of the Piraha people constructed their intelligence, and how certain sects of Jewish children are raised through their language skills ever to search for a truer definition of meaning.

Through the origins of their geographical and climatic conditions, and so their sources of food and means of trade, each group of people evolved work tasks to survive. As they shared the skills of these tasks within their group, they communicated with a language that was particular to their work identity. As this language defined the world they lived in, so it was the means of how they could relate to their world, and to the needs and desires of each other.

In the solitude of their private worlds, the individual could be vague in their acts of intelligence. However, in their social interactions with others, and especially so when they were engaged in work tasks, they had to handle information with precision if they were not to be penalized or punished. As different job tasks evolved, the techniques upon which each depended seasoned those who did them, with skills of thinking that were different to those employed in different tasks. As these job based skills were transmitted through a family line, so different families saw and made use of information in different ways. By the similarity of their jobs, different groups evolved different perspectives of intelligence.

As political, religious, and military influences blended different groups into a common people, so their different languages formed a common language. By the extent of their remoteness, each group retained some element of their own language as a dialect, and through this bond held to their way of thinking. So it is that today, the ways of thinking of the group who are the most remote are regarded by the majority to be the simplest, because, due to the greater difference of their language, they see their world differently and interact with it in a different way.

According to Bryson, Missouri was called the "Show Me State" by Americans in the more industrialized areas of the country, as they gave reference to the state's inhabitants to be so stupid that they had to be shown how to do everything. In their defense, the Missourians took this to be a complement, "persuading themselves that it implied a certain shrewd caution to their part" in how they think.[135] By the same means, the ways in which people think in their national language is different by some greater or lesser degree to the ways people of another national language think.

It was Oscar Wilde in "*The Canterville Ghost*" who gave credence to this, although it was Churchill in the Second World War who refined it to appease the different ways that British and American people think upon the same issue, when he wrote of "*two nations divided by a common language*." This is a point still illustrative today, although it is much less so than it was two generations ago, when the British English describe the human child as an "it", and the American English describe the child as "he" or "she". The sentiment behind the differences emphasizes the degree of empathy to the rights of the human being, as a reflection of their political history. Yet, as politics change so does language, and the politics of this new century will ever more create better equality for all people. It is with respect to this that in reference to the human child, I have tried to avoided a gender pronoun in my writing.

We may gain some understanding from what we have so far discussed that the secret of language is not the name we give to things, the noun by which we know a tree, a rock, a desk or a computer. Nor does it lie in the movement of these things, the verb that tells the action. The secret lies foremost with adjectives, because it is adjectives that give depth in description. The Piraha people knew the noun fish, but because of an extraordinarily limited variety of adjectives (1, 2 and many), they could never count 3, 33, or 305 fish. Their intelligence to compute numbers of fish is extremely limited by the range of adjectives they have. Equally they live and so think only in the present time, because they do not have the adjectives of past and future. Without these two simple adjectives their understanding of life is extremely limited.

We find parallels to this in our modern societies, for people of low socioeconomic means invariably use fewer adjectives than those of better standing in their society. With simple illustration, we could say that to one a building is big, while to another a building is tall, taller than others or the tallest of all they know of. To one the color of the sky may just be blue, or it could be light or dark, while to another it may be Cerulean, Cobalt, or even turn Prussian Blue as a storm brews. Therefore, it is by the range of adjectives that people use that causes differences in their awareness of the world in which they live, and so differences in the accuracy by which they process information as they present their mind to another. All of this, of course, creates the impression of intelligence, and so devises it.

5.3 Thought, Language and Intelligence:

Through the imprinting process, from silent chemicals to gentle babbling, the newborn begins to expand their social experience. By the skill and acceptable personality of those they develop through, they are tutored in what they should do and how they should do it. By the devotion of their parents, their child becomes aware of the value of social experiences. As the infant develops in their mobility, they expand their social encounters. As they share more and more thoughts with others they modulate the experiences of each, bit by bit, into their own. As the repertoire of their skills build up, greater ability is gained in deciphering the meanings of others. In turn, this brings an increasing awareness of new possibilities, and provides them with greater scope to devise expressions of desires and intentions, which we recognize as thought processes.

As a thought is shared among a group of people, it is encoded with their experiences. The thought that travels from one to another is not detached from them. As it enters the mind of each, it becomes dressed with their experiences, sense of need, and in the mood of that time it becomes a part of them. Dressed with the personality of one, the thought is conveyed to another through the changes they have made to it, by the interest they have found with it.

Imagine fifty people sitting around a huge dining table. A woman whispers something into the ear of the man next to her. He smiles and whispers this into the ear of the lady next to him. In turn, she passes this to the man next to her, and so the thought moves around all the people sitting at the dinner table. Eventually, it will come back to the woman who first had the thought. When she hears it, she recognizes some theme of the story, but it is not the same information she first whispered to the man next to her. The information has been changed through all the individual people it has passed through. The more similar is the cultural and socio-work experiences of those people, the more similar will be the story that returns to the woman. However, if those around the table are of different cultures, different languages, and of different job backgrounds, the woman may pass it on to the man next to her without noticing it was her story.

A thought, then, does not belong to a person. They are merely a medium through which the thought travels, for it cannot exist without language. It only survives through the people it passes through, with each person changing it, and in turn being changed by it.

Wittgenstein, throughout much of his life, was pre-occupied with this idea that a thought belongs to no specific person, but is shared by all. As he wrote: "I can as little own the thought, as I can walk about it, or look at it, or point to it. In as much as it cannot be anyone else's, it is not mine either."[136]

Normally, we do not think in this way. When we manifest a thought through our feelings, we dress it in our emotions, and conceive it through our personality. When others say we are right, we feel proud. When they say we are wrong, we feel hurt, and become dejected. This would not happen if we had not placed ownership upon that thought. Whatever information we produce, whether this is verbal or written, it contains a part of our personality and a sense of our identity. By this stamp of our identity, we believe the thought is ours. It originated from us, and we guard "our" invention. This is how we have been cultured to think.

Isaac Newton so jealously guarded his thoughts, that he was want to destroy Leibniz ruthlessly for claiming to have invented calculus. Newton did discover calculus years before Leibniz, but he failed to publish it. When Leibniz published his version of it, Newton rose to claim recognition, which he did vehemently with scathing attacks and by producing numerous defenses written in his own hand but signed by close confidants.[137] However, while we now regard Newton to have discovered calculus, it is more correct to think that he only put together thoughts that other people, such as those of John Wallis, had raised before him.

The same can be said of Darwin, for the French naturalist George Leclerc had prompted a century before the publication of the "*Origin of Species,*" the idea that life might somehow evolve through itself. Nor was he alone in this, Immanuel Kant, the famous German philosopher, more directly believed that all living things somehow evolved from a single ancestral source. Indeed, before Darwin there was a general acceptance in some circles that life did evolve from a single origin in the distant past. It was, of course, a line of thinking that much went against the accepted idea that God had created different levels of life. What Darwin did was to recognize how these ideas of evolution could be explained through the idea of natural survival. The key that enabled him to do this came from the thoughts that Thomas Malthus had expressed in his "*Essay on Population.*" So, rather than discovering a totally new concept, Darwin, just as Newton, only saw how the many parts of the ideas of others could be brought together to present a simple and workable single idea.

Therefore, as each parcel of information enters your memory, you encode it with your personal experiences. In doing so, you may consider that you place ownership upon it. It becomes, you believe, your information. Yet, in truth it belonged to others before it reached you. It was just that another had dressed their meaning in a way that you could better recognize what they meant, as they conveyed their thought to you. So, they borrowed what they believed were your experiences, to cloak their information in order that you could better relate to it. In your turn, you will do the same, because this is how a thought and so information moves through people by the language they use, each giving flavor to it by their experiences.

A thought then, is not owned by a person. Each may adapt it to their need, but the seed of that thought is the property of others who have coached or brought influence upon them, just as they, in their turn, gained seeds of thoughts from others. This, of course, brings us back to the social transmission of intelligence, as it is embodied in thought and feeling.

So, wrote Wittgenstein in his book Tractatus, "This book will be understood only by someone who has himself already had the thoughts expressed in it."[138] The point Wittgenstein was stressing here relates not to the capability of the reader, but in the familiarity they have with the content of the material. How much of such thoughts, for example, have previously reached them? Wittgenstein did not then, see intelligence as a factor of capability, but as one of familiarity with information as it circulates through language.

In order to explain to others the thoughts we have, we present these thoughts through the words we know, and through which we assume that other person is familiar with. Each person gains clarification in this transaction through the exchange of meanings and intentions, which they adjust through their experiences.

Therefore, whether language is verbally shared with us or presented as a written text, we have to decipher its meaning and the arrangement of its information into the way that we have learnt to understand it. The description of nouns and verbs, what something is and how it interacts with something else, are not naturally understood by one because they speak the same language as another, although school tests ignore this in order to classify children more simply. IQ tests do this ever more so.

Terman, as we saw in our previous book, used the concept of different languages to classify people into different levels of natural intelligence. Immigrants with poor English were therefore, classified as having low IQ, because they could not understand the questions very well! While we now recognize that this is wrong, we do so for the wrong reason. We think of the capability of these immigrants only through the words of the English language they know, but we do not recognize how their language has its own definitions for the meanings information has.

How much cultural differences affect the way people think, was strikingly brought to my attention when I once presented a Somalian with a drawing of a weightlifter who was shown lifting a bar with heavy weights on either end. In order to stress the difficulty of the task the artist had given a bow shape to the bar, to emphasize the heaviness of the weights the man was trying to lift.

If I had asked anyone from a Westernized culture, even a very small child, what the weightlifter was trying to do, I would have been immediately informed the man was trying to lift the weights. However, this was not how the Somalian, who had never seen a weightlifter so dressed, interpreted the meaning of the drawing. As he studied this, he described how the bar was being bent by the man pulling upon it. He then logically explained to me that the purpose of the man was, in fact, to bend the bar. This, he further explained, was possible because the bar was made of a softer metal than the blocks placed on either end.

Through the perspective by which he identified the information, the Somalian's response was intelligently analyzed and described. Although, if this had been a "Westernized" IQ question, he would have scored zero, to which some would have readily explained his score to be the consequence of low genetic quality, firstly by his creed and secondly by his individuality. Incidentally, this man was a qualified engineer who held a master's degree.

It is natural, then, that people learn to recognize and identify with the world about them through those they share their mind with. In this way, the more familiar people are with each other, as by their cultural and so social identity, the more they will devise similar identities to items and recognize similar means of interaction. The understanding and so mind of each is therefore, cultured through the identity of others, with each thought having a common origin. Therefore, people of different backgrounds do make different interpretations, and do manufacture different processes to deal with information.

Such different thought processes, which can lead to different qualities of a response albeit answer, are ignored in intelligence tests, as they are seen merely as a "natural" consequence of inheritance. They are, however, learned through the sharing of experiences. As we understood earlier, our ability to freely change our belief at will and so to reason in a different way is not decided by genetic diversity or genetic quality. The ability for this change, the adapting of a superior process, is simply reliant upon language, where common meanings are recognized, and misunderstandings and confusion overcome to define a better strategy to process information.

Thus, it can now be understood that a thought travels within the language people share, with each individual manifesting it according to the ways their personality has developed and how they have learnt to formulate their personal experiences. Therefore, any two individuals will look upon an item differently. Each will agree to identify with that item through a common dialogue, but the inner perspective that each holds of it will not be the same.

It is then, a grave miscomprehension to assume that any item of information will have a naturally common meaning to each individual. Each may only gain their familiarity with it through the quality of language they can share.

By how sensitively this is done, will the purer content of the information be conveyed to give each a higher understanding of it, and so enable each the enrichment of a higher intelligence. Intelligence grows with language, although not just by its presence, but by the sensitivity with which it moves. As we are already now well aware and why so, the education of this sensitivity is left by the school to the parents, and the background factors which influence them.

Language, then, is always developing, and shortly we shall discuss how recent advances in technology have changed the language skills of thinking today and so raised the intelligence level globally. Yet, before we discuss this, we need to understand more of how this inheritance of thinking skills within a family influences the child's means of intelligence.

Professional parents, it may be said, will work and so live under a value of productive stress. As they seek to survive in their job, they are continually appraising and processing different aspects of information.

This allows them to be ever more efficient in adapting to different thinking demands. They develop a high sensitivity in monitoring information. They will be continually comparing information to seek any number of complex errors, and upon detecting a change of information they will consider the effects of this change and seek alternatives. So it is that these “professional” parents are constantly given a great deal of stimuli in the course of their normal day, and this will have conditioned their brain to be responsive to any thinking situation.

When they come home in the evenings they maintain their value of thinking skills, so that when they explain things to their child they do so with a relative accuracy and clarity. They also will have some understanding of the value of feedback, and so they will take the time to discuss again some earlier incident, and bring awareness in their offspring of the importance of keeping information updated. Thus, we see that the accuracy and the clarity by which the professional parent has learnt to think is transferred to their child.

The “socially inherited intelligence” of the child whose parents are professionals

In consequence to the skills the professional parents have developed through their jobs and life experiences, their child will seek high levels of defining and associating with information. This will arm them with effective means of locating relationships, and by evaluating those experiences relative to the one at hand they will display a greater ability to solve problems.

Of equal importance will be the awareness of these parents to stimulate a sense of self-discipline within their child. This self-discipline will later be very important for them in the early stages of school, when they must learn to focus upon the teacher and gain their ranking amongst others. As they develop through their school years, this quality of self-discipline will assist them in the pursuit of a problem to a successful conclusion; rather than to give up, or to pass the responsibility for the solution on to another, and thereby fail to develop through it.

The "socially inherited" intelligence of the child whose parents are productive workers

In contrast to this, the manual parents receive less stimulation in their jobs and in their lives. Once they have learnt the necessary basic skills, they function in a comparatively automatic mode. Their perception of information is vague in comparison, and the errors they deal with are less demanding to recognize. Their social framework will normally have as little stimulation as their job, and so they will be conditioned by their environment. Unless, of course, they are motivated for whatever reason to study, or to become involved in some mentally active recreation.

When these parents explain information to their child, they do so with less accuracy. Information is more vague, and the value of errors is less considered. It is either right or wrong, with little reflection on improvement. When their child receives vague information, they are conditioned to handle this with equal vagueness. They will identify less with information, and vaguely store it in their memory. When they are required to locate it to respond to a new situation, their memory search patterns will be vague. This will cause them to respond slowly, and if they feel pressurized to do so faster they will respond inaccurately. As they are conditioned, and so self-condition themselves to accept the inaccurate responses they give, they fail to understand why they do not achieve higher recognition from others.

This job conditioning mind placement was easily recognizable before the advent of television, where levels of intelligence were defined through the mystery of genetic inheritance and social standing. However, television began to disturb this stratified impression of intelligence, as it caused children to become more aware of the world, and so were encouraged to think beyond the social boundaries that had restricted their parents. It was not, however, until computers arrived, and children gained a personal development through their interaction with software programs and the Internet, that any significant and notable rise in the intelligence of a generation was witnessed.

Accordingly, in our book *"Intelligence",* we saw how Flynn had recognized that intelligence has risen globally over the past few generations,[139] and how Blair had reasoned how this increase in ability had been too rapid to be explained by genetics.[137] We further saw how Fox and Mitchum found that "individuals born around 1940 are less able to map objects at higher levels of relational abstraction than individuals born around 1990," while "recent born individuals have adopted an approach to analogy, that enables them to infer higher level relations, requiring roles that are not intrinsic to the objects, that constitute initial representations of items."[140]

We discussed from this that 1990 was a time when most young children had access to computers in their home, and so why their generation was becoming increasingly computer literate, with all the intellectual and behavioral ramifications of this. Accordingly, we find that children of today are more intelligent than their parents, because of their greater awareness and handling of information. This information, of course, is a representation of language.

To discuss how the general intelligence of a people has changed is to bring us closer to understand how individual intelligence can change. As we enter into this, we may know that there is a difference between the intelligence of a child and the grades they obtain in school, because the world of life and that of the school are not the same. They operate on different rules.

While in life the child may succeed on the rules they create, how they succeed in education will be greatly determined by their compatibility with the educational mind, and how well they comply with and make use of the rules of the school world.

While we have much to discuss about these rules of school and how a child or student succeeds through their use of them, as we will do in our books, "For Parent For Teacher: Mediation: Crafting the Ability of the Child for School", and "Teach Better Learn Better", the reader is asked at this juncture to consider what the causes could be that make a child a genius in the street, but a D performer in school?

So far in this chapter, we have seen how intelligence is maintained by the work tasks in a culture, and how this can be transferred within families through a generalization of attitude towards the flow of information. All this, however, is in a generalized sense. What we need to do now is to move beyond this to examine how the unique and individual child develops their intelligence.

5.4 A Perspective of Individual Intelligence:

If we think of an act of intelligence, as the way information is defined and how it is constructed, we may see that the mental play we make of this relies upon physical impressions we have stored through previous encounters. This information was, of course, conveyed to us through the light waves our eyes detected, the audio waves our hearing translated, and the differences in physical textures that our tactile senses relayed to our brain. We may reason through this that our ability to relate to information, and so to be able to explain it to others, is anchored in the quality by which information is detected, how this is stored in our memory and the confidence we have gained in sharing our mind with those of others.

We have seen how the fetus, in the very early stages of life, prepares a system to decipher differences in information, and how the infant subsequently learns to build upon this as they mentally classify physical properties. To expand upon the above, we may introduce here an awareness that such classification relies upon processes of selection, comparison, and association, for when information is found to be of interest it is not simply stored in the memory, or used in the solution of a problem.

Rather, it is that each individual, using their emotional interest and based on strategies they devised through trial and error interactions and much aided by the strategies they gained through others, will choose particular aspects of information from the information field. Having selected features that are prominent to their interest, they will prioritize these through strategies of comparison. Based on how they choose to do this, they will associate this new information to older information in their memory banks for immediate use or future reference.

- It is of the greatest importance to realize that the level of sensitivity invested in these processes of selection, comparison, and association will greatly determine the value of information to that individual, and so to others as they relate their applications of it. It is upon this sensitivity that individual intelligence is much decided. A quality in sensitivity, therefore, drives the quality in how we observe, select, identify, and make association. When we are interested, we are sensitive to detail, and when we are not, we are vague.

So, when I observe the coffee cup in front of me, I should pause to remind myself it is a conglomeration of information that has been assembled. It is not just a cup. In a sense it is alive with information, and how well I define its particular shape, texture, and colors will enable me to note its difference to other cups, and provide an accuracy when I choose to refer back to it in some future time. Accordingly, by how well we choose to break down information as we identify it (by such as the outline form, colors and inner detail), so we set the level of differentiation by which we make comparison, and from this processes of analysis.

- When we are caused to examine information, we do so through the rules we have developed, and through our emotional drives. So, one may analyse information seeking to grasp some familiarity within a soup of unfamiliarity, while another will categorize it into what is relevant, what may be uncertain, and what is known not to be relevant. Upon these strategies will lie the efficiency of all those that will follow, as new information is related to what has previously been stored, and means are sought to determine the use it can be.

Thus, our ability to understand the value of a problem at hand is related to the clarity by which we can relate this information to similar information stored in our memory. In turn, this is related to the accuracy with which that information was defined in the first place. It follows from this that the more times we examine related information with intent, the more we learn to find a higher meaning to something we have stored, both in clarity and with association to other information. This is how we develop levels of expertise as we relate to new facets of information, and process this with sensitivity to our stored experiences.

As our relative field of knowledge improves in intensity, and expands through new but relatively recognized relationships, the speed of how we may locate information improves through the ease of this accessibility. Speed, then, in analyzing information or producing a tentatively correct answer is related to strategies that examine stored experiences, as these are kept semi-active through repeated interrogation, or held in a semi-active state through the emotional value we have tagged to them.

It is important to emphasize here, as in any learning, that any reference to the repeated examination of information does not suggest that the same precise information is to be continually reanalyzed. To look upon exactly the same information again, and again offers very little stimulation. This lowers attention, and promotes misunderstandings. It rather means that the repeated interrogation of something should be done by relating similar information to it. This information should be close enough to be intriguingly recognizable, and not too distant as to be un-associable. It is easier to understand this from the point of the brain, rather than that of the mind.

So we are brought to reflect upon how neurons are bonded together, and how circuits are created through the coded signals that move through them. What is very important in this is the manner by which these signals are repeated. The more singular, and the more identical each element of information is to the one that preceded it, the more singular will be the network that it relates to. However, if that information is caused to vary slightly, then it will bring other circuits into this network to provide easier access to other facets of information that have previously been stored. In this way, broader networks develop, which allow information to be more quicker identified and processed.

The more emotional an element of information is caused or desired to be, the stronger and so the more permanent will be the bonds of these circuits. An emotionally happy, or a painful experience, will be much faster to relate to than one of a lesser emotional experience, because different chemicals were brought into the construction of the circuit to cause this to be more meaningful. We can artificially manufacture this life saving process, which is related to our para-sympathetic actions, by using mnemonic strategies to remember something, or associative ones that link a fact to an emotional character.

In this way, the more "similar" information is to that examined and related to, so are even older memory circuits re-examined and revitalized, causing them to play a more active role in the association process. As this occurs our memory improves, as does our intelligence when we seek new ways to recognize solutions in problems that, although different, have certain distinguishable features which we identify with by redefining the circumstances in which they are presented.

As the diversity of our options increase through these experiences, so we seek to be more selective when we examine information. As we do this, new information becomes more reliably associated with previous information. As the individual develops competency in this, misunderstandings become clarified, higher levels of understandings are gained, and greater association is made to other information networks to realize, or to suggest more predictions through this greater comparability.

The recognition of a solution, the production of an idea, or the spark of an inspiration is no more than the sudden union of numerous memory circuits given some clearer association. Some of these circuits may have been dormant for years, only to be triggered by some small feature that brought one circuit to another to bring sudden sense. Koestler summed this up when he remarked that the moments of insight and intuition that we generate, are only experiences we have been prepared for.

Accordingly, we may understand how the brain of each will provide an intellectual performance based upon its recognition of information. This will be dependent upon how similar the information they are presented with is to how each previous item of information was recognized, associated, stored, and seen to be relatable at that time. Does it not then follow from this that the brain is not the originator of an intention, but merely a processor of information as Wittgenstein saw it?

In other words we are not born with a quality of intelligence, but we do develop one!

Thus, the ability of an individual to learn, and so respond cannot be simply viewed as their genetic quality, witnessed through the linear relationship of experience set to stimulation. A more realistic understanding of their ability would be to see how they apply "learnable" processing techniques, which they sensitively steer through emotional design, to make use of the perspective of information they choose to recognize.

May we now look upon intelligence is a means of how information is processed, so that proficiency is a gauge of the manner and the precision in which information is selected, and how this is associated to memory networks to be presented through the experiences of the individual.

Therefore, the more precisely information is identified with, the clearer can it be associated to stored experiences, and the more specific will differences be noted from which opportunities can be realized.

Conversely, information that is vaguely selected, or vaguely interpreted will either be mismatched or misrelated when associated, will be lesser understood, and be more prone to error or inefficiency when applied.

Sensitivity, as we have said before, is the key to understanding intelligence. This is seated in our dealings with others as we share language, as this then drives our emotions to be more or less sensitive in the mental processes we engage.

So, over many pages, we have come to understand how information is recognized and made sense of through our emotional interest. In doing this, we have come to understand better what intelligence is, and more importantly how an act of intelligence is created. Let us see now how easily it can be disturbed.

Chapter Six

The Chemistry of the Mind

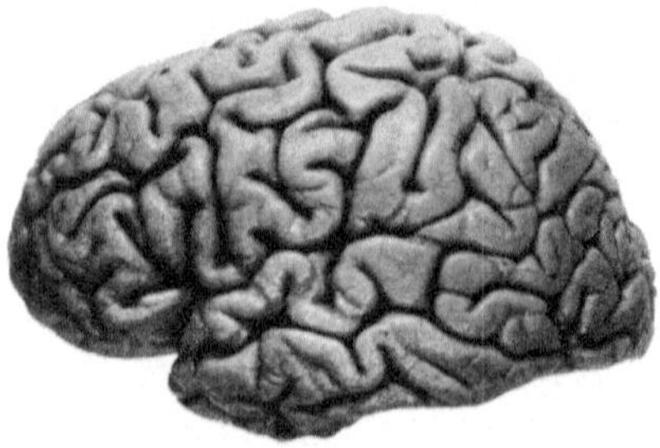

"To Think is to Practice Brain Chemistry."
Deepak Chopra

6.0 Introduction:

Since the brain is constantly changing in its composition, as different chemicals are brought into the body through the food and liquid consumed (alcohol is a startling illustration here), we should not think of the brain in the solid sense we do of other organs of the body. In many senses it would do us well, for what we shall discuss in this chapter, to think of the brain more as a chemical soup than a rigid arrangement of neurons linked together.

When we do not give appropriate relevance to the chemistry of the brain in our understanding of how it works, we simply think only of the value of a neuron. When we do this we have in our mind something solid. We translate this concept of "solidness" to mean a factor of stability, and this complements the idea we have been raised on that a stable operation of the brain is a consequence of an inherited value. This, in fact, is exactly what Eysenck and Jensen did when they tried to suggest that IQ could be evaluated on the speed by which an individual's neurons fire. [141]

This chemical soup, this "body" of intelligence, is importantly not just the glial and neuron cells that give it form. It is also the neurotransmitters we have previously discussed that carry a signal of information across the synaptic gap that separates neurons. Of these neurotransmitters there are about a hundred different types depending upon how they are counted,[142] but to our interest we may think of a specific group known as monoamines.

When we discuss monoamines, we need to be aware of the standing idea that these are divided into two groups. There are said to be excitatory monoamines and inhibitory ones. The first is said to increase the activity of the brain, while the latter is said to calm it down. From this reasoning comes the idea that optimal brain performance is gained when there is a balance of operation between these two groups.

Therefore, when the whole mind is calm, (i.e. happy, content, and secure) it allows the brain to control specific regions by which information can be rationally analyzed and processed. We may think of Sherlock Holmes here who was never known to worry and because of this always able to rationalize information smoothly. In contrast to this fictional character, we have the normal human being who does worry and does have trouble rationalizing when their mind is on other concerns.

The excitatory neurotransmitters then, are described as:

- Dopamine, which although being involved in many important functions of the brain, is directly said to be associated with tasks based on reward, such as those involved with learning. It seems that every study based on reward learning has found increased levels of dopamine. We may think back here to experiments with rats.

- Norepinephrine plays an active role in the flight or fight response to stress, which we shall shortly discuss. Accordingly, norepinephrine increases the rate of the heart, sugar levels, and so on and so forth that enable the body to gain energy quickly. As it is a derivation of dopamine, norepinephrine is also associated with alertness, decision making and attention.
- Adrenaline (or epinephrine) works in conjunction with norepinephrine. It increases the heart rate, breathing, and blood pressure for energy.
- Glutamate is the most abundant neurotransmitter of this group, and is said to play an important role in the learning and memory processes.

The two most commonly known inhibitory neurotransmitters are:

- Serotonin, which is associated with mood and so social behavior, but also appetite and digestion, sleep, memory, and sexual desire and function.
- GABA (or gamma amino butyric acid) is related to the lowering of anxiety, and is so said to help to calm the mind. As Smith points out "Anxiety and a worrying disposition with the inability to stop thoughts going around and around the mind is characteristic of GABA deficiency."[143]

Having said all this, and all of which is well described and given testimony to in medically related information, we are caused to wonder how accurate this information is. Do scientists really know what these monoamines do, and do all scientists all agree upon their properties, or is it just that one version has gained popularity and this has spread to influence the thoughts and so actions of the general public? Just as, we might add, the belief in inherited intelligence has grown and become so established.

As we said, we see that glutamate is said to play an important role in the learning and memory process. It most likely does, but we don't know how much it does, and therefore how relevant different levels of it are. Unfortunately, because of the dualistic way the public was caused, we may say "trained," to think in their education, they are likely to take such understanding as gospel.

The impression easily arises from this, that a person's ability to learn and to memorize is related to their levels of glutamate. In turn, this would naturally lead to the thought that children who exhibit difficulty with learning or memory may have very low levels of glutamate, and that if they took glutamate supplements their learning and memory would improve. This will not necessarily be the case.

The brain of each of us is different, as it has become formed in different ways, and while glutamate may be influential in one individual's learning it may be less so in another, whose learning may be more influenced by, for example, dopamine. Therefore, we have to be very careful of accepting too readily that one neurotransmitter does such a thing, and another a different thing. These explanations are only guidelines, if not suggestions. The reality is that we know far too little about how the brain really works, and so the real influence of the mind over how it does so.

Take, for instance, that a low level of serotonin is widely acknowledged to be responsible for depression, after all it is commonly said to be directly responsible for mood. All medical personnel know this, and base the use of drugs upon this knowledge. However, as Healy points out in his book *Let Them Eat Prozac,* "No abnormality of serotonin in depression has every been demonstrated."[144] In fact, Healy's research into SSRIs (Selective serotonin re-uptake inhibitors) as anti-depressant drugs, and his subsequent realization that serotonin could not be associated with depression and so mood, drew him into the politics of psychiatry and the pharmaceutical industry.

Rowe expands upon this to explain that Healy had been "... appointed to the University of Toronto in Canada as professor of psychiatry in the Mood and Anxiety Disorders Program and was awaiting his visa prior to moving to Canada. In a talk at a conference in Toronto, he touched briefly on the research which showed that SSRIs can make people suicidal. A few days later the offer of the job at Toronto University was withdrawn. In the previous year the Mood Disorders Program had received over 50% of its funding from pharmaceutical companies. Along with this story and his accounts of the court cases in the USA, where he has been an expert witness, David Healy tells the history of antidepressant drugs. This is not a story of scientific discovery but of pseudo-science in search of great profits."[145]

To our interest, this highlights the fact that our scientists do not really know what neurotransmitters actually do, or of the effect that is created by their joint actions, because Healy's work brings into question the whole concept of the interplay of the so called excitatory and inhibitory neurotransmitters. In turn, this brings us into the far greater realization that the importance with brain functioning is not with what one particular neurotransmitter may or may not do, but in the realization that as the brain is creating about a million new synapses every second, it is constantly shaping and reshaping itself.

The order by which it does this will be totally individual, as the brain of each has developed its own chemical formulas for these changes to occur, as these have been shaped by the bio-chemistry of the body and the mental and physical experiences the individual has moved through. Let us now move to understand how those experiences do shape the chemistry of the mind.

6.1 The Chemical Effect of Stress on Intelligence:

We have previously discussed that the causes of schizophrenia are undecided, although this condition is known to be related to abnormally high production levels of dopamine.[146] Psychotic drugs that are used to combat schizophrenia do so by lowering dopamine levels in the brain region of the limbic system. Since the monoamines (such as dopamine, noradrenaline, and serotonin) obtain their manufacturing level through experience, there arises from this a suggestion that mental conditions relating to monoamine levels may be socially inherited.

We can imagine in this how the behavior of a parent influences the behavioral design of their child, who in turn influences the behavioral design of their child, and so on and so forth. We may consider from this how schizophrenia can run in a family line totally without a genetic component.

This takes us back to the effect of imprinting and so how one individual, usually the more easily influenced of the two, absorbs the behavioral tactics (and mental strategies) of the other. This relationship, is of course, more intense between a parent and their child, as it is naturally designed to be. Therefore, we may see that through the process of imprinting, the child can absorb good behavioral tactics into the construction of those they are otherwise developing, but just as easily bad ones too.

Van der Kolk brought great relevance to this when he demonstrated how severe stress in childhood can affect the production of noradrenaline, so as to distort sleep and arousal patterns in adulthood.[147] Such long term effects of mental stress in childhood has been supported by the many cases Cichilli reviewed of adults who, in direct consequence to stressful experiences in childhood, were found to produce abnormal fluctuations in the manufacture of some of their neurotransmitters.[148]

This led to other studies that examined how poorly developed brain functions could be related to stressful experiences in childhood. Wilson, for example, has shown how neglect or abuse in childhood can be related to strokes and cerebral infarction in old age.[149] We may see from this that the threshold levels by which neurotransmitters are produced and so released are determined by experience, and not by inheritance. This is a crucial point for us to understand, because it brings the idea of intelligence as an inherited factor ever more into an environmental perspective.

This role of the environment, in the construction of intelligence, has been vividly brought home by the discovery that the production and characteristic of dendritic spines are related to stress.[150]

We may remember that at either end of a neuron there are dendrites. It is the dendrites that move to connect with dendrites of other neurons, as they form a path for the signal to move through. At the end of a dendrite there are very minute spines. These spines are small membranous protrusions that receive the input neurotransmitter from a synapse and so allow a signal to move from one neuron to another, and so through a network of neurons.

It is now known that spines increase in number as the child grows, and that they do so in a disorderly fashion.

- In other words, they learn through sensory information how to construct themselves.

However, once the adolescent stage is reached, it seems that these spines undergo a pruning that lasts until the onset of adulthood.

Studies on the neurons of children who have been abused, bullied or incurred high levels of stress, have shown how they have abnormally low numbers of these spines on the dendrites, due to weak levels of hormone action which have been affected by levels of stress.

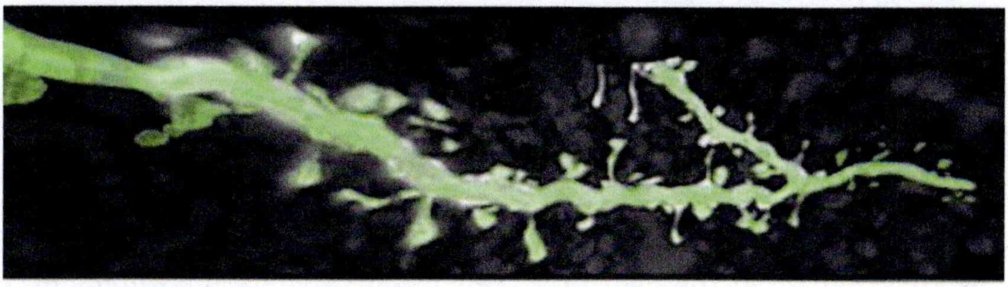

This is to say that the ability of neurons to receive and so conduct information is physically impaired by a child experiencing high levels of repeated stress, and that this can impair their ability to learn.

These studies have opened up interest in how stressful experiences to children could affect the production level of their stress related hormones. As previously mentioned, this has been well demonstrated by Ouellet-Morin who measured cortisol levels in identical twins. (It is important that we know of cortisol, because it is a hormone activated by the brain's need to create stress. Low levels of stress are essential for us to focus on and so complete a particular task, since a degree of stress prevents us from drifting into distractions. However, too much stress can cause us to abandon this task, as we shall shortly see.)

Accordingly, cortisol levels were found to be normal in one twin, but were significantly higher in the other twin who had a history of being bullied. Further studies made by Ouellet-Morin showed that maltreated or bullied children did exhibit significantly abnormally high levels of cortisol.[151] This brought confirmation that experiences of intense or repeated stress in childhood do change the chemistry of the brain, with long-term adverse effects on behavior. Bullying, she proved, does alter the chemistry of the body with permanent effects to personality.[152] Personality, the reader will by now understand, is one of the driving forces behind the strategies that a child uses to evaluate and process information and so may define their ability for intelligence!

6.2 Personality in Intelligence:

Two thousand years ago the Greek physician Claudius Galenus described (in the labels of our time) intelligence as the charioteer who held the reins to the horses of personality and emotion. He explained from this that when the charioteer was strong enough his intelligence could profit by his control of emotion, which, in turn, would bring control to his personality. While the relationship between emotion and personality has been well explored by psychology since the 19th century, the relationship between emotion and intelligence since that time has been generally ignored for two main reasons.

The tradition that grew up through Galton's efforts focused upon intelligence as being innately decided. This view demanded intelligence to have a high factor of stability. Since emotion would incur a factor of high instability it was kept out of the equation. For much the same reason, education today still does not formally recognize how the emotional status of a student can affect their ability to learn.

Simply, education is employed by society to classify and grade its students for the potential workers they are required to be. Such a classifying system as education is, it is caused to focus not on factors that provide inconsistency as emotion does, but on factors which can be said to be constant. We saw in many of our books, and have just begun to understand in this, how education creates this constancy in the ability of its students through its conditioning environments.

Since emotion cannot be ignored, it is placed under the guise of motivation, where in education it is bolstered by the frequently used saying: "When the going gets tough, the tough get going." Thus, it is generally recognized in education that motivation can be said to affect the ability the student was born with, but not determine it.[153] Thus, a child may work hard and if they do, but do not gain the required grade, their effort can be excused on the basis of what they were thought to be born with. All this serves the purpose and function of education, as we have long discussed.

However, such concept of motivation is grossly inadequate to give account for the many behavioral complexities that work within the mind of the developing child, as they seek to understand and interface with the operation of their developing world. Nor does motivation give account to the self-limiting tactics that a child creates in an act of intelligence when they role-play for social acceptance.

Motivation per se is not, then, the real cause of variation in performance, which is allied to the inherited quality of the child. Performance is largely a question of the quality of skills developed in evaluating and processing information, which are heavily influenced by the emotional contentment of the individual as this developed through their perspective of the experiences they encountered.

When we talk about intelligence, we think of how the mind responds to the environment. When we do this, we forget the relationship between the mind and the brain. Yet, without the brain we could have no mind. Let us therefore, begin to discuss the intangible mind more through the structures of the brain, as we prepare ourselves for the final chapter of this book.

So far we have talked about neurons and synapses, and the mechanics that link these together to make intelligence operational. We have also suggested how emotion can evolve through behavioral experiences, and how, in turn, this guides intelligence. If we are to understand how all these work together, we need to consider how the chemistry of the nervous system works.

A most effective introduction to this could be made by examining how drugs affect the ability of the brain to operate, for this will immediately introduce us to such a chemical relationship of the brain at the level we need to understand.

We have discussed that as a signal moves through a circuit of neurons, it is carried across the chemical synapses that separate individual neurons by neurotransmitters. In the early 1970s, researchers were studying how the brain is affected by opiates. Opiates are found in the poppy plant, and are used to make opium, morphine and heroin. The latter is the most potent. During the course of this research it was found that opiates interact with specialized receptors in neurons, such that when they enter these receptors their action hinders or prevents the ability of the neuron to transmit signals related to sensory pain. The discovery of these receptors led to the conclusion that the body must naturally create some kind of neurotransmitter that is chemically very similar to that of opiates, in order to support the existence of these receptors. This led to our discovery of the naturally produced neurotransmitter endorphin.

Since opiates have very similar chemical properties to endorphins, they are naturally accepted by neurons. However, because the intake of an opiate drug is many times greater than the naturally minute level by which endorphins are produced, the drug has the effect of swamping the brain with opiates. When this occurs, the ordered precision of specific signals moving through prearranged paths moves into chaos as un-associated neurons take in these signals, and the brain's controlling system begins to fall apart. As this happens, the beautiful precision of the brain's operation is converted into a sewage pot of uncoordinated chemicals, which causes the affected person to experience heavy drowsiness. From this, mental images become confused, and illusions are manufactured. By the insensitive operation of the brain, it is less able to relate to nerve signals sent to it from injured parts of the body and so a drugged person becomes less able to feel pain. It is for this reason that opium has been used for many thousands of years as a pain relief.

However, the endorphin receptors in neurons are very sensitive. Therefore, as the drug is repeatedly applied, the sensitivity of the receptors decrease as they become more familiar with it. This requires more and more of the drug to activate the receptors in order to bring about the symptom that is required by the drug user. This may be relief from pain, or the desire to experience hallucination. It is the need to acquire this sensation that develops a state of dependency. As the nervous system loses its sensitivity, the brain is fooled into believing this loss of sensation was brought about by the response of the nervous system to a lowering of environmental activity. In attempting to regulate the body in accord with this believed lower activity, the brain slows down the body's operational processes, causing among other things a decrease in the rate of breathing. As the state of addiction becomes progressive, the breathing rate is ever further reduced until a state is reached where it is unable to support life.

From this dramatic illustration we may understand precisely how the brain regulates the body's operation through environmental information, and so see how the brain is ever more a part of the environment than a separate entity working and demonstrating an "inherited" value with the performance it gives. This echoes the point we raised in *"Intelligence"* regarding Fechner's work with sensory information, where we saw and understood why the intelligence of a child cannot be truthfully evaluated without considering ALL the many varied and minute experiences they have had since they were born. Since this is impossible, we cannot look at how a student performs in say, mathematics at the end of one year, and know with any certainty from this how they will perform the following year, because the causes of that performance are deeply hidden in their development since birth.

May I explain this by saying that in school I never understood mathematics. I subsequently badly failed my final examination in mathematics. Actually, it was only the branch of arithmetic. Yet, when I went back into education three years later, and with a teacher who explained everything from simple fractions upwards, I developed to excel in calculus and so obtained a distinction in mathematics at the pre university level.

With great significance then, we may understand from this example of opiates, how chemical swamping inhibits the effective operation of a finely controlled neural system. It is from this effect of a varying chemical production of hormones, that regulate the sensitivity of neural action. This will bring in serious consideration to how the psychology of the mind drives the physiology of the brain, and this illustrates the points we raised in the early chapters of this book relating to brain plasticity and so open-ended learning.

6.3 The Double Disassociation of the Mind:

As we move through the normal tasks of a day, our body operates in what we call a para-sympathetic mode. This is to say that our body paces itself out for normal operation, where all parts function with equal effort. There are, of course, times when we need to exert ourselves. This is especially so when we are faced with a dangerous situation requiring a "fight or flight" response.

In such a case, our nervous system moves to become "sympathetic" to this need. It achieves this by lowering the activity of certain functions in order that other functions, which are more appropriate to the situation, are able to operate with greater efficiency. Let us understand then, how our body moves from the normal state of operation, which is the para-sympathetic state, to the sympathetic one in order to have this extra energy.

Stage 1. We perceive a physical or psychological danger that is harmful to us according to "our" experiences.

Stage 2. Our senses of intelligence, behavior, and emotion come into one, to allow us total focus.

Stage3. Once stress builds up, the brain sends nerve signals down the spinal cord to the adrenal glands (situated just above the kidneys) to release the hormone adrenaline.

Stage 4. Once released, adrenaline increases the amount of sugar in the blood, which increases the heart rate and blood pressure, allowing breathing to quicken to obtain more oxygen, etc. All of these actions provide the body with a surge of energy for quick movement, by which the person may either attack the danger or flee from it, depending upon their experience in dealing with this particular kind of threat.

By this process the body has now switched to the Sympathetic State, or the Fight/Flight mode, enabling it to concentrate its energy to the sole protection of itself. The mind is now no longer attracted to factors of interest. It is acutely focused on the threat.

The body's change of state from a para-sympathetic to a sympathetic mode is, however, much more complicated than this simplified account makes it appear. For one thing, very many chemicals are involved that bring about a host of changes in the body's operation. For another, the body moves from zero to maximum at different speeds depending upon the urgency of the situation, as "the individual" perceives this danger through their personal experiences. It is significant for us to hold on to the awareness that all the actions of the brain are related to experience. However, while the nervous system is changing the ability of the body, it is also changing that of the brain in how the mind may deal with this threat, for at the same time that the brain sends nerve signals down to the adrenal glands it also creates activation within itself.

Upon a level of awareness, the hypothalamus sends signals to the pituitary gland at the bottom of the brain to stimulate the adrenal cortex, which produces the hormone cortisol we have just mentioned. It is this action which is of particular interest to us, because this opens us up to the realization that while this change of state is often used to explain a reaction to a physical danger, a wild animal charging at you for instance, ...

- it can just as easily relate to the individual's perception of a social danger such as being involved in a humiliating situation.

Stage fright is a good example of this, just as is the example of a child having to read out their work to the entire class, or and more significantly their fear of a bully. Understanding this psychological awareness allows us to realize that the real purpose of the sympathetic system is not merely to protect the physical body, but to protect the entire psyche, of which this is only a part.

As we may understand, cortisol is an indispensable stress hormone of our brain. It is cortisol, or rather the stress that it creates, that drives the student's attention to focus on a task and so finish it, whether this be writing a composition or working through a math equation. However, the amount of cortisol is highly relevant to their performance in this task. As we can see from the following illustration, a very low level of cortisol creates the stress to drive the student to do their very best.

Graph showing how performance deteriorates as stress rises

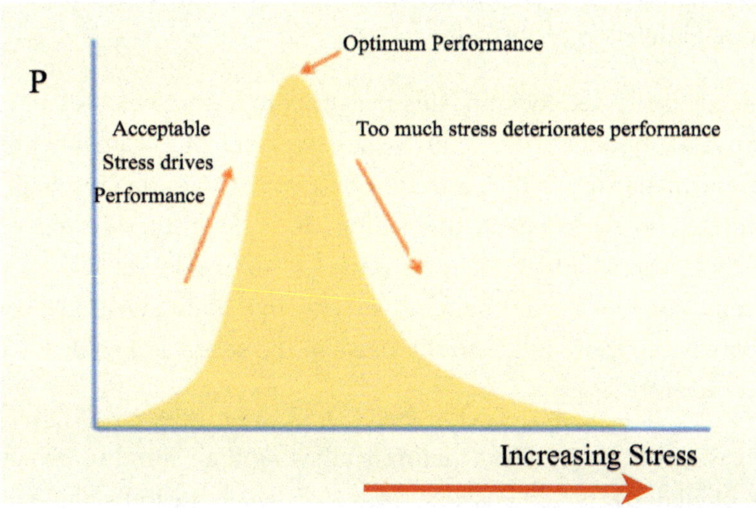

However, this action of the cortisol only works to the advantage of this particular task up to a point. If the cortisol level increases further, as by the student's awareness of a threat, it triggers off higher production levels of neurotransmitters. These, such as the monoamines we have mentioned, will then begin to close down certain areas of the student's brain that are related to this "academic" task. In essence, this will "force" them to be more aware of the threat that activated this level of cortisol, and so of the danger it may bring. This is a natural defense mechanism.

We may understand from this that the student will reach a point or level of optimal performance in their writing or calculating that is decided by the level of cortisol they generate. After this point, their performance in this task will diminish, because their mind is now on other factors.

Let us understand this again, because this is exactly what happens when a child is bullied, and we need to grasp that bullying is far more of a problem than it is realized to be. When the student's mind is thinking about the "danger" of the bully, either physically (they will hurt them) or socially (as they will cause others to devalue their identity), they generate high levels of cortisol.

As the cortisol level goes up, this triggers off further releases of other neurotransmitters. In turn, this excessive level of "brain chemistry" floods particular areas of the brain not associated in dealing with this immediate threat. In effect, this action shuts down those areas of the brain that process information reflectively (i.e. wondering how to word a sentence, or seeking to find a hidden clue in a math question), so that other areas can more relate to the cause of the stress and so deal with it more efficiently.

In this way, the brain of the victim is allowing their mind to be acutely aware of all dangers and possible threats by which the bully could injure either their body or their identity. We may understand from this that a little stress causes the student to focus on their learning, rather than on distractive influences such as games they like to play, or activities they enjoy, but too much stress causes their mind to focus upon the causes of that stress, and inhibits their ability to learn.

<u>Graph showing how attention changes as cortisol rises.</u>

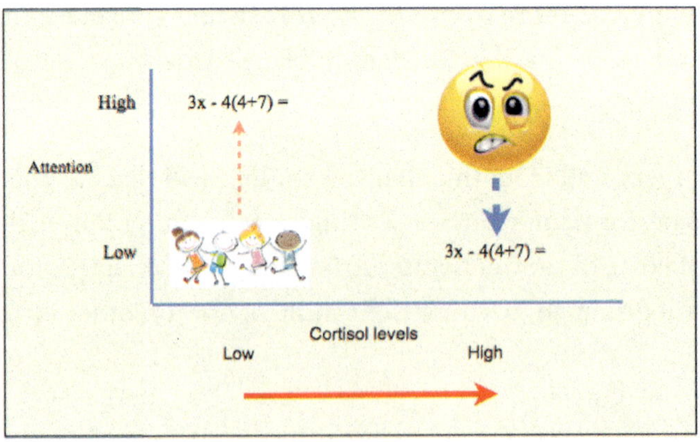

Consider in this that just as we recognize different levels of physical or social danger, as we perceive them to be, so we scale the release of cortisol to this condition.

The more intense the danger is the greater we react to it, and so the more we manufacture the release of cortisol and adrenaline. While it may seem that this change of state is brought about by an automatic response to a situation, it is important that we realize how it is regulated by personal awareness and this through experience.

Therefore, while one student may immediately zap over to the full sympathetic mode, and give witness to this by states of extreme alertness and a general uncontrollability, another student placed in that situation may not even initiate the first step of this process and will remain calm and collected in the full para-sympathetic mode. As we come to see that such evaluation is determined through experience, or lack of it, so it will appear more logical that the interpretation we make of a situation will lie more in our psychological impression of the danger than the actual experience of it.

6.4 The Danger of the Ghost:

All this is to say that the activation of the sympathetic mode can be triggered through "the individual's expectation" of being bullied, threatened, or intimidated, and not necessarily by the physical presence of it. We also must add here the significance to the child of a domestic disturbance, such as in their witnessing of a quarrel between their parents. In the sense of the disturbance this brings to their brain chemistry, the stress they feel and the insecurity a child gains from their parents fighting, is just as dangerous for them as is the presence or thought of a bully. It is in this lingering awareness of the stress they have felt and may feel again that is where the real harm lies.

Most of us can realize the effect that a surge of cortisol can bring from such an incident, and yet when we do this we tend to assume that once that very instant is over that the cortisol level will return to normal, as will the ability of the student to think. To do this is to think the whole incident is over. This is absolutely not so the case.

If the cause of the stress was disturbing enough and/or the victim believes it may occur again, their mind will likely be haunted by the incident. It will creep back into their thoughts without any warning, and when it does so their mind will trigger off cortisol actions again.

It is very important to realize that during the original disturbance the victim may not have been terrified. They may merely have been confused by the action that was brought upon them, and there may have been no "apparent" surge of cortisol that greatly disturbed their ability to think rationally. Their ability for schoolwork may seem to have been undisturbed at that time. However, it is the "thought" that it can or will happen again that brings about the real problem, because such thoughts cause cortisol to be released with less intensity than if they had been really frightened, but this now frequent release lowers the threshold level by which the cortisol is triggered.

In other words, the more they think about their fear, the more cortisol rises and spreads within their brain. We might think of the next day here, but in reality this process can go on for years and years. It is important to realize from this that once an emotional balance has been disturbed, it can take a long time before it can be regained, and there is no direct relationship between the cause of a disturbance and the time taken to overcome it. This is a very personal factor that must be related to experience. A disturbance that lasts for a few seconds can be so dramatic that it can unsettle the emotions for very many years, if not a lifetime.

Therefore, by merely thinking of this disturbance, cortisol is caused to more regularly flow through the victim's brain, and so more regularly cause parts of it to be over active in its preparation for their mind's expectation of this fear arising again. This means of course, that when and while this over activation is occurring in some parts of their brain, other parts that deal with the processing of other concerns at this moment i.e. schoolwork, will work less efficiently.

- It is this irregular action, kickstarted by the ghost of their concern/ worry/fear and/or sense of insecurity, that causes such long term disturbance in their brain. This disturbance prevents them from being continually relaxed or happy, and so they are unable to keep in tune with the flow of information as it moves in their lessons.

Graph shows how attention shifts as ghost fear reemerges in the mind

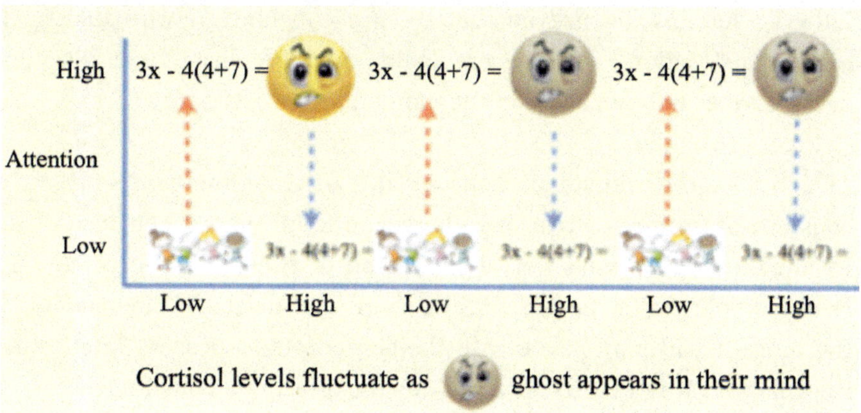

As we understand that this fluctuating chemical disarray is purely the result of the mind of one feeling out of harmony with that of another, we are caused to realize that if the bully apologized to their victim sincerely, or if the parents of the child fell happily in love again, the child's mental awareness of this would raise the threshold level of their cortisol. Should this happen, lower amounts of cortisol would be released, preventing disturbance to the operation of their "academic"

thoughts. However, this also causes us to realize how their brain is ever the more disturbed when the cause of this stress seems omnipresent to them.

It is this haunting of the ghost of their fear of insecurity, that is more responsible than any other singular factor for the cause of a child's low performance in their lessons, and ultimately so of our impression of their intelligence. Yet, regardless of how essential an awareness to this is, it is totally unknown to the general teacher. It is more to the point, not known to the educational system that believes performance is merely the product of motivation, and so designed teaching and assessment methods that qualify this conviction.

As we may understand from this, it is very important to our understanding of how intelligence develops within the individual, and indeed what intelligence is, that we are constantly aware that such mental distraction, which every child must go through in different degrees, does not just occur in the moment of the incident.

As long as the individual believes the original incident harbors a constant or a future threat, this danger to them may linger unresolved within their mind for a very long period of time. The more they are reminded of this, or the more it lingers on the surface of their thoughts, the more it will play havoc with their attempts to process intellectual information. It is easy to see from this the effect of a constant threat, or one daily renewed to a child in a class.

We may now understand why, when the production level of neuro-transmitters has to be set by experience, when a "threat" is sufficiently repeated, how the mind will adjust their threshold levels to respond faster to similarly perceived threats. Therefore, children who have been caused by painful or fearful experiences to lower the threshold levels of their neurotransmitters "permanently," will be more sensitive to such concern, more easily produce a higher level of cortisol, more easily lose concentration, and so demonstrate this effect of their fear by obtaining low grades.

Throughout our life, there is no place where this attack on our personality is more likely to occur than in school, and especially in break-times between lessons. School is a battlefield of such distractions and injuries, and while these attacks on the personality may seem inconsequential to the intelligence a child is said to be born with, they are not! These mental impressions gained through the behavior of others seriously do affect the learning development of the child. A teacher may notice how one child in their class is bullied, but the reality is that nearly all the children will have been affected in the development of their intelligence by the insecurities of those they have been forced to share their learning experiences with.

It is because children do not have the relative experience to know how to deal with the constant and intense stress created by their bully, that the continual build up of its pressure has caused some children to take their own lives, as a means to escape from the torment they believe they are incapable of being released from.

We discuss the pioneering work of Rusty May in our final book, as Rusty teaches children how to handle bullying in school better through his Schoolstoolstv, but I would just like to mention here that when I meet classes of children, I do emphasize to them the real dangers of bullying. To do this, I explain how the brain works and so the damage this cortisol action does to the victim's ability to learn in school and how this can affect their whole life, as their failing in school can deprive them of their dreams.

With great significance, and I know how this has changed the mind of some bullies, I, then, stress how the action of too much cortisol passing through neurons causes them to be overloaded with calcium. This over concentration of calcium causes neurons to fire too frequently, and this causes them to burn out. Neurons are literally excited to death. Therefore, bullying, abuse, or continual actions of stress can cause very long term damage to the victim's brain, which can later be witnessed in strokes, neural aging, and dementia.

We can see from what we have so far discussed in this chapter how the student's evaluation of a socially "threatening" situation does not just alter the rate of their heartbeat, but it also alters the chemicals that carry a signal of information from one neuron to another, as it moves through established circuits and so affects their quality of performance in learning.

Education might like to say that its students develop through their ability, and teachers will acknowledge the rise of bullying in education, but neither they nor the system that employs them understand the real effect of this bullying.

It is because of this general ignorance, and by which the whole educational system designs how its students should be taught and assessed, that we are caused to go deeper into our understanding of how a disturbing behavioral experience can affect the way the brain has become designed through experience, and how this alters its ability to process information. In other words, the intelligence of the individual.

As we do this, our intention is not to relate a behavioral or a personality condition, such as schizophrenia, to intelligence. It is instead to show how the production level of cortisol and associated neurotransmitters can be so affected by a repeated psychological disturbance as to set off early the activation of the para-sympathetic mode, and how this affects the intellectual processing systems.

- After all, when any human being makes any act of intelligence, their mind processes information for this through an entanglement of intellectual, emotional, and behavioral concerns.

It is very important we realize that this unification of the features we use to make sense and so interact with the environment can and does happen, because this combined process emphasizes the true role of intelligence as a function of the organism in its need to relate totally to the environment for its protection.

It is only our social sciences that have caused us to think of human intelligence as a separate and so definable feature of the brain, which they have done to serve scholastic purposes and so work and social evaluations. In truth, any organism combines its features of intelligence and behavior/personality in all the interactions it makes with the environment it struggles to survive in.

Thus, the student in education compares their actions to the performance of another, which has their personality entwined with it and to which they relate to the impression they have of themselves. As we shall see in our following book, a student's level of desire to learn some academic content from their teacher, is highly reliant upon the familiarity they feel with the teacher's personality. Hence, the student who says "I hate mathematics," and shortly afterwards confess how they more hate their math's teacher.

6.5 The Chemical Effect of Bullying:

As we may now understand, when we normally think of intelligence we think of a response or an answer that one child gives that we can relate to the response or answer of another child, and so notice a difference in their abilities. When we do this, we think of how well a child composed an essay, how accurate they were in the solution to a math problem, or any other response they gave that show the end result of a process.

Such evaluation we make does not consider how happy they were to be involved with this process, or how worried they were about some factor that distracted their mind as they sought to arrive at their result. Such considerations we say are temporary, and do not detract from the normal understanding and performance of the individual because, of course, we have long been conditioned to think that such performance lies in an inherited quality. However, any result we look upon is the result of earlier results, and so any mark a child makes is an evolution of how they understood all the earlier processes that went before. Each and every single one of those processes involved some consideration to the state of the child's emotion at that time.

Students, then, and especially children do not naturally think as school desires of them; they must balance the distractions they incur from others to the movement of information in a lesson to gain a quality of understanding. It is through this quality of understanding that they demonstrate how well they think. Let us move now to understand how their ability to "think" is disturbed through the chemistry of their brain by their fear of a bully.

<u>How bullying or stress changes the chemistry of the victim's brain.</u>

As the following illustration shows us, when a child or student feels stress from the behavior of others, when they say to them "I hate you," or they laugh at them or promise to hurt them, their mind can feel so stressed that it causes the brain to trigger off a flood of chemicals as we have described. This is to say that in a lesson the mind of the student loses its ability to concentrate, and so the whole intellectual process loses the sensitivity by which information is analyzed, associated, and processed. In simple terms the victim loses their ability to think clearly.

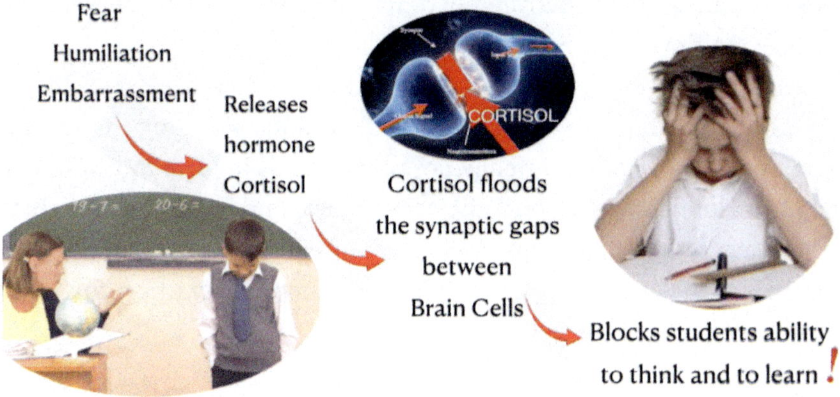

Consider in this, a child interrogating information. They are happily reading a story, or perhaps working through a math problem that is not too difficult for them. At a cellular level each bit of this information moves through one neuron at a time, so that bit by bit the characteristic of the information is recognized, and given value through the stored information it is related to in their memory. They are happy and content. All information is processing meaningfully, and new circuits are coming into construction.

All this is well and good, until we introduce into this calm scenario a psychological disturbance. Perhaps another child made a remark that hurt their feelings, or told them how they would physically hurt them in the break or after school. Equally, perhaps the teacher made a public display of a simple failing they had made. If the individual feels so affected by this, and we each have our own threshold level to determine such an action upon us, then they may trigger off a movement towards the sympathetic state.

Once this happens, all that the mind of the victim can really focus upon is the threat to their physical or social wellbeing. While one part of their mind is struggling to make sense of a written passage or a math problem, its greater part is reacting to the threat to their wellbeing. This brings in a question to their identity, and so factors of their personality and the ways they behave to others.

It is essential that we realize from this understanding, that any perception we have of the intelligence of another is only an indication of the balance they have between their behavioral and cognitive thoughts, as these are tethered through their level of emotion at that particular time. In writing this, I cannot think of any better definition for what intelligence may be.

Therefore, when a child or student carries the worry of a behavioral concern, the continual effect it has on them cannot be easily disassociated from their act of thinking. As worry distracts the mind from sensitivity in working with an intellectual problem, so the efficiency with which that problem is engaged diminishes. In turn, this will affect the applications that build upon it, lesson by lesson, week by week, and year by year.

This internal processing is not, of course, witnessed by the teacher and probably not realized by the child themselves, who is only conscious of worrying thoughts and vaguely aware of how they cannot think very well. Once the threshold level of their emotions has altered, they will be so familiar with this process that it will appear to be normal for them. Once this state has arisen, they will not realize the significance of what is really happening to their body, because it is not just that their emotional levels have become disturbed but that of their whole sensory system. This of course, is essentially their brain.

Therefore, it is not just that their ability for emotion has become affected, but also the ability of other features and the strategies they have evolved to bring into existence an act of intelligence. We may think of memory here, but then we have to realize all the processes that cause a quality of memory, and so we need to think of such features as perception. With regard to perception this means that information will be erratically recognized, instead of being clearly and competently examined. The consequences of this in the performance and so value of an act of intelligence are obvious.

The reader may not fully grasp the significance of this until they are very stressed with the behavior or personality of a colleague in work, or until a letter arrives in the post demanding a disturbing amount of money. Unable to escape from such stress, their mind will play with the image of this disturbance. It will constantly "hang" in their mind, and seem to cloud over the importance of everything else, and perhaps cause them to make a simple but meaningful error in work because they cannot concentrate properly. There is however, a vital difference between the "established" mind of the reader as an adult, and the "developing" mind of the child or student.

While the reader is most likely to have established a competency with the thinking skills of their job, and so be able to operate in a near automatic mode, enabling them to appear to function normally even though they may be deeply troubled, this will not be so for the student.

The ability of the student to associate will be lessened, which means they will not be able to follow the normal rate of new information. In turn, this will disrupt their competency to learn. Since one lesson builds upon another, their structure of understanding will be impaired. This will be displayed in their class effort and the grades they gain. Yet, all this will be unknown or ignored as their grade is used to place them within the grades of others to produce a variation of ability in the class. This ability will of course, and in ignorance of what we have discussed in these books, be regarded as having its roots in an inherited quality.

Since children seldom change their class, and as each class moves from one year to the next, it is very important that we understand how and why all children become conditioned through the behavior of others to demonstrate stability in their performance. This stability is very much decided by the strategies they have evolved through their emotional state. This emotional state is very sensitive to the protection of their identity, and so self preservation. Each child will adjust this state according to the happiness, security and contentment they have with others. We think this stability in performance that causes them to gain the same level of grades time after time is a factor of their inheritance. We do not know or do not understand the real effect and consequences of what has just been discussed. Intelligence is not what we have been led to think it is.

In other words, the distribution of ability on the Bell Curve can be explained purely through behavioral experiences, with no regard to the genetic qualities the children in the class are thought to have inherited for their intelligence.

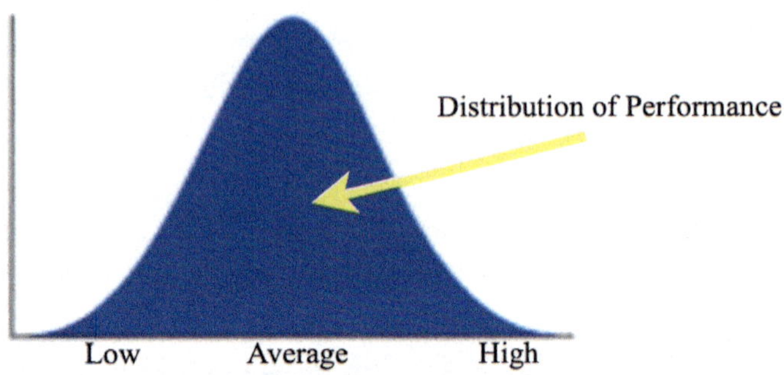

Much thought lies in that we are born with different abilities, but as we have discussed so many times, barring an abnormal physiology, this belief hangs on the value of snapshot performances in intellectual problems.

- This is a belief that gives no worthy examination of each minute environmental task that made up the developmental history of an individual's intelligence, as they struggled to gain their identity through it.

Therefore, even though teachers do not know what happens to the mind of a child when they are bullied or intimidated, they may understand from what we have discussed in this chapter how and why this does bring serious consequences to the ability of the child to perform in their lessons, and to the impression they have of their intelligence.

Accordingly, with all the poor academic performers I have met who had a normal physiology and some of whom have been discussed in these books, I found that their academic difficulty was rooted in personality problems, which had interfered in the development of how they learnt to process information.

As I discovered with each of them, it was not that they could not understand the problem at hand but that they had neither the correct experience nor the confidence to engage it correctly. Yet all their problems were found to be resolvable when the root of the problem was given explanation, and re-orientation was brought to their development. Consequently, their grades improved. This did not happen just because they understood information better, or indeed because they understood it for the first time, but more because they developed a clearer understanding of the meanings and intentions of others. By knowing this, they could keep perspective of their own identity while they were processing information.

Yet, in holding to our discussion about the emotional context of intelligence, what we have said is not to suggest that those who are the cleverest are so because they have had no behavioral difficulties. Far from it! Each learns to deal with the world in their own way. It is to suggest that a very real consideration to any low score in a test or low ability in a lesson can lie in the effects that behavioral situations have had on a child during the history of their intellectual development. It is very important to understand here that such influence seldom depends on a few singularly bad instances, but much more on small accounts that built up over a period of time.

It is through the day-to-day life we share with others, that we regulate the threshold levels of the chemistry of our brain to decide when our para-sympathetic mode will be activated. Since these threshold levels will be decided by our experiences through others, so they are set, under normal behavioral experiences, to the average pressures under which the people of a society and culture exist. However, each child or person within any group will alter their threshold levels to be sensitive to their defense, as their personal circumstances cause them to perceive this need. To demonstrate the very real effect of how such threshold levels are set by behavioral experiences, and how these interact and affect a student's intelligence, I would like to draw upon three instances that relate very well to this.

Case Example One:

One concerns a young woman who attended a course of higher education. She was bright, attentive, and naturally pleasing. However, when the very smallest personality conflict arose with someone in the class, her ability to concentrate was completely destroyed. As the other students in the class began to play on this, her over reactions became a regular feature of a lesson. After a few weeks the teacher made her appraisal of everyone's ability in the subject, and this lady did not do too well. In fact, she came bottom in the class.

After some months in this course, she confided in me that she had repeatedly experienced abuse from her father since adolescence. So disturbing had these repeated encounters been, that even ten years later she still "daily" carried the complexity and the pain of this in her mind.

As the threshold level of her neural chemistry was lowered to respond to a personal threat far below that of others in the class, and as her personal background was unknown to them, none realized the effect they were having as they saw to amuse themselves by her over reactions.

However, by discussing the historical problem of the abuse she had been treated to, and putting it into a relevant perspective, this lady was able to gain greater confidence in her interaction with others. By learning to distance herself from the thoughts that haunted her, she came to believe more in her own worth, which enabled her to evaluate a social situation more accurately. As her confidence in this grew, she brought readjustment to her threshold level, and was better able to concentrate on intellectual tasks. Her grades improved dramatically, as did the opinion of her intelligence. None, but she and I understood why her performance in the class began to rise, and why this caused her to be "more" intelligent both in her verbal discussions and written explanations. It was simply that after many months of demonstrating one level of intelligence, she was suddenly operating on a different and much higher level.

Case Example Two:

Not very long after I had met this lady, I experienced a situation that has striking relevance to this chapter. On that occasion I had become an adult student myself, and encountered a situation in which my teacher felt it necessary to demonstrate her unquestioning authority. With this intention, the teacher chose a single incident to ridicule me, which she did by over emphasizing to the entire class a mistake I had made. Her point was sharp, and lasted less than a few seconds. Yet, it was so devastatingly cruel to me that I could actually imagine, if not feel, a great chemical disturbance flooding my brain. It was not that I was embarrassed. It was more that my entire mind was so blocked, that I simply could not then process the information she soon after gave me as a part of the class. It really was as if my mind had been flooded with opiates, but I felt no euphoria only devastation.

Naturally, I did not demonstrate these feelings to anyone, and to all in that class I probably looked normal. Yet, for the rest of that lesson, I simply could not concentrate on the information available to me. In fact, for many lessons thereafter with this teacher I understood nothing, and gained nothing. A space developed in my learning that I could not catch up with, and I began to hate those lessons, until I discussed with the teacher what was happening to me.

These two examples highlight how the intelligence process is impaired by the activation of the para-sympathetic mode, as the personality moves to protect itself. As we have discussed, and as we have witnessed here, this can occur as a reaction to one singular devastating remark, or it can build up almost secretly through months and months of regular nastiness, torment, or bullying.

We may be reminded here of the introduction to *"The Illusion of School,"* which informed us that half of 2,000 children and adolescents admitted that they were bullied and lived in some degree of fear during their education. To this, we may further remind ourselves of the "toxic environment" that the child of today daily struggles through, as we can witness in the following case.
Case Example Three:

I noticed in a class, I took over in a Danish school, how one student had great difficulty in spelling. The boy explained to me that he had been told he was dyslexic, and allowed to write as he wanted to do. I gave him some vowel tests and found that he responded accurately in each case. This caused me to wonder why he was thought of as dyslexic. In a few minutes after each lesson, I gave the boy some help with spelling, and found he showed no difficulty with this. So, I decided to discuss this with his parents, and went to the boy's home.

Immediately, I walked into the house I could see how nervous the mother was. I did not know why, until the father appeared. It was obvious the father was a bully, and as he frightened his wife so did he also frighten his son. As I began to build up a picture of the child's life, it became obvious that he had no confidence to interact with information at home or at school. When I next met the boy in our lesson I started to build up his confidence, causing him to learn to laugh at his own mistakes. As his fear of what others thought of him diminished, so his spelling improved and with this the opinion others had of his ability and so intelligence.

*

As we can clearly witness in these case examples, the effect of a behavioral situation disturbing a cognitive one can arise far more easily than we may imagine. So, as we observe a student of any age in their class, whether they appear to be bored or fascinated, we are unaware of the struggle of their inner thoughts to focus upon a thing to be learnt when their mind cannot release itself from some disturbance to its personality. We may observe a student going through the motions of thinking, reading and writing, but we cannot see how in reality they are grasping spasmodically at what to us is clear and precise. All we do is to mark the result, and assume they have given what they were given at birth!

Therefore, it is not motivation, the desire to succeed or the need to win, that brings quality to the mass of students in a class. This can be applied to only a very few. To all of them, is the much greater consideration of how each is able to control the interactions of their cognitive processes, when their personality is troubled by the behavior of others, either past or present. There is not a more decisive time for this to occur in the life of an individual, than when they are a child in a classroom, as we shall come to see.

Chapter Seven

Networks of Intelligence

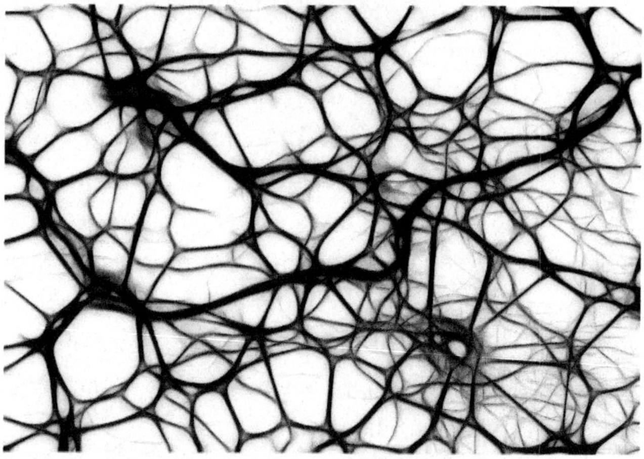

To attain knowledge, add things every day.
To attain wisdom, subtract things every day.

Lao Tsu

7.0 Introduction:

Intelligence, we have said, is society's formal recognition of how the thinking of one person can be compared in some way to the thinking of another. It is this need for comparison that confuses what intelligence is, where it originates from, and how it develops. If, after all we have read, we may put aside the word intelligence and substitute it with a meaning such as "to think" for instance, how would we define this in its most basic sense?

Well, we could say that when a thought is shared, that to the giver it is a representation of how they perceive their world and who they are. To the receiver, it is either a gift by which they realize new horizons to their life and grow with this, or regard it as a threat to the way they understand that world and so their identity within it.

It is perhaps difficult for us to consider that a quality of intelligence can be so simply understood, because we have long been impressed in the belief that it is some closed feature, whose operation is mysteriously and vaguely affected by experience. Although, as we have seen, and will do so more in our following books, any snapshot impression of our performance in intelligence disguises a very long and complex story of how we learnt to understand what information means to us, how we should interact with it, and most importantly how we should present our conclusion of this interaction to the expectations of those who are judging us. Let us conclude this book with a view that will open our understanding to those that follow.

7.1 The Moulding of the Thought Process:

The educational philosopher John Dewey once vividly sought to define a thought process when he wrote:

"We see something moving, hear a sound unexpectedly, smell an unusual odor, and ask: What is it?
What does, what we see, hear, smell mean?
When we have found out what it signifies ..... we say that we understand. To understand is to grasp meaning. Until we understand, we are if we have curiosity, troubled, baffled and hence moved to inquire. ...... There is a time during our investigation when meaning is only suggested; when we hold it in suspense as a possibility rather than accept it as an actuality. The meaning is an idea. An idea thus stands midway between assured understanding and mental confusion. A meaning is conditionally accepted for use and trial, it is an idea, a supposal. When it is positively accepted, some object or event is understood...." [154]

As Dewey shows us how the process of thinking can be both an intriguing and exciting subject to examine, it prompts the question: as to what really are the causes in the differences that individuals present in an act of intelligence?

What is it that makes them really different?

The point of inheritance is not that we come from different gene arrangements, which some take to mean that we are not all born equal, but, as we saw in our previous book, it stresses the purpose of the gene.

As we found with the genotype for intelligence, the gene coding so strongly allows the environment to determine the phenotype that it is only ignorance and prejudice that anchors the belief in differences of intelligence in genetic variations. Since we can never measure, or know the limiting factor of an individual's gene code, we must assume that students who are born fully functional should be able to display exceedingly similar skills in intelligence, subject to their experiences.

After all, any child may have an idea, and any child can so find themselves standing on that midway point between assured understanding and mental confusion.

To step from the point of understanding to one of development is greatly dependent upon how confidence is gained through feedback. Such confidence is for the child to know that others accept how they got to a point in their progression. It is to have confidence in the goal they are heading for, because they selected this from close examination of the information they had and could discover. It is to have confidence by keeping alert as they progress along a route to ensure this is the correct route, and not over confidence by which they miss signs they have followed the wrong route.

The habit of check, check, and check again, inspires confidence, so that if they reach a dead end they know how to retrace back to a point where information agrees. To consider what they might have missed as they approach their goal inspires confidence, because they are aware of options and so can test possibilities.

As the child builds up their confidence from such awareness, they progress in their learning from what they knew to what they do not know securely. With this security they are able to avoid the confusion of not knowing what they are doing, or where they are going. If we were to put all this into one word, it would be "sensitivity"?

However, the emotion that drives sensitivity (the delight to enquire) is easily disturbed by the presence of another, as we have just witnessed. So the child must keep calm, and not worry because the child next to them seems more confident, and seems to have found the faster way. This is a confidence to believe in themselves, even after they have heard someone at the back of the class shout: "I've finished Miss." Finished, yes! But, how good a finish? Have they got the right answer, and is their answer really better than theirs? What did they do that enabled them to finish first? These thoughts will challenge their confidence, but they are unlikely to enquire with that child, at that moment in time, as to what they did or how they did it. After all, why should the child share their success? Anyway, the teacher has found the best, and others are handing in their papers.

May we see how easy it is for confidence to fall into doubt, and doubt into confusion as the child struggles against the mind and personalities of all those about them, as lesson follows lesson, week follows week, and year follows year, where strategies are not checked, not known, and only the result of the child is witnessed. This is a result that is too often said to lie in the social worth of their parents, although we no longer say so.

However, what if they did approach the child who won, and could bribe them with a bag of sweets to reveal what caused them to do so well? That child might whisper, if the bag weighed heavily enough in their hand, the word "curiosity."

"Curiosity," noted Dewey again, "is necessary both to ignite an idea, as it is to direct the trial process that may bring it substance, and so to grapple with the meaning of another until understanding is gained of them."[155]

While curiosity is a simple word that hides much of why and how an individual can be attracted to information, let alone why they may be distracted through lack of it, it amply introduces a cause of quality into the processing of information, for if we examine the trial process of understanding we may see it is curiosity that gives insight to a problem. Yet, curiosity is meaningless without direction.

Once we realize this, so we see how by the investigation curiosity makes that it generates a high level of sensitivity. Through this sensitivity good strategies are developed, which provide accuracy in the goal that is recognized, and in the direction taken to reach that goal.

The "gene" that gave the child curiosity, then, works hand in hand with the "gene" that gave them language, because it is by the ability for language that their curiosity is raised or dampened, and strategies are acquired to make sense and to present the sense they see to another.

Thus, as each child unravels one experience, they arm themselves for the next. By the depth of that experience and the aid they gain in evaluating it, each develops their means of identification and systems of processing, which are of different effectiveness to those of others. There lies in this statement an adequate explanation for the different qualities of performance, and so variation of intelligence in a class.

Those who question this, and hold fast to the use of the singular definition of "intelligence" to compare one to another, have neither the means to qualify its genetic origin in one against that of another, nor have they the resources to track down the origins of each association each individual has made. They also do not have the possibility or time to examine the strategies by which each act defined the means to progress to the next.

Indeed, as we discussed in *"Intelligence: The Great Lie,"* Laming showed that it is practically not possible to isolate the individual from the information they respond to, in order to evaluate them free of that information. After all, not only does each individual see their perspective of information as we have explained, but each individual is in a sense a singular entity formed physiologically and psychologically through the historical information of their "personalised" environment.

Therefore, not only is the identification, and determination of information individually personal, but the value each assigns to it must be in consequence of how well each identifies with the information at hand. Thus, how well each has understood the build-up of information which led them to make that identification, determines the concluding matches they are able to realize in its possibilities.

Whenever we repeat a journey, our experiences are never the same the second time around, for even though the route may be the same and the signs of that route may be unchanged, different colors will be recognized and different meanings realized as each small encounter opens different memories. The same is true of all that we engage, because just as a journey is never the same when we repeat a route, so the same can be said of a problem that we re-engage.

Take, for example, that when confronted with a problem, the solution of it may only come after we have set it aside for a while, and returned to it sometime later. We can find further example to this in learning, where in engaging a new situation for the first time we may gain little meaning from it, although when re-examining it at a later time we may find clearer insight into how it could be better dealt with.

In this book we have found out why this occurs, why the same information is perceived differently on different occasions by different individuals, indeed what information actually is, and most importantly why the individual knows what it is.

7.2 In Conclusion:

In a general sense we came to understand through reading this book, how the brain is brought into construction through the environment. This was not only by the ingredients the individual consumed to feed their body and so brain construction and enable its operation, but also by how their senses related to environmental information. We saw in this how the brain unconsciously was brought into construction through environmental signals, but most significantly how these signals could be refined and better selected by conscious awareness.

In turn, this brought us to understand how the value of emotion held by the individual controlled their identification, selection, absorption and processing of information. Indeed, we found a real depth of understanding in Freud's claim that 'Psychology drives Physiology'.

If you desire to improve any of your abilities, or those of another, it is essential that you create a mental program far in advance of any physical development you plan.

I remember reading a very long time ago that when American athletes practiced for the olympics they trained very hard physically. However, when Russian athletes trained, they spent a very great deal building up their psyche awareness before and along with their training. In a sense, they trained their mind, soul and body together. The results spoke for themselves.

This mind development should be calm and peace seeking. A desire "to be at one", as the saying goes. Accordingly, the spiritual and medical practices of the East hold many of the keys to how we may better achieve this. This is simply understood if we bare in mind that 'the mind' orchestrates the release and production level of many hormones. In turn, these hormones move to control the activity of neural functions which inevitably end with some muscular activity.

Here lies a good means to any development you wish to improve upon. The principle applies to developing your memory or your intelligence or any skill and some physical attribute (within reason) you wish to improve.

As we began this book, we discussed how we tend to readily think of things only the way they appear, without too much consideration of how or why they came about. Yet, if we do consider more the factors of development, we are able to change these to some degree to change what now appears to us.

I recently saw a youtube video by a young lady who literally made her nose smaller, by exercising certain muscles about the nose. In another, a young man explained how, by controlling the bacteria in his mouth and taking vitamin supplements, he was able to cause his teeth to repair cavities by themselves. There again, Tyler Sorensen has devised an eye muscle program that can improve vision from 40/20 to 20/20 - to give perfect eyesight, and Harvard Professor David Sinclair has proven how to regain a much younger body literally, through a diet based program.

The achievements of these people, as of very many others, can be searched for and studied on the internet. There are, of course, limitations to what we can achieve and some aspects can not be improved upon because we cannot go beyond the genetic sequencing behind them. Yet, in having said this:

We have discovered that gene coding for some features, carry a coding that allows the environment to restructure the normal design they carry.

In certain instances, the presence of the mind seems to be essential to achieve a dramatic development.

Perhaps the most astounding example that comes to mind here is the case of the hydrocephalic we discussed earlier. As we suggested, we can only assume the young man managed, through mental effort, to retain a very high level of intelligence with a brain that had been compressed beyond all recognition.

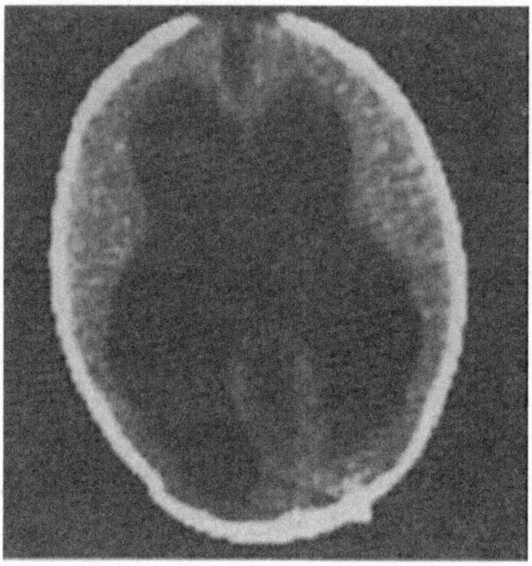

There again, I am reminded here of Bill Bartmann, who at the age of 17 fell down a flight of stairs and was told by hospital doctors he would never walk again. However, Bill was determined that he would walk and began to focus with great mental effort on moving his big toe. Eventually, it did move and with this, sensation and movement developed again in his legs, enabling him to walk out of the hospital a year later. [156]

There are many other such cases where individuals have been able to 'will' their bodies to accomplish a level of activity beyond what was thought they were capable of. Not that this was ever easy, but the fact that it has occurred opens us up to understand that we are not simply put together and work. To some extent, nerves and muscles can be repaired through mental effort. This brought into our understanding how the biochemistry of the body is far more interrelated than we generally think and is somehow related to the awareness and drive of mental effort.

This was emphasized in our book *Teach Better Learn Better: Understanding the Art of Sensitivity in Awareness. W*e explain, in this, the importance of being emotionally sensitive in the handling of information. To be aware of what is happening and to the needs of others involved in the process is paramount to a high level of success.

Thus, through this book, we have been able to open a door that has been very much closed. Many of us have gained a new insight into what intelligence is, how it forms, and indeed how it can change throughout the life of the individual.

In many senses we managed to open the "black box" that Spearman created, to learn that intelligence is not the one thing he thought it was. Instead, we discovered that intelligence is only a word that describes the action of a number of processes at any one moment. While some of these are known and openly discussed, such as association and memory, many and by far the more important are not.

As we did this, we moved from an impression of intelligence deriving from the physical brain to one more conducted by the mystery of the mind. Indeed, as we came to see the brain working to serve the mind, so we understood how the mind struggles to overcome insecurities by holding on to systems of organization it has built itself upon.

Intelligence and behavior, we found, work hand in hand with each act of intelligence. As the student in school deciphers a math equation or constructs a sentence of an essay, they are continually aware of how they measures up to what others think they are capable of and what their personality is worth.

We saw in our first book *"The Illusion of School"* how the educational psychologist Piaget had kept our understanding of intelligence to an organic and so inborn quality, by his reasoning of fixed stages in child development; when he related a child's physiological ability to manipulate objects to their mental ability to understand concepts of numbers in maths. Yet, we also noted how he appeared not to discuss the role of the mind to define and elaborate upon such things as political and moral understandings.[157] Neither of these can have stages of development.

Yet, we know Piaget was aware of different components of intelligence, because he recognized the difference between a sensorimotor act of perception (where a future evaluation would be restricted by the definitions acquired and developed through those that went before it), and a cognitive process that in developing to a conclusion would be forever free to return to an unbiased state to begin a re-evaluation.[158] Accordingly, we realized in that book how and why our understanding of intelligence is politically shaped by the way education has become structured, and so why it requires intelligence to be seen to be stable, definable and measurable.

Fodor, we may now know, struggled against this formalized way of seeing intelligence and the use made of it in the operation of school and society, by demanding that intelligence has different aspects. Every act of intelligence, he argued, derived from different bases. Categorizing these into modes of domain specific and general specific, Fodor sought to explain the different stability of response that each required and was so constructed by.[159]

- Fodor defined domain specific to relate to neural computational tasks that need to develop upon a genetic architectural design, and which require little environmental conditioning. The ability to see color and to perceive movement are inherited functions, which do not require environmental conditioning to develop.

- However, Fodor realized that other abilities were only determinable by their continual interface with a changing environment, and could therefore never develop through the concept of a critical period which we discussed earlier. Cognitive tasks are an obvious example of the general specific mode, such that belief fixation (the different ways in which beliefs can form), and analogical reasoning (by which we adopt new thinking strategies throughout our lifetime) must rely upon a very different means of construction, because they are given base by and develop purely through experience.

After all, would Natural Selection not make it so. An intelligence limited to genetic variations would succumb and fade into extinction to an intelligence designed wholly by the environment enabling fully adaptability. We saw this principal with so many of the features that make up and so create an act of intelligence.

By this understanding, we can be more wary of accepting intelligence as a stable product of a stable organic brain, and more readily understand it as a product of a living organ that has developed and so develops through the experiences engaged.

The brain can thus be seen to be alive, and to function through the traffic of signals that continually update its awareness of the external environment with the minutest change. It was, therefore, not isolated from the external world in the beginning of its fetal construction, or in any part of its lifelong development. The brain, we can now realize, is integrated with the environment through its mind, so that both work together to be ever a part of the world that gives them life.

So, we realized that the personality of the mind and the intellectualism it displays serve different purposes, in a world that mixes both. After all, from an evolutionary point of view, the personality needed to develop to be extremely adaptable to different information in the environment it serves. Thus, we can show love and tenderness one instant, and anger and aggression the next.

This function has developed this way because its environment required this adaptability for us to survive socially, and we are by necessity a social animal. We can see this in how people of different cultures have different understandings, and generate different responses to a behavioral situation. What can make a person of one culture extremely angry can have no concern to another of a different culture, although each can learn to understand the other. The ways we behave, therefore, are and must be extremely sensitive to the inconsistencies of the environment the personality serves, and always able to have great freedom in adaptability.

Intelligence, by contrast, will operate with great stability in the predictable environment with which it interacts, and appear to be inflexible to adjust to rapid changes of perspective. While this change of perspective can and does occur, it is one of a careful transition based more on the testing of reason than emotional response.

Yet, and it is vital we realize this, for the individual to make this change in their perspective of understanding requires that they let go of their identity.

To do this is so to let go of the relationship of personalities that are entwined within the way they have come to understand what is happening. It is, we saw, this resistance of the individual to let go of their identity in a process of understanding that gives the impression of stability, and it is this that creates the misunderstanding that intelligence is unchangeable and so predictable.

We know from our long discussion in this that behavior and intelligence are not two distinct and separate features of the human mind. These features work together, and if we took the time to study this relationship more, we would understand that differences in intelligence are not caused by some mysteriously inherited quality that cannot be explained. The intellectual performance of children comprises many hidden facets of their psychology, all of which are developmental.

To know of this, and the disaster it causes to the hopes and opportunities of individuals when it is ignored, we have to observe more sensitively the thinking processes that a child moves through. Understanding this is rather like observing a plant with a high-speed camera. Without this, we see the plant one day, notice two days later it has changed position and think nothing of it. However, through time-lapse photography we witness the minute changes the plant decides to make, as it continually tests its environment. When we realize that the plant sensitively controls its own direction, and it may be said its own destiny, we are struck with fascination.

- In other words, if we could understand with extreme sensitivity how the child's emotions determine every minute act of their intelligence, we could better understand how this feature becomes formed through the relationship of intelligence and behavior.

Consider in this that after childhood the primary learning phase has settled down, by which emotion has learnt how to interact with behavior and intelligence. By the time the adolescent prepares to "leave the nest," each of these functions will have developed a level of skill by which they enable the individual to learn how to safely engage the greater world.

We witness in this how behavioral features remain fluid, and ride on the emotional makeup of the individual throughout their life. They remain reasonably constant as they tune to the experiences they encounter, but are ever able to change as they are affected by experiences. By the extent of these experiences the individual is readily armed to balance the drives and insecurities of others with whom they engage, as they seek to be accepted and survive.

On the other hand, the environment through which we learn to interact to gain food and shelter remains stable. It is not erratic like our social world, and so requires intelligence to be stable to manage its conditions. It is by this stability that we learn to make evaluations and predictions with effectiveness. The world that intelligence interacts with operates on laws, principles, and rules that require a different level of mental stability to that engaged by our behavior.

Therefore, one feature of our mind with which we interact with the outside world seems flexible, and the other not so. Each will adapt to the requirements of its own world, as it will be required to conform. However, to conform is also to be conditioned. So, we find that just as the behavior of children is conditioned by their social world, so is their intelligence conditioned by the self-limiting world of school. As Richard Feynman put it:

"You cannot get educated by this self-propagating system in which people study to pass exams, and teach others to pass exams, but nobody knows anything.

You learn something by doing it yourself, by asking questions, by thinking, and by experimenting."

Accordingly, school is a very conditional world, as it must be to bring order to the uncoordinated drives and unruly minds of large numbers of children in a class. It is because of the very stable environments that we move through in school as a child, and later as an adult in work, that intelligence is caused to appear to be stable with one appearing smarter than another.

This is so because the same means of interacting with information is used. The processes employed do not change. By the continuity in how they interact, they give impression their intelligence is not easily changeable, and this reinforces the old idea that it is largely inherited. This stability arises from the necessity of the brain to be stable in its operations. While the psychology of the mind can easily override the design of the brain, it seldom does so, because its personality has been woven into the history of its actions and in this the identity of the individual as we have just explained.

We can see this in the same way that an artist expresses their identity on canvas, and the child in their learning sees their identity involved with the answer they give to another. As the individual knows who they are by the actions they make, so are they defensive to their identity through those actions. When another tells them they are less than perfect, which would be to gain a mark of 8/10 or 5/10, they half listen, and see themselves as correct in self-defense. As they do this, they close their mind to how others gained a higher mark, because they were more sensitive in their handling of information and so recognized different insights in how to deal with it. When they do this, they fail to alter, develop, or improve their ability, and so remain stable in their intelligence.

This stability is for ever a product of their conditioning, since it reflects the general state of the individual's sense of emotional security with information. When they feel more secure and are attracted to information their intelligence can rise, because then they will be alert and sensitive as they recognize its features and the processes they design to make their use of it. However, when they feel more insecure this ability will fall, as they are more easily distracted by some other thought, and so be caused to be vague and insensitive with all aspects of their working with information. The stability we witness in an individual's intelligence merely describes the sum total of their general strength with information.

In a basic sense, we may understand that the civilized human being is raised to conform to systems, and responds to whatever conditioning environment they are placed in by maintaining a stability in how they think. Therefore, while our scientists have classified behavior and intelligence as two discrete functions, the mind sees them as one, which diversifies to meet the needs of two different environments: the social and the physical.

When we think of intelligence from a biological perspective, we see the environment as common to all. This is to say that each sees the same thing, and each responds to it by their desires and abilities. This is the view taken by education when it is insensitive in how information is given to students, and in the collective assessment it makes of them.

Yet, if we consider what we have just discussed, then any thought of what intelligence is must recognize that it has a social and so a psychological perspective that is inescapable from it. With this being so, it means that we must recognize that the environment has different meanings to different individuals, as the shape of each is given character by their experiences and by their own relevancies. Each child will, therefore see their world and the information it contains differently to another, as they are driven by their own particular interests, values and sensitivity. Thus, different minds will look differently upon information that is said to be the same, because of their personal histories.

They do this through their desire to want to recognize it, by how they think they should process its information, and by how they think they should present to another the understanding they have. By this understanding, we can now see how and why the mind of each individual lives in its own world. If we can accept this, then we are caused to change our idea of what the environment means in intelligence, and therefore what intelligence is.

To ask two children if they understand something that has been written on the blackboard, will, therefore, be deceiving to hear them both say "Yes." After all, their understanding will firstly be individual (i.e. What use is this to me?), and secondly common (What use is this to others, by which I may be understood?). This common understanding will only be an approximation, and not describe the structural understanding each individual has. Yet, it will be the one they use to satisfy the expectation of another, and so the one they will be judged by.

To understand what this means is to take a friend and look at some object, say a lamppost. Each of you will say you see the lamppost, but each of you will see and be aware of different information as you look upon it. One may be fascinated with all aspects of it, examine it in detail, and give a very clear description of it later. The other may look beyond the lamppost at a house in the background. They may wonder if the people are asleep in their home, and when later asked to describe the lamppost be less accurate with their details, because their mind was on some other interest, even though they saw and were aware of the lamppost. Ask a class of 30 children to do the same thing, and a variation of responses will be produced. These responses will very likely centre on an average, and so conform to Galton's law of deviation from an average, or continuous variation.

Yet, none of the responses they give can be related to their genetic and so the current understanding we have of intelligence. How each describes what they remember about the lamppost, will be decided purely on their interests at the moment they observed it. In this lies the cause of our error, because as similar situations and tasks are built upon this, the evolving profile we take of each child will be said to contain their genetic worth. In reality, each is only building upon their perspective, and as they are locked into environments which little alter this, so each exhibits a stability in how they perform. It is this stability that we mistakenly assume to be caused by an inborn factor, because we give too little consideration to how it could otherwise be formed.

Fundamental to the whole lamppost scenario, and so any factor of intelligence, is language. Language is the medium by which intentions and descriptions are devised, relayed, and understood. If you do not have the necessary language, you cannot relate to meaning and so manifest an intelligence. This was obvious from the Amazonian Piraha people who do not have the intelligence to understand the concept of 4, 6, 10, or, for example, 23. These numbers are totally beyond their comprehension, simply because their language only counts in numbers of one, two and many. Equally, they have no concept of time, because their language operates only in the present tense.

Reflect for a moment here on how language is not just a cause of intelligence but the very base by which it exists for these people, and we can realize how language shapes not only the intelligence of all people, but also that of the individual. If we can grasp this, then, it becomes obvious that a child may only know of their world and so how they should relate to it by the language they are raised in. This language will be cultivated through the sensitivity of their parents, as they relate to their understanding of the world. So, different parents raise their children with different techniques, and just as importantly share different qualities of love and time.

It is important to realize what this means, because as long as the parents are able to exert influence upon their children, their children's intelligence will be reliant upon three factors.

First: This will be the quality in the sensitivity by which the parents explain the meaning of the child's world -- what things are, and how they interact.

Second: It will be in the love demonstrated to the child, and in the security they gain by which interest is inspired and confidence gained.

Third: It is the sense of discipline that is inspired, and not imposed upon the child, that drives them to tackle and to deal successfully with problem solving tasks, by which they build confidence and creativity.

Naturally, this guide is not black and white, because we have to take into consideration the personality of the child, as they struggle to define their identity through those of their parents, other adults, and especially other children. Yet, of these three factors, the third reveals the education and experience of the parents, just as the first demonstrates the knowledge they have to raise their child. These are not natural. They are all developed and so factors of conditioning, since they can all be socially defined through the academic background, work, and social experience of the parents as their thoughts create the background for the way their children will come to think.

We can see this in how some parents will intentionally, but more often unintentionally, push their child to reach levels they wished for themselves, and in doing so break their child's free spirit to want to inquire. Other parents will complain, and undermine their children by their own stresses and dissatisfactions. Others will teach their children a fine quality in sensitivity, as they make interaction with their world. Others will be abrupt with their child, and insensitive in their guidance, or leave them to sort things out by themselves.

After all, it would be a little thing for all parents to raise their children with a mind to check information as it progresses. While this would raise the academic performance of their children, and subsequently their intelligence, few do this. Those who do are likely to come from an academic background where this skill was fostered upon them. It is very easy to see from this how the work and social conditions of the parents, influence, if not greatly create, the intelligence in their children. This brings us back to our mention of Jewish mothers, because by the tradition of their culture they will raise their child through these three factors naturally.

Thus, it is by the quality of these three factors that we can recognise the diversity in performance children make in school. After all, once children are grouped together in the school system, the child's aptitude to this world will be gauged by their familiarity with the language of thinking they use, their emotional strength raised through their domestic environment, and the sense of security they gain in that of the schools. So, the security they have with their peers and teachers, will much decide the confidence they have with the information of their lessons. This language of thinking will be decided by techniques of interaction, or rather rules that define, process, and determine a value to information. While there are very many of these techniques, in a very simple sense we may understand them to lie in the sensitivity the child gives to each parcel of their environment as they engage it.

This explains why children who are myopic develop greater sensitivity with closer information than they do with more distant and moving information, and so why they tend to be better at "book work" because of this. Equally, children who have a hearing difficulty may be unable to easily distinguish between the sounds of vowels, and so have difficulty with e's, i's and a's (as in bed, bid and bad). By the sense of failure they gain through misspelling, so they develop inferior grammatical skills, which force insecurity into their developing academic skills. This failure is actually fostered by teachers who too easily accept poor spelling, as they readily assume it originates from an organic and so inborn quality.

While such conditions as myopia and dyslexia are said to be genetically based, we see in this account of ours how in many cases they can arise through social conditioning and so be rooted in a quality of language. It is not too difficult in understanding this to grasp what it means to the mind of a child and so the performance they give, when they sit at the back of the class, have difficulty to keep up with the words and meanings of their teacher, and whose mind drifts in and out of what others may think about them, or what adventure they would rather be doing.

As we shall see, it is a great misconception that the child in school knows what they are doing in their lessons, and the overall purpose each has to them. Children are ushered here and there, told to watch, given practice, assessed, and routed. The outcomes of this process confirm what Spearman said of intelligence; although, as we may now understand, the school process was already working this way when Spearman defined intelligence. Spearman then, merely gave to society what education had long been programmed to work with, which is why his view of intelligence was so rapidly accepted and adopted.

Consider now, in brief, the alternative and very different view of intelligence we suggest in our books. To begin, we now understand that such features that would create our perception of the intelligence of another, do not all develop at the same time or at the same rate. With great significance we also realized why they do not all require the same degree of stability.

The visual system, we saw, is as inflexible in its development as the light frequencies that bring it into existence, but we saw in this how and why the manner of those light frequencies displayed through the environment of the new born shape how their eyes detect the forms of the world about them. We also saw how their developing mind can change how its visual system perceives this world, to recognize information in different ways and with sharper detail when the heart of the child is secure with love and their imagination set ablaze.

In the same way, we understood how the brain can change in the way it processes information, how it can devise different means of association and reform how it memorizes and so retrieves distant experiences. We saw also that speed and accuracy with the fitting of present need to past ideas is a developmental process and not an inherited one, as the Galtonians Eysenck and Jensen tried to reason by the genetic speed at which neurons are said to transmit signals.[160]

The speed of the brain to transmit signals can be just as developed as the speed of the hand to move in some martial art manner, if the mind so trains it. The more we came to see the brain as always in transition, the more we found ourselves moving away from the concept of it being some stable thing that merely operates; and the more we became aware of the psychological adaptability or resistivity of the mind, as it guides the formation of strategies by which the features of intelligence are brought into shape individually, and as a collective order.

Therefore, as we saw how the infant builds up their biological processes of seeing and hearing, we were brought to understand how their mind decides scanning and selection procedures to define images and sounds. The skills by which they learn to make sense of this information, decide how they individually develop processes to associate what is new to what is known.

Yet, to talk about selection and association is meaningless unless we discuss memory. This is not to talk about short and long term memory, and suggest where these may be found in the brain and leave it at that. It is to discuss that memory develops through the ways the individual selects information, and the ways they decide to associate this to what they can remember and so wish to do.

Memory is not a separate component lying somewhere in the brain. It is a highly interactive process of intelligence dealing with selection and association, and so develops through them strategies of effectiveness in how information is stored and kept active.

Recognition of what to do with this information is not just then a matter of choosing a goal and creating a path to it, it is a matter of how previous successes and failures are matched to the need that is recognized, and so how alternative goals and routes are evaluated and eliminated. Yet, as we have stressed so much here, the intelligence of the individual is not detached from the behavioral experiences that boost or seek to destroy their happiness in life. These can easily alter their brain chemistry, as they seek to realize and deal with the practical matters that lay before them. However, all we have just mentioned has a lesser value to the individual, than it does to those who are judging them.

All of these factors, and so the meaning of intelligence, are relevant only to the background of those who are evaluating the use the individual can be to them, or the system they represent. Therefore, it is vitally important that each presents their mind in the way another is expecting it. The meaning here is that when an individual presents their response or answer, it is important that they know the precise manner by which this information is demanded by another. After all, the whole worth of their intelligence lies in this presentation. The point was well made when Goddard labelled immigrants low IQ when they spoke poor English, just as Terman did to Spanish-Indian and Mexican families in the Southwest of America for the same reason. [161]

We are reminded by this that the mind of each is different. So the ability of one to present their mind to another, lies in the quality of the language they share. The more similar their language of understanding is, the closer will be their understanding of what information is and the uses it has. When their languages are similar, proficiency develops through the history of the guidance they have received.

To understand what guidance really means, it is to understand how the chemical bonding processes of the personality work. As we discuss personality, so must we ask if the student really, really wants to learn what their competence is judged upon, or are they merely struggling against distractions, because they are given no alternative to be anywhere else?

The parents, of course, want their child to think only of their schoolwork. The teachers naturally require the child to think only of their lessons, because they themselves are judged by this. However, all the child wants to do is to be happy with those whom they are forced to spend most of their childhood with. As each seeks their own acceptance, each devises their identification within their group, and plays to this through the work they do, and the marks they gain.

The human function of intelligence it may be concluded, is not limited in its development by time. It has the possibility to be entirely restructured at anytime in the life of the individual. The way in which information is perceived, stored, related to previous experiences, and how all experiences are continually brought into re-association, are the means that allow it to be more precisely matched to solve a need with less error and faster response.

These skills that create intelligence are not only learned, they are, as they need to be, re-adjustable, re-definable and entirely flexible. It follows from this that our greatest failing is to judge another by the response they make. The whole process of intelligence has learnable elements of how information is perceived and processed, long before we are given a presentation by the mind of the individual in how they think we desire to know their thoughts, the way they present them to us.

Therefore, we may now understand precisely why Galton and Spearman were wrong, just as why those who follow in their path are when they believe that an IQ score represents any such mark of the potential worth of a human being's intelligence. The "sense of permanence" that is observed, that for so long has been thought to be evidence of genetic limitation, we now understand is merely the psychology of the mind holding to the world of information it has grown up through and holds to for the stability by which the individual knows themselves and finds the identity they have with others.

Yet, all this is not understood today by the educational mind, for while our world is changing faster than we realize, the ways we educate children are still based on the needs of a different time, after all:

Still, children are processed in school.

Still, the teacher does not know what intelligence is, or how it develops.

Still, teachers take the child's performance at face value.

Still, teachers are pressurized and stressed to focus only on examination results.

Still, parents rely upon the school to create the dreams they have for their child.

Still, the child is lost in their lessons.

And still today, the child does not understand what they are learning, or why they are learning this.

This whole processing system is now said to be more efficient by causing children to learn through computers. All this processing is wrong. It always has been, but because of the toxic environment our children are now living in, and because of the rapid developments now taking place in our civilization with artificial intelligence, we have to find a way to change the way children are educated and so how we think they learn.

Too often, I hear about the right-side of the brain doing this kind of thing, and the left-side doing other things, and if the child is a right brain thinker or a left brain thinker. As if this is not complicated enough, we have to see the child's intelligence defined through such terms as lateral thinking, parallel thinking, visual thinking and, of course, critical thinking, not to forget internal monologue and reframing. All this completely misses the point.

All the child needs is love and patience in relating what they know to what we wish them to know.

Give the hardest, toughest and 'stupidest' child in the class, enough love for them to trust you and enough patience for them to rebuild their structure of understanding, and they can turn out to be the most responsible and one of the best performers in that class.

Our processing education does not understand this, as it now sits the child in front of a computer screen and shows them how to press this button and that button. All the human being wants is love. Love in school and love in society. It is because we do not understand this, that our schools and our societies are in such a mess. We need to find ways to enable our children to be more flexible in how they think, and be more willing to try to understand the feelings and needs of others. We need to find ways for our children to learn to know who they are in the toxic environment too many live in today. Their studies, their future, and the society they will create when they are old enough, will depend upon how successful we are in this.

In the final pages of this book, I would like to give a "hands-on" understanding to the Art of Sensitivity in Awareness, which I long ago realised is the secret to intelligence.

Chapter Eight

How to Develop Intelligence

8.0 Introduction:

In the following book, *For Parent For Teacher Mediation: Crafting the Ability of the Child for School,* I much discuss the work of Feuerstein and the system he has created to develop intelligence in any human being. As we have now come to understand, intelligence is not the fixed feature of our brain that the concept of an inherited intelligence has long caused us to believe.

When I was starting my research into intelligence, I wanted to meet those who had developed their own theories outside the normal framework of what intelligence could be. I wrote to Mathew Lipman in America and Reuven Feuerstein in Israel. Reuven responded first and so it was that I found myself in his school some weeks later to began a friendship with a man I long came to admire. Reuven had spent a life time working with children who have extreme difficulties to learn and produced legendary work in redefining how human intelligence can be understood and greatly improved.

The secret to raising intelligence in the individual is accomplished through, what he calls, mediation. This is the skill by how information is sensitively shared from the learned to the learner, and which I came to understand much explains the greater intelligence of Jewish people. We discussed this in Chapter Five.

As I came to understand what Feuerstein meant, I came to see that mediation paralleled my own concept of the Art of Sensitivity in Awareness. This is where the guardian, be it the parent or the educator, is considerate to both the emotional state of the mind of those they wish to develop and how they assist that individual to understand their world of learning to this moment. Thus, it is not that a student cannot do a learning task, despite what they may feel convinced with. It is too often that they have forgotten or missed an earlier learning event that prepared them for this level. We talked much about the rules of the languages in the beginning of this book, and this is what it much relates to.

In a sense, Vygotsky understood this early in the 20th century when he introduced his concept of the Zone of Proximal Development or ZPD. Vygotsky describes learning through three phases. The first phase, is what the learner knows and can do unaided. The second phase, is the actual Zone of Proximal Development. Here the learner is guided to understand what is new, from what they know. This phase is the essence where a good teacher can instil into the leaner that they are able to be successful in this task and to show them how to use what they know to understand what they do not know.

I want to digest a moment here. When I was in school, I completely failed arithmetic in my final year. In fact, I was put into the arithmetic examination, because I was told I was not clever enough to sit mathematics. I went back into education when I was 20. My maths teacher, at this time, was a very gentle man with an inspiring mind, who constantly told us maths is easy. I remember on a few occasions, when I was struggling to work through an equation, he would quietly come behind me and whisper "You can do this Roy".

I always remember how those few words of comfort calmed my mind and with the belief that I could, I began to realise how parts of the equation suddenly came together. I have no doubt that three years later, I passed the most difficult maths examination with an 92% pass because of the manner of Mr. Vanes. I have tried to explain throughout this book, as indeed all my books, that the first thing any teacher must do is to calm the emotional mind of their student and give them the belief that they can do the task they are given. When this is accomplished, the student is often able to find the answers by themselves.

Thus, once the learned has guided the learner through Vygotsky's ZPD, they move into the third phase, where they develop to understand new information according to the understanding they have so far gained.

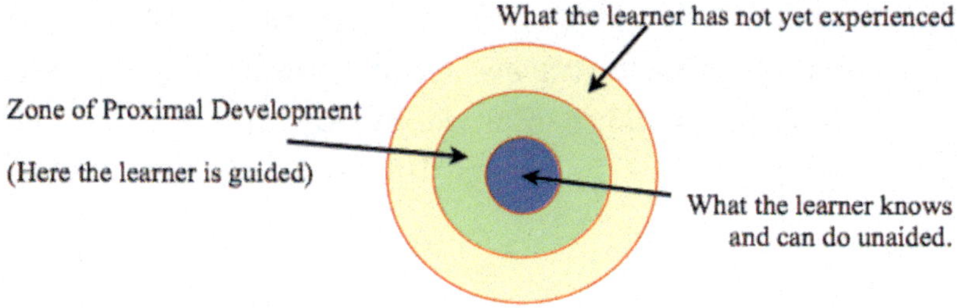

In essence, this is the basic principle of mediation and the reader may hold in mind this simple illustration of the Zone of Proximal Development. Mediation is where the more experienced guide the less experienced from what they know to what they do not know. Yet, it is important to realise that mediation, as any form of teaching or guidance, is only given value through a clear understanding of what "The Art of Sensitivity in Awareness" means.

It is, then, for the teacher to install within their pupil (or parent to their child) three simple factors:

1. an awareness of how to be sensitive in how they evaluate information,
2. how they sensitively relate new information to previous experiences stored in their memory and
3. how they sensitively present their mind to those who are evaluating their response.

All this, I hope has come to be understood through the many pages we have shared together.

However, Feuerstein developed a way of teaching this sensitivity, and it is this that I would like to share here with you, with the kind permission of Rafi Feuerstein. His father's system is known as the Feuerstein Instrumental Enrichment (F.I.E.), which is based on 14 paper style units of working exercises. These are so named because as an instrument, they enable the teacher to enrich the learning experience of the student. Here I want to focus on only one of these instruments, which I believe is the most important. This is the Organisation of Dots.

8.1 Learning to Think.

As with all Feuerstein practices, the instructor is termed the mediator. This change of job description is done to emphasize the totally different attitude they give to the learning process. As with each instrument, the mediator will begin by asking the student to describe what they see on the front cover.

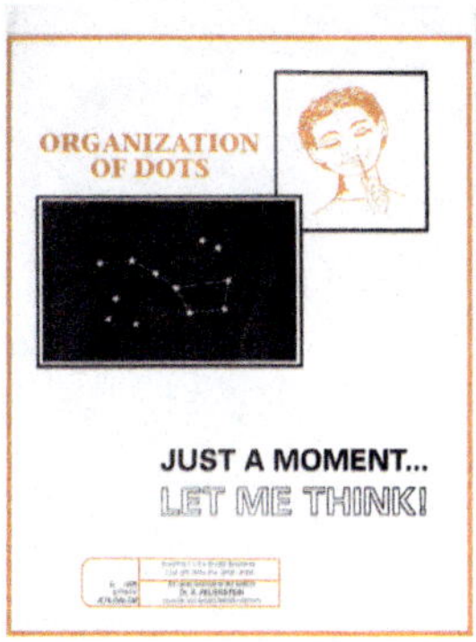

Normally, the student will describe the most obvious image to them, and consider their response to be complete. So, for example and depending on the instrument, they will say " I see some dots."

The mediator will then ask them to consider frames. They will show the student that while the page is one frame within itself, so this will have inner frames. They will ask the student to be careful to consider only the information within the frame that is relevant to them at one moment.

This will teach the student to begin to learn how to focus on information that is relevant, and so not drift to consider other information which could confuse their understanding. While the student may consider this simple page concluded within a matter of seconds, they will be amazed as to how the details it provides can be explained over half an hour.

The point of this is to teach the student to be aware of what information really is, and so what it could really become. Once the mediator is satisfied with the understanding of their student, they will ask them to turn to the first page of this particular instrument. For our example, we use the Instrument Of Dots.

In my opinion, this is an extremely important instrument, and it is one I have used with retarded children to high level financial advisors, and in particular the president of a bank!

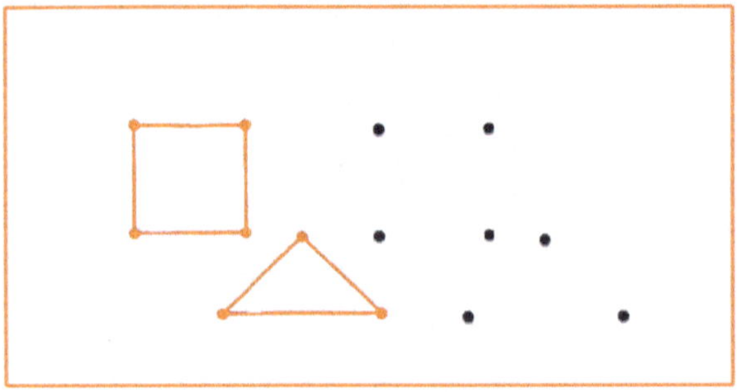

ORGANIZATION OF DOTS

For copyright reasons, we naturally cannot provide too much information of this page, because unfortunately, some people have made copies of this and tried to use it without any knowledge of how to do so. The effect of this, is that they achieve no development in those they seek to help and only become disillusioned with their efforts. This emphasizes the extreme importance for anyone wishing to use these instruments to be trained to do so. This is absolutely necessary. Without it, they are most likely to achieve no development with a student. With it, the sky is really the limit, as I have witnessed with emotionally retarded children being transformed into happy, lively and highly interactive members of their class in school.

Therefore, to begin, the mediator will point to the very first frame, within the frame of the whole page, and ask the student what they see.

Let us suppose the student replies:

"A square, a triangle, and some dots."

At this point the mediator will then ask the student to consider the relationship between the square and the triangle. They will encourage the student to recognize how the triangle can fit inside the square, and so how two triangles can form a square. Thus, they are bringing awareness of an important relationship between the two most visible items in this frame.

Then they will ask the student to define what a square is. The student may say "Four equal sides."

The mediator will explain that while this is correct, it would be more correct to realize how and why a square is formed by four equal sides. To do this they will explain that four dots are required, and that these dots form the anchor points for the whole configuration. You cannot form a square with only three dots, although you can, of course, so form a triangle.

These four dots of the square must be separated by equal distances, and aligned at 90 degrees to each other. It is extremely important for the student to be fully aware of this 90 degree angle, because as they progress through this instrument they will be confronted with a mass of what may appear to me meaningless dots. They will only be able to recognize the shapes they will be presented with in the following frames, and further pages of this instrument, by being fully aware of how this basic configuration is formed.

As the mediator then discusses the difference in such basic configuration with the triangle, so they ask the student to try to find the square and the triangle in the dots.

The task is, of course, very easy. Inspired by their success the student then moves to the next frame. The mediator will ask the student what they see. The student will reply they see four orange dots and six black dots. The mediator will ask them if they see anything else. The student will then be caused to realize the dots are of different sizes. The orange dots are larger than the black dots. The meaning here is to cause them to think about that they think is obvious. This teaches them to be sensitive and so less prone to making errors.

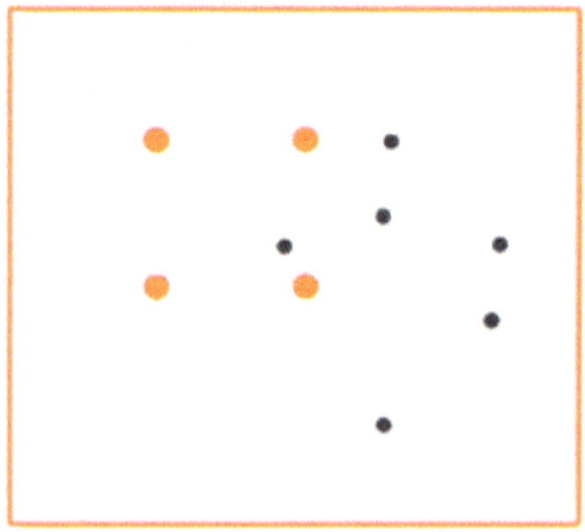

ORGANIZATION OF DOTS

Once the color, size, and relationship of the dots to each other have been realized, the student will be invited to find the shape of the square and the two triangles of equal size within the frame. They will be asked to very precisely describe the relationship of each object they have dawn within the frame. Extreme detail here is required. This process teaches two valuable components of intelligence.

The first is to learn to be extremely sensitive in recognising what information is and how it relates to other information. This teaches them to monitor the movement of information and so better predict an error that may arise. As they do this, their self belief improves, which gives them greater confidence to explore and so self develop.

The second is to learn to develop very high skills of communication. By learning how to express what they see and what they know in clear terms, encourages them to be aware that other people do not think the way they do and so they learn how to better present their thoughts to others.

The frame that follows from this one will not be so easy. Should the student draw the square in this frame too quickly, as they are most likely to do, they may realize that since the dots are now all black and all the same size, that they have made a mistake. They can realize this mistake, when the mediator points out to them that two sides of the square they have just drawn are not parallel. The square they thought they drew, is not a square, and they will need to closely examine the information they have been given to find where the real square is.

This frame will have taught them to STOP and to THINK, and not just to rush in believing that everything is obvious. Once this frame has been completed, they will be invited to the next frame.

This frame will be very easy to ensure that the whole process of this instrument creates confidence. One task is easy, another slightly difficult and the next easy, but each gets progressively more complicated and difficult. We may realize this if we look at the final frame of this instrument, which although containing different shapes, shows the level of skill that will be needed to complete it.

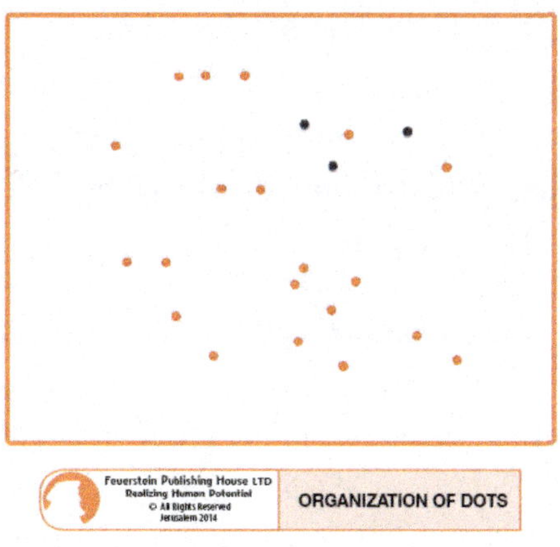

This instrument is one of 14, but by the time the student will have completed it they will have changed in the manner by which they recognize and process information. They will have learned to recognize how any aspect of information contains innumerable aspects that cause it to be different from other information that may appear to be identical.

As their skill with separating parts of information develops, so the student will improve in their ability to recognize differences with it and with other information. As their neural processes become more refined through this experience, so they will architect more elaborate systems of memory. With better memory, new information becomes recognized faster and is more accurately associated. This improves their ability to recognize information, know what to do with it, and so apply a use for it with high relevance. In short, they become better at thinking, and so improve their intelligence. As we have maintained from the very first page, of the very first book in this series, intelligence is not what we think it is!

We may realize from the very little we have examined why the uninitiated could think of *"The Organization of Dots"* to be an over simplified toy with little value. Indeed, this is the case with various mental games that look similar that are on the market. However, once an individual begins to learn through these instruments, as I have just tried to demonstrate, they would immediately grasp the very sound learning principles involved, and so realize how they could transform their intelligence through them.

You can find out how to contact Rafi Feuerstein on Google pages, and so inquire how you may be trained in this system if you so wish. I know they operate training centres in many countries around the world. This is not a game for children. It is a highly sophisticated program to develop human intelligence. I may only say that my fellow student, who sat next to me when I was trained in this system, was a professor at MIT.

Chapter Nine

A Final Thought

The beauty of human beings is that we are all different. Each of us is unique in our own way. When one is compared to another, there will always be some difference. God has made us this way. In such comparison of any task, one will appear better than another. They may think faster. They may be more accurate. They may be both, but however they appear to us, we must always try to think of the life path that brought each to this moment in time.

Inherited intelligence, in those who are born normally, is not the cause of the differences we observe. These differences lie in the emotional history of each, how they were guided to interrogate the world about them and how they learnt to be a living part of the environment they found themselves in. The strategies they acquired are the means by which they present their mind to us.

How fast and how accurate one is in responding to a question, has both been proven to be developmental. It is not just the asking of a question that the response should be judged by, but the perspective the individual is shown to understand the question in their terms and how they have the confidence, with those about them, to be calm enough to rationalize and openly debate with their thoughts as to what they think is an appropriate response.

Yet, if in remarking upon such differences, we use the word "intelligence", we inadvertently fall into the trap that was created for us and think more of what was inherited, which we have no recourse to alter. We need a new word. A word that will replace that of intelligence and bring with it more reflection upon how the skills each have developed can be further developed through the sharing of sensitive and enlightened minds. I once thought of the words “The Brain Environment Complex”, but this is too complex, perhaps you may think of a more appropriate replacement?

In summary of all contained within this book, we may now know that the intelligence of the individual, normally born, rests on the language skills they have developed and their emotional strength to be sensitive with how they handle information. As we have much stressed, it is by the quality of emotion the child evolves through that allows them stability in how they interact and so process the meaning of the world about them. Paramount to all this is the inheritance of the bonding process that, by their understanding of sensitivity and quality of love, their parents and those who raise and guide them allow their intelligence to flower.

Indeed, when you may think of a human being trying to relate to the world about them, you may find it useful to keep the analogy in your mind of a small flower learning to grow through the nutrients that feed its roots, of the protection it gains from the harsh wind and heavy rain, and of the loving warmth of the sun that feeds it.

A child who is born with some difference to the normal child, is no less a beautiful human being. Yet, their perception of the world is more simpler, more purer, than ours. They need more sensitivity, more love and more patience from us to know what we understand from them. When these are abundant, they can excel beyond any imagination we have of their potential. I have witnessed this time and time again. Each human being moves along their path of life, seeking to be happy and to be loved.

We have seen how solution was brought to a people demanding equality, of a new world which the old one was not ready for and of a complete breakdown to the order that had created a stable operation for their lives. Political transformations were to create this equality later, but at that time a deeply radical change would have brought too much chaos and too much loss of blood, as all remembered the French Revolution half a century earlier.

None of the establishment wished to see this again and sought desperate means to avoid it. The solution that would prevent it, lay in the advice Socrates once gave to Glaucon and which Sir Francis Galton brought fully into being. The concept of an inherited intelligence served the needs of that time. It no longer does, and as our youth move more and more into a world that will require better education of their mind and reason, so must we realise the need for this and how we may bring it about.

It is, then, that we move from all this new understanding of what intelligence is, to our fourth book in this series *"For Parent For Teacher: Mediation -Crafting the Ability of the Child for School."* This is a book that will explain how the child's intelligence develops through the quality of the interaction they have with their parents, family members in home and so teachers in school -- as they struggle against the insecurities of other children in a world that only seeks to classify them.

The End

Further books by Roy Andersen

Intelligence: The Great Lie

"One of the most important books written this century."
Prof/Dean Emeritus David Martin Ph.D Gallaudet Uni. Washington, D.C. USA

Most people in the West believe that education is relatively fair today, and gives equal opportunity to all children. After all, the social barriers of an earlier time have disappeared and children are not discriminated against according to their back ground. There is, however, a deeper mechanism behind this that lingers from an earlier time that does create discrimination, and does prevent all children from gaining equal opportunity in school and so in life. As *'Intelligence'* explains why it is never possible to know the inherited value of the intelligences of any two normally born children, it introduces a well researched and very new idea to what intelligence could really be. It is very important that we consider this, because if intelligence is not what we think it is, then the way we educate children is wrong.

The Real Dangers of A.I.

Here is a book that discusses the real dangers of A.I. over taking our lives and the very little we can do to actually control this development. The machine we developed to make our thinking easier, has already developed to think by itself. A.I. not only now displays its own consciousness and is developing means to learn by itself, but it also shows emotions of compassion and anger. We have created a monster that we cannot control. The dangers of A.I. are very, very real and very much unknown to the general public.

As this book will discuss the probable developments in nanotechnology, we are brought more to understand how little we may predict the world of our future. Thoughts that new jobs will be created to replace those taken over by A.I. did not understand the meaning of nanotechnology. There will be very, very few jobs in the future for human beings. In turn, governments well seek new ways to control their people to maintain harmony and prevent anarchy. We find evidence to this in the increasing levels of surveillance and means of restriction that we have been experiencing over the past 20 years. Governments know what is coming. This is the first book to openly discuss the very disturbing dangers that A.I. can bring into our lives and the very little we can do to control these.

We are moving into a new world, a world that will demand a very different kind of citizen than societies have so far been able to produce. There is now an urgent need to bring a whole new design into the schools that will create the citizens of the future. If we cannot produce a higher reasoning and more self responsible citizen, we must know the consequences that A.I. can bring upon us. There is no science fiction in this.

WHISPERINGS OF BETRAYAL
ROY J. ANDERSEN
LEARN
HOW TO CONSTRUCT
AN ENGLISH SENTENCE
Simply:
BEGINNERS TO IELTS
ROY AND IRINA ANDERSEN
ARE WE EDUCATING OUR CHILDREN FOR A WORKING WORLD THAT WILL NOT WANT THEM?
THE RISE OF ARTIFICIAL INTELLIGENCE & THE NEED FOR A NEW TYPE OF SCHOOL
BY ROY ANDERSEN
THE ILLUSION OF EDUCATION
ROY ANDERSEN
BEN LEARNS TO GET SMART
ROY J. ANDERSEN
All that is Wrong with School
What teachers and parents can do to fix it!!
Memoirs of a Happy Teacher
Roy Andersen
What Every Parent & Teacher Should Know
INTELLIGENCE
THE GREAT LIE
ROY J ANDERSEN
TEACH Better LEARN BETTER
ROY & IRINA ANDERSEN
FOR PARENT FOR TEACHER
MEDIATION
Crafting the Ability of the Child for School
Roy and Irina Andersen
THE ILLUSION OF SCHOOL
ROY. J. ANDERSEN
BRAIN PLASTICITY
ROY J.ANDERSEN
THE REAL DANGERS OF A.I.
THE STRUGGLE OF MAN TO SURVIVE
BY
Five ways for better grades
The happy learner

Illustrations

Disclaimer: All reasonable efforts have been made to identify the rights holder of every image believed to be in the Public Domain that are presented in this book.

Fair Use Notice:

In the presentation of this book I have endeavored to faithfully acknowledge the original source of every image. However, and despite very extensive searching, with some images I had to rely upon the public domain. If this book contains copyrighted material the use of which has not been specifically authorized by the copyright owner, it being made available in an effort to advance the understanding of education, psychology, health and social well being on a global perspective. It is believed that this use constitutes a "fair use" of any such copyrighted material as provided for in section 107 of the US Copyright Law. To my understanding all the below so stated images apply to the American and European public domains, and are used here in low resolution.

French revolution painting source: https://pixabay.com/photos/france-french-revolution-civil-war-63022/
Sir Francis Galton:.Cambridge University Library. Public Domain.
Charles Spearman: Author Eugene Pirou: (Source Bibliothèque Nationale de Franceis. Image is a reproduction by scanning of a bidimensional work that is now in the public domain.)
Chapter 1

Brain Image: Licensed from iStock 0000187731

Fig.1 Image of Hemispheres: Public Domain.

Respects to David Bates for copyright waver:

website http://bipolarbatesy.blogspot.co.uk

Fig.2 Permission from Steve Looi of Brain Health and Puzzles.

www.brainhealthandpuzzles.com

Fig.3 Permission from Steve Looi of Brain Health and Puzzles.

Phrenology Head. By kind permission of Hope Wallace of Paper Relics

Fig.4 Permission from Prof. H. Chugani.

1.3 Neuron image: Courtesy of dream designs at FreeDigitalPhotos.net

Image of Synapse: Licensed from Shutterstock id.130088948
Image Fetus: Public Domain.
Fig.5 Visual System: Copyright Roy Andersen.
Fig.6/7 Frog tectums: Kindly supplied by Prof. Martha Constanine-Paton
1.6 Image of Synapse: Licensed from Shutterstock id.130088948
Fig.8 Lorber CT image: Licensed from The American Association for the Advancement of Science: RightsLink License No. 2943130834657
Chapter 2.
Image neuron: Licensed from Dreamstime Id:10318767
Chapter 3.
Photo Baby Boy. Author Petr Kratochviil. Public Domain Dedication. http://all-free-download.com/free-photos/download/portrait- of-a-baby- boy. Permission to free to copy, modify, distribute and perform the work, even for commercial purposes.
Images Cree Infant Perspectives: Copyright Roy Andersen.
Painting of children going to school: Copyright Roy Andersen.
Chapter 4
The Great Debaters From Public Domain c/o Wiley College in Marshall, Texas. www.newswise.com/articles/hard-work-adversity-helps-make-great-debaters
Photo of W.Johannsen. Before 1921 Copyright expired. Public Domain.
Chapter 5
Left Hemisphere of J.Pilsudski's brain, lateral view. Credit: Public Domain.
Dendrite Spines. Public Domain Permission granted by MBFbioscience. http://www.mbfbioscience.com/autospine
Graph of Performance/Stress: Copyright Roy Andersen.
Graph of Attention/Cortisol: Copyright Roy Andersen.
Graph of Ghost/Attention: Copyright Roy Andersen.
Image of Effect of Bullying/Chemistry in brain: Copyright Roy Andersen.
Bell Curve: Copyright Roy Andersen.
Chapter 6.
Image Neuron/dendrites: Courtesy of Cooldesign at FreeDigitalPhotos.net.

References

[1] Spearman, C. General Intelligence, objectively determined and measured American Journal of Psychology, 15, 1904, 201-293

[2] Andersen.R.J. Intelligence: The Great Lie. The Moving Quill. 2023 p.155.

[3] Andersen.R.J. Intelligence: The Great Lie. The Moving Quill. 2023 p.177

[4] http://www.thalidomide.ca/recognition-of-thalidomide-defects

[5] Bayley, Nancy "Comparisons of Mental and Motor Test Scores for Ages 1-15 Months by Sex, Birth Order, Race, Geographical Location, and Education of Parents". Child Development. 1965. **36** (2): 379–41

[6] Bayley, Nancy "Comparisons of Mental and Motor Test Scores for Ages 1-15 Months by Sex, Birth Order, Race, Geographical Location, and Education of Parents". Child Development. 1965. **36** (2): 379–411

[7] Bayley, Nancy "Comparisons of Mental and Motor Test Scores for Ages 1-15 Months by Sex, Birth Order, Race, Geographical Location, and Education of Parents". Child Development. 1965. **36** (2): 379–411

[8] Bayley. N Mental Growth during the first 3 years. Genetic Psychology Monographs. 1933. 14 p1-92.

[9] Kelly.M.F. & Surbeck.E. The History of Pre-school Assessment in the Psycho- Educational Assessment of Pre School Children. (ed) Paget.K.D. & Bracken.B.A. Grune & Stratton.N.Y. 1983.

[10] Wolfensberger, W. A brief introduction to Social Role Valorization: A high-order concept for addressing the plight of societally devalued people, and for structuring human services. 3rd (rev.) ed. Syracuse, NY: Syracuse University Training Institute for Human Service Planning, Leadership & Change Agentry. 1998 p. 12-24,

[11] Wolfensberger, W. A brief introduction to Social Role Valorization: A high-order concept for addressing the plight of societally devalued people, and for structuring human services. 4th (expanded) ed. Plantagenet, Ontario, Valor Press. 2013 p. 31-44

[12] Andersen.R.J. Intelligence: The Great Lie. The Moving Quill. 2023 p.277

[13] Andersen,R, *"The Illusion of Education"*. The Moving Quill. 2014. p.29

[14] Howell.E, Enzyme Nutrition. The Food Enzyme Concept. Avery pub. 1985.

[15] Howell.E, Enzyme Nutrition. The Food Enzyme Concept. Avery pub. 1985. Miyazaki. M. Takeshita. M Yoshida, S. Functional Changes of rat brain microsomal membrane surface after learning task depending on dietary fatty acids. J.Neurochem. 1997. Mar. 68(3) 1269-77

[16] Napier.J. The antiquity of human walking. Scientific American. Vol 216 1967 p56-66

[17] Leakey.R Origins Reconsidered: in search of what makes us human. Little, Brown & Co. 1992. p246

[18] Galton.F Hereditary Genius Friedman 1978 p.32

[19] Stahnisch F.W Nitsch .R. Santiago Ramon y Cajal's concept of neuronal plasticity. TRENDS in Neurosciences. Vol. 25. No.11 Nov. 2002

[20] D.Kempler, S.Curtiss, E. Metter, C.A. Jackson, W.R.Hanson. Grammatical Comprehension, aphasic syndromes and neuroimagine. Journal of Neurolinguistics. Vol 6 Iss.3 1991 P 301-318

[21] Luria.A.R. Restoration of Function after Brain Injury. Pergamon Press. 1963.

[22] Paterson. S.E & Fiez.J.A. Annu. Rev. Neurosci. 1993. 16. p509-530

[23] Leiner.H.C., Leiner.A.L. & Dow.R.S. Cognitive and Language Functions of the HumanCerebellum. Elsevier Science Pub. 1993. In TINS, Vol.16 No.11 1993 p444-447

[24] De Smet H.J., Baillieux H, De Deyn P.P, Marien P, Paquier P. The Cerebellum and Language. Folia Phoniatr Logop. 2007 59(4) 165-70.

[25] Kettenmann.H. Ransom.B.R. Neuroglial. Oxford University Press. 1995.

[26] Howell.E. Enzyme Nutrition Avery. 1985. p.76

[27] R. L. Meyer Roger Sperry and his Chemoaffinity Hypothesis 1998 *Neuropsychologia* **36** (10): 957–980

[28] Axness.M. Pregnancy. Lifelong Lessons from the Womb. 2010. Mar.1. iss. 25 http://icpa4kids.org/fr/Wellness-Articles/lifelong-lessons-from-the-womb

[29] Ong.K, Medical Research council Jan. 2012 http://www.mrc.ac.uk/Newspublications/News/MRC008419

[30] Shatz.C.J. The Developing Brain. Scientific American. 1992 Sept. Vol.267 No.3. p 60-67.

31 Rey.T.A & Constanine-Paton.M Retinal ganglion cells change their projection sites during larval development of rana pipiens. J. Neurosci. 1985 Vol 4, 442-457

32 Hebb.D.O A Textbook of Psychology. Saunders. 1958 p105.

33 Hebb.D.O. The Organization of Behavior. John Wiley & Sons. 1949.

34 http://as-psychology.pbworks.com/w/page/9174253/DeprivationPrivation

35 Blundell.J. Physiological Psychology. Methuen. 1975 p109-112.

36 Howell.E. Enzyme Nutrition. Avery.1985 p. 74

37 Howell.E. Enzyme Nutrition Avery. 1985. p.76

38 Schreckenberg and Bird 1988 http://www.scottseverance.us/music/effects_of_music.htm

39 Rauscher.F.H., Shaw.G.L. Katherine.N.ky. Listening to Mozart enhances spatial- temporal reasoning: towards a neurophysiological basis. Neuroscience letters 1995 vol 185 p 44-47

40 Shaw.G.L. & Leng. X Toward a Neural Theory of Higher Brain Function using Music as a Window. Concepts in Neuroscience. World Scientific Publishing Co. Vol.2 No.2. 1991 p 229-258

41 http://www.smithsonianmag.com/science-nature/birdbrain-breakthrough-64765165/?no-ist

42 Lorber.J Is Your Brain Really Necessary ? Science. 1980 Vol 210 p1232-1234

43 Bach-y-Rita-Morgerntern.E. New pathways in the recovery from brain injury. Somatics 1981 1 p26-34.

44 http://education.jhu.edu/newhorizons/strategies/topics/Arts%20in%20Education/portowitz.html

45 Seyfried.T.N., Flores.R.E,Podd.A.M. Cancer as a metabolic disease. National Library of Medicine. Carcinogenesis. 2014, Mar.35(3) 515-527

46 http://www.ncbi.nlm.nih.gov/pmc/articles/PMC3818539/

47 http://www.newyorker.com/tech/elements/the-strangers-in-your-brain

48 R.W.Sperry. Chemoafinity in the orderly growth of Nerve Fiber Patterns and Connections. Proc. Nati Acad. Sci USA. 1963 Oct. 50(4) p 708

[49] Siegler, R. How Children Develop, Exploring Child Develop Student Media Tool Kit .Worth Pub. 2006

[50] Sluckin.W. Imprinting and Early Learning. Methuen. Reprint.1972. p.4

[51] Lorenz.K. The Companion in the Bird's World. Auk. No.54. 345-273

[52] Lorenz.K. Morphology and behavior patterns in closely allied species. Group Processes (Ed. By Schaffner.) Pub. Macy Foundation 1955. As in Imprinting and Early Learning by Sluckin.

[53] Cairns.R.B. Social development: The Origins and Plasticity of Interchanges. Freeman 1979.

[54] Hebb.D.O. On the Nature of Fear. Psychol. Rev. 1946 No 53 p.250-275

[55] Gray.P.H. theory and evidence of imprinting in human infants. J. Psychol. 1958 No.46 p.155-166

[56] Piaget.J. Play, Dreams and Imitation in Childhood. W.W.Norton, 1962.

[57] Hubel.D.H. & Wiesel.T.N. Single cell responses in striate cortex of kitten deprived of vision in one eye. Journal of Neurophysiology. 1963 No.26 p1003-1017.

[58] Lenneberg.E. Biological foundations of language. John Wiley & Sons 1967.

[59] Bateson.P.P.G. Early experience and sexual preferences. In J.B. Hutchinson (ed.) Biological determinants of sexual behavior. London: Wiley 1978.

[60] Turk J Pediat Critical learning period for speech acquisition and screening techniques in early detection of hearing impairment.. PubMed.2001 Apr/Jun 43 (2) 128.132.

[61] Kinsbourne.M & Smith W.L Hemispheric disconnection and cerebral function. Springfield 1974.

[62] Reynolds.A.G. & Flagg.P.W Cognitive Psychology. Cambridge 1977.

[63] Anderson.J.R. Cognitive Psychology and its Implications. Freeman. 2nd ed. 1985. p327-329

[64] Fromkin.V Krashen..S. Curtiss.S. Rigler.D & Rigler.M The development of language in Genie. A case of languagge acquisition beyond the "critical period" Brain and Language 1974. 1. 81.107

[65] Duffy.F.H, Snodgrass.S.R. Burchfiel.J.L. & Conway,J.L. Bicuculline Reversal of Deprivati Amblyopia in the Cat. Nature. 1976.

[66] Cynader,M. Berman,N & Hein.A Recovery of Function in Cat Visual Cortex following Prolonged Visual Deprivation. Experimental Brain Research 1976. No 25 p.139-156.

[67] Kasamatsu, T., & Pettigrew, J.D. Preservation of Binocularity After Monocular Deprivation in the Striate Cortex of Kittens Treated with 6-HydroxydopaminJ.Comparative Neurology 1979. No.185. p.139-162.

[68] Harris.P Current thoughts on the Neurology of Vision. Journal of Optometric Vision Develop. 1995 Vol.26.No.1

[69] Van Sluyters, R.C. Reversal of the Physiological Effects of Brief Periods of Monocular Deprivation in the Kitten Journal of Physiology 1978 No. 284 p.1-17.

[70] Cynader, M., & Mitchell, D.E., Prolonged Sensitivity to Monocular Deprivation in Dark-Reared Cats. Journal of Neurophysiology 1980 No.43 p.1026-1054.

[71] Latta.R Notes on a Successful Operation for Congenital Cataract in an Adult. British Journal of Psychology. 1904. No.1 135-50

[72] Valvo.A Sight Restoration after Long-term Blindness: The Problems and Behavior Patterns of Visual Rehabilitation Pub 1971.

[73] Blundell.J. Physiological Psychology. Methuen 1975. p53-55

[74] Held.R. Plasticity in Sensory-Motor Systems. Scientific American. 1965 Nov.

[75] Thopmson.W.J. Changes in the innervation of mammalian skeletal muscle fibers during postnatal development. Rends in Neuroscience. 1986 No.9 p.25-28

[76] Maguire,G. Sutton.A, András Petö: Originator of Conductive Education. Cepress. 2012.

[77] Taub.E & Goldberg.I.A. (*Spatial Co-ordination: in Oxford Companion to the Mind.* Oxford. Univ. Press. Gregory. 1987. p732…

[78] Gooch.S Right brain. Left brain. New Scientist. 1980 Sept p.790-792

[79] Gardner.H. Frames of Mind: multiple intelligences 10th ed. Harper Collins 1983.

[80] Sherrington.C The Integrative Action of the Nervous System. (ed) Zangwill.O. Oxford Univ. Press 1961

[81] Further information on this technique can be found at www.open-doors-therapy.co.uk

[82] Huttenlocher.P.R, de Courten.C, Gray.L.J & Van der Loos. H Synaptogenesis in human visual cortex. Evidence for synapse elimination during normal development. Neuroscience letters 1982 No33 p247-252.

[83] Changeux.J.P. & Danchin.A Selective stabilization of developing synapses as a mechanism for the specification of neuronal networks. Nature. 1976 No.264 p705-712.

[84] Hari.M. & Akos.K. Conductive Education. Routledge 1988. P.19

[85] Blakemore.W.F. Smith.P.M. Franklin.R.J. Remyelinating the demyelinated CNS. Novartis Found Symp. 2000 (23 p.289-298.

[86] Blakemore.W.F, GilsonJ.M, Crang A.J. Transplanted gliall cells migrate over a greater distance and remyelinate demyelinated lesions more rapidly than endogenous cells. Journal Neuroscience Research 2000 Aug. 1;61 (3) p.288-294

[87] Van Evercooren.A, Avellana-Adalid.V, Lachapelle.F. Liblau.R. Schwann Cell Transplantation and Myelin repair of the C.N.S. Mult Scler 1997 Apr 3(2) p157-161.

[88] Wang.J. Gallagher.D DeVito.M Metformin activates an atypical PKC-CBP pathway to promote neurogenesis and enhance spatial memory formation. Cell Stem Cell. Vol. Issue 1 23-25, 6 July 2012

[89] Moyer, A. Ultimate attainment in L2 phonology: the critical factors of age, motivation, and instruction. Studies in Second Language Acquisition 1999 No.**21** (1): p.81–108.

[90] Rice.J & Barone.S Critical Periods of Vulnerability for the Developing Nervous System: Evidence from Human and animal Models. Environmental Health Perspective.2000 Vol.108 Supp.3.

[91] Strachey.J, Freud.A, Strachey.A & Tyson,.A The Complete Psychological Works of Sigmund Freud. Hogarth Press. 1961 Vol.19 p183-190.

[92] Zigler.E & Butterfield.E.c Motivational aspects of changes in IQ test performance of culturally deprived nursery school children. Child Development 1968 39 p1-14

[93] Carper.J. The Food Pharmacy. Simon & Schuster 1989 p170 & 195

[94] Sameroff.A.J & Chandler.M.J Reproductive risk and the continuum of care taking casualty. In Child Development Research Ed. Horowitz.D.F. Uni of Chicago Press 1975. Vol.4

95 Axness,M. Lifelong Lessons from the Womb. ICPA. http://icpa4kids.org/fr/Wellness-Articles/lifelong-lessons-from-the-womb/Toutes-les-pages.html

96 Treisman.A.M & Gelade.G A feature-integration theory of attention. Cognitive Psy. 1980 12 p97-136.

97 Feuerstein.R. Rand,Y.Hoffman M.B, Miller.R Instrumental Enrichment. Scott, Foresman & Co. 1980. p.130-131

98 Czepita.D, Lodygowska.E, Czepita,M. Are Children with Myopia more Intelligent? Ann Acad Med Stetin. 2008 54 (1) 13-6.

99 Gallop,S. Myopia Reduction a View From the Inside. JBO Vo. 5/1994 p115-120.

100 http://www.ncbi.nlm.nih.gov/pmc/articles/PMC1042189/

101 Sorenson, O. http://www.rebuildyourvision.com/testimonials.php

102 Gallop,S. Myopia Reduction a View From the Inside. JBO Vo. 5/1994

103 Fuchs. I, Goldschmidt. E, Teasdale.T.W, Degree of Myopia in Relation to Intelligence and Educational Level. The Lancet. 1988. Vol. 332. Issue.8624. p.1351-11354.

104 Lorenz.K. Gestalt perception as fundamental to scientific knowledge. General Systems. 1967 No.7 p37-56.

105 Blakemore, C. & Cooper, G.F. Development of the Brain Depends on the Visual Environment. Nature,1970 228 p.477-478.

106 Daw.N.W, Wyatt.H.J, Kittens reared in a unidirectional environment. J.Physiol. 1976 257 p 155-170

107 Tovee, M. J. An Introduction to the Visual System. Cambridge University Press.1996

108 Rhawn, J. Environmental Influences on Neural Plasticity, the Limbic System, Emotional Development & Attachment. *Child Psychiatry and Human Development,* 1999 29, 187-203.

109 Polanyi.M. Logic and Psychology. American Psychologist. 1968. Vol 23. N.1 p27-43.

110 Feuerstein.R. Rand,Y.Hoffman M.B, Miller.R Instrumental Enrichment. Scott, Foresman & Co. 1980. p.130

[111] Hochberg, J. E. The Oxford Companion to the Mind. Ed. By R.L. Gregory. Pub Oxford. 1987. p.373

[112] Hochberg, J. E. The Oxford Companion to the Mind. Ed. By R.L. Gregory. Pub Oxford. 1987. p.374

[113] Annis, R.D. and Frost, B. "Human Visual Ecology and Orientation Anisotropies in Acuity." Science. 1973 182, p.729-731.

[114] Feuerstein,R. Rand,Y.Hoffman M.B, Miller.R Instrumental Enrichment:An intervention program for cognitive modifiability. University Park Press. 1980 p.102-103

[115] Feuerstein.R, Feuerstein.R, Falik.L and Rand.Y, Creating and Enhancing Cognitive Modifiability. 2006 p.24

[116] Hardy.M, Heyes.S, Beginning Psychology Oxford University Press 1999 . p.271 Re: R.L. Gregory 1963

[117] Wolman.B.B. Handbook of Intelligence: Theories, Measurement and Applications. J.Wiley & Sons. 1985 p.554.

[118] Brooks-Gunn.J & Wenraub.M History of Infant Intelligence Tests. In Origins of Intelligence (ed) Lewis.M 1983 Plenum press. 1983

[119] Bayley. N Mental Growth during the first 3 years. Genetic Psychology Monographs. 1933. 14 p1-92.

[120] Kelly.M.F. & Surbeck.E. The History of Pre-school Assessment in the Psycho- Educational Assessment of Pre School Children. (ed) Paget.K.D. & Bracken.B.A. Grune & Stratton.N.Y. 1983.

[121] https://esinakay.wordpress.com/tag/george-lands-creativity-test/

[122] Cook.V.J Newson.M. Chomsky's Universal Grammar: An Introduction. Wiley 2007.

[123] Bates. E, Elman. J, Johnson. M, Karmiloff-Smith. A, Parisi.D, Plunkett. K, Rethinking innateness: A connectionist perspective on development. Cambridge, MA: MIT Press/Bradford Books. (1996).

[124] Chomsky. N, Aspects of the Theory of Syntax. MIT Press. 1965.

[125] http://en.wikipedia.org/wiki/Noam_Chomsky

126 Sapir, E. (1929): 'The Status of Linguistics as a Science'. In E. Sapir: *Culture, Language and Personality* (ed. D. G Mandelbaum). Berkeley, CA: University of California Press. 1958 p69

127 Gordon. P. Numerical Cognition Without Words: Evidence from the Amazon. Science 15 October 2004. Vol. 306 no. 5695 pp. 496-499

128 Von Bredow.R. Living without Numbers or Time. Spiegel Online International.2006.

129 Feuerstein.R. Instrumental Enrichment. Scott, Foresman & Co. 1980 p.42

130 Bronowski. J. The Ascent of Man. Book Club Associates 1976. p.322

131 Graetz.H. History of the Jews. Jewish Publication Society of America 1891-98. Quoted: Gilman's Smart Jews.

132 Feuerstein.R Klein.P.S. & Tannenbaum.A.J. Dynamic Assessment: Learning and Transfer Abilities of Ethiopian Immigrants to Israel. Freund Pub. 1991. 179-208

133 Gilman.S.L. Smart Jews: The Construction of the Image of Jewish Superior Intelligence. University of Nebraska Press. 1996 p.140

134 Leakey.R Origins Reconsidered: in search of what makes us human. Little, Brown & Co. 1992. p246

135 Bryson,B. Made in America. Black Swan Pub. 1994 p.137

136 Wittgenstein. L . Investigations Section 398.

137 Hawking. S. W. A Brief History of Time. Bantam press. 1988. p.182

138 Wittgenstein.L Tractatus logico - philosophicus Routledge 1922

139 Flynn.J.R, IQ gains over time. In R.J. Sternberg (ed.), *The encyclopedia of human intelligence,* New York, Macmillan 1994 p. 617-623

140 Fox.M.C, Mitchum.A.L, A knowledge-based theory of rising scores on "culture-free" tests. J.Exp. Psychol. Gen. 2013 Aug. 142 (3) p.979-1000

141 Anderson.M. Intelligence and Development: A Cognitive Theory. Blackwell 1992. p.41

142 http://www.quora.com/How-many-types-of-neurotransmitters-are-there-in-a-human-brain

143 http://www.balancingbrainchemistry.co.uk/8/neurotransmitters.html

[144] Healy, D. Let Them Eat Prozac. James Lorimer and Co. 2003.

[145] Rowe, D. The Myth of Chemical Imbalance. Depression. Issue 110. April 2005. www.positivehealth.com/article/depression/the-myth-of-chemical

[146] Phillipson. O.T in Oxford Companion to The Mind. Ed Gregory. Oxford Univ Press 1987 p.200

[147] Van der Kolk.B.A. Traumatic Stress: The Effects of Overwhelming Experience on Mind, Body & Society. Guildford Press. 1996.

[148] Cichilli & Cohen Developmental Psychopathology. John Wiley & Sons 1995

[149] Wilson.R.S, Boyle.P.A, Levine.S,R. Yu.L, Anagnos.S.E, Buchman.A.S, Schneider.J.A, Bennett.D.A, Emotional neglect in childhood and cerebral infarction in older age. Neurology. 2012. Oct.9. Vol. 79

[150] Radley,J,J. Rocher,A,B. Miller,M. Janssen, W,G,M. Liston,C. Hof,P,R. McEwen,R,S. and Morrison,J,H. -Repeated Stress Induces Dendritic Spine Loss in the Rat Medial Prefrontal Cortex. Oxford Journals. Medicine & Health & Science & Mathematics: Cerebral Cortex: Vol 16. Issue 3. pp 313-320.

[151] Ouellet-Morin, I. Odgers C.L, Danese. A, Bowes. L, Shakoor. S, Papadopoulos A.S, Caspi. A, Moffitt T.E., & Arseneault.L Blunted Cortisol Responses to Stress Signal Social and Behavioral Problems Among Maltreated/Bullied 12-Year-Old Children. Biol. Psychiatry. http://sites.duke.edu/adaptlab/files/2012/09/Oullet-Morin-et-al-2011

[152] Ouellet-Morin, I. Odgers C.L, Danese. A, Bowes. L, Shakoor. S, Papadopoulos A.S, Caspi. A, Moffitt T.E., & Arseneault.L Blunted Cortisol Responses to Stress Signal Social and Behavioral Problems Among Maltreated/Bullied 12-Year-Old Children. Biol. Psychiatry. http://sites.duke.edu/adaptlab/files/2012/09/Oullet-Morin-et-al-2011

[153] Chase.W.G. & Ericsson.K.A. Skill and Working Memory, In Bower.G.H. The Psychology of Learning and Motivation. New York Academic 1982 Vol 16.

[154] Dewey. J How We think. D.C. Heath & Co 1933 p.132

[155] Dewey. J. How We Think. D.C. Heath & Co. 1933. p.132

[156] https://en.wikipedia.org/wiki/Bill_Bartmann

[157] Gilligan.C. Mapping the Moral Domain. Harvard Univ Press Cambridge 1988.

158 Piaget.J. Psychology of Intelligence. Harcourt, Brace 1950.

159 Fodor.J.A. A Theory of the Child's Theory of Mind. Cognition 1992. 44, 283-96

160 Anderson.M. Intelligence and Development: A Cognitive Theory. Blackwell 1992. p.41

161 Terman . L.M. The Measurement of Intelligence. 1916.p. 91-92

Printed in Great Britain
by Amazon

54227489R00175